Histor

for the IB Diploma

Interwar Years: Conflict and Cooperation 1919–39

Allan Todd, Jean Bottaro and Sally Waller
Series editor: Allan Todd

Cambridge University Press's mission is to advance learning, knowledge and research worldwide.

Our IB Diploma resources aim to:
- encourage learners to explore concepts, ideas and topics that have local and global significance
- help students develop a positive attitude to learning in preparation for higher education
- assist students in approaching complex questions, applying critical-thinking skills and forming reasoned answers.

CAMBRIDGE
UNIVERSITY PRESS

University Printing House, Cambridge CB2 8BS, United Kingdom

Cambridge University Press is part of the University of Cambridge.

It furthers the University's mission by disseminating knowledge in the pursuit of education, learning and research at the highest international levels of excellence.

www.cambridge.org
Information on this title: www.cambridge.org/9781107640207

© Cambridge University Press 2013

First published 2013
Reprinted 2014

Printed in the United Kingdom by Latimer Trend

A catalogue record for this publication is available from the British Library

ISBN 978-1-107-64020-7 Paperback

Contents

1 Introduction

This book is designed to prepare students for the Paper 3 Section 8 topic, *Interwar Years: Conflict and Cooperation 1919–39* (in HL Option 5, Aspects of the History of Europe and the Middle East) in the IB History examination. It discusses the history of the period between the First and Second World Wars, looking at the main attempts to achieve international co-operation and collective security – and the various economic, political and diplomatic challenges these attempts encountered. In particular, the book examines the impact of the problems resulting from the Great Depression, and the rise of fascist and right-wing regimes in Italy, Germany and Spain. It also considers the various responses of the main democratic states to these developments, including support for the League of Nations, attempts to revise the peace treaties of 1919–20, and appeasement. Lastly, this book examines the final steps leading to the outbreak of the Second World War.

A map showing Europe after the 1919–20 peace settlements

5

Themes

To help you prepare for your IB History exams, this book will cover the main themes and aspects relating to *Interwar Years: Conflict and Cooperation 1919–39*, as set out in the IB *History Guide*. In particular, it examines the main political, economic and diplomatic developments in the period 1919–39 in terms of:

- the political, constitutional, economic and social problems of Weimar Germany in the period 1919–33
- the rise of fascism in Italy after 1919, and Mussolini's main domestic and foreign policies in the period 1922–39
- the impact of the Great Depression around the world in the period 1929–39 and, in particular, how this affected foreign policy
- the main political and economic factors behind the outbreak of the Spanish Civil War, foreign involvement in the war, its outcome, and its impact on diplomacy during 1936–39
- Hitler's rise to power in Germany, and his main domestic and foreign policies
- the attempts to achieve collective security in the period 1919–39, the policy of appeasement, the failure of international diplomacy, and the outbreak of the Second World War in 1939.

A case study will focus in more detail on the impact of the Great Depression on Germany.

Theory of knowledge

In addition to the broad key themes, the chapters contain Theory of knowledge (ToK) links, to get you thinking about aspects that relate to history, which is a Group 3 subject in the IB Diploma. The *Interwar Years* topic has several clear links to ideas about knowledge and history. The subject is one that is much debated by historians – especially where it concerns responsibility for the eventual outbreak of the most destructive war in history.

At times, the controversial nature of this topic has affected the historians writing about these states, the leaders involved, and their policies and actions. Questions relating to the selection of sources, and the way historians interpret these sources, have clear links to the IB Theory of knowledge course.

For example, when trying to explain aspects of particular foreign policies, political leaders' motives, and their success or failure, historians must decide which evidence to select and use to make their case, and which evidence to leave out. But to what extent do the historians' personal political views influence them when selecting what they consider to be the most important or relevant sources, and when they make judgements about the value and limitations of specific sources or sets of sources? Is there such a thing as objective 'historical truth'? Or is there just a range of subjective historical opinions and interpretations about the past, which vary according to the political interests of individual historians?

You are therefore strongly advised to read a range of publications giving different interpretations of the operations of the League of Nations, the foreign policies pursued by different leaders, their attempts to form alliances, and the significance of different historical events during the period covered by this book, in order to gain a clear understanding of the relevant historiographies (see Further information, page 236).

IB History and Paper 3 questions

In IB History, Paper 3 is taken only by Higher-level students. For this paper, it specifies that three sections of an Option should be selected for in-depth study. The examination paper will set two questions on each section – and you have to answer three questions in total.

Unlike Paper 2, where there were regional restrictions, in Paper 3 you will be able to answer *both* questions from one section, with a third chosen from one of the other sections. These questions are essentially in-depth analytical essays. This is reflected in the time available, which is 2 hours 30 minutes. It is therefore important to study *all* the bullet points set out in the IB *History Guide*, in order to give yourself the widest possible choice of questions.

Exam skills

Throughout the main chapters of this book, there are activities and questions to help you develop the understanding and the exam skills necessary for success in Paper 3. Your exam answers should demonstrate:

- factual knowledge and understanding
- awareness and understanding of historical interpretations
- structured, analytical and *balanced* argument.

Before attempting the specific exam practice questions that come at the end of each main chapter, you might find it useful to refer *first* to Chapter 11, the final exam practice chapter. This suggestion is based on the idea that if you know where you are supposed to be going (in this instance, gaining a good grade), and how to get there, you stand a better chance of reaching your destination!

Questions and markschemes

To ensure that you develop the necessary skills and understanding, each chapter contains comprehension questions and examination tips. For success in Paper 3, you need to produce essays that combine a number of features. In many ways, these require the same skills as the essays in Paper 2.

However, for the Higher-level Paper 3, examiners will be looking for greater evidence of *sustained* analysis and argument, linked closely to the demands of the question. They will also be seeking more depth and precision with regard to supporting knowledge. Finally, they will be expecting a clear and well-organised answer, so it is vital to do a rough plan *before* you start to answer a question. Your plan will show straight away whether or not you know enough about the topic to answer the question. It will also provide a good structure for your answer.

It is particularly important to start by focusing *closely* on the wording of the question, so that you can identify its demands. If you simply assume that a question is *generally about this period/leader*, you will probably produce an answer that is essentially a narrative or story, with only vague links to the question. Even if your knowledge is detailed and accurate, it will only be broadly relevant. If you do this, you will get half-marks at most.

Another important point is to make sure you present a *well-structured and analytical argument* that is clearly linked to *all the demands of the question*. Each aspect of your argument/analysis/explanation then needs to be supported by carefully selected, precise and relevant own knowledge.

In addition, showing awareness and understanding of relevant historical debates and interpretations will help you to access the highest marks and bands. This does not mean simply repeating, in your own words, what different historians have said. Instead, try to *critically evaluate* particular interpretations. For example, are there any weaknesses in some arguments put forward by certain historians? What strengths does a particular interpretation have?

Examiner's tips

To help you develop these skills, most chapters contain sample questions, with examiner's tips about what to do (and what *not* to do) in order to achieve high marks. These chapters will focus on a specific skill, as follows:

- Skill 1 (Chapter 2) – understanding the wording of a question
- Skill 2 (Chapter 3) – planning an essay
- Skill 3 (Chapter 5) – writing an introductory paragraph

- Skill 4 (Chapter 6) – avoiding irrelevance
- Skill 5 (Chapter 7) – avoiding a narrative-based answer
- Skill 6 (Chapter 9) – using your own knowledge analytically and combining it with awareness of historical debate
- Skill 7 (Chapter 10) – writing a conclusion to your essay.

Some of these tips will contain parts of a student's answer to a particular question, with examiner's comments, to give you an understanding of what examiners are looking for.

This guidance is developed further in Chapter 11, the exam practice chapter, where examiner's tips and comments will enable you to focus on the important aspects of questions and their answers. These examples will also help you avoid simple mistakes and oversights which, every year, result in some otherwise good students failing to gain the highest marks. For additional help, a simplified Paper 3 markscheme is provided on page 225. This should make it easier to understand what examiners are looking for in your answers. The actual Paper 3 IB History markscheme can be found on the IB website.

This book will provide you with the historical knowledge and understanding to help you answer all the specific content bullet points set out in the IB *History Guide*. Also, by the time you have worked through the various exercises, you should have the skills necessary to construct relevant, clear, well-argued and well-supported essays.

Background to the period

To understand developments in the period 1919–39 fully, it is necessary to have some knowledge of the First World War and its immediate impact. The war lasted from 1914 to 1918, and at the time it was the most destructive conflict the world had ever seen. Several factors contributed to the outbreak of the First World War, including a rise in nationalism, and economic and colonial rivalries between the most powerful nations of Europe. These rivalries were accompanied by arms races and secret diplomacy, as countries tried to strengthen their position in Europe and around the world.

By 1914, two major alliances had formed. On one side was the Triple Alliance (Imperial Germany, Austria-Hungary and Italy) and on the other was the Triple Entente ('entente' is French for 'understanding' or 'agreement' and is applied to diplomatic agreements between states). The Triple Entente was made up of Britain, France and Tsarist Russia. In June 1914, a clash of imperial interests and the rise of nationalism in the Balkans (south-eastern Europe) resulted in the assassination of the heir to the Austro-Hungarian throne. Within two months, the countries of the rival alliances were at war.

Revolution and the end of empires

In addition to widespread physical destruction, the First World War also had significant political effects. In particular, the pre-war nationalist tensions led to the break-up of the old Austro-Hungarian (or Habsburg) Empire, and to the emergence of nationalist groups demanding the right to form independent countries.

The Russian Empire also collapsed as revolution spread across the country. Russian soldiers mutinied against the horrors of modern warfare and overthrew the tsar (emperor). After a second revolution in October/November 1917 – led by the communist Bolsheviks – Russia withdrew from the First World War and a revolutionary Marxist government was established. The Bolsheviks called on soldiers and workers in countries around the world to overthrow their governments and end the war. The new Russian government also demanded self-determination (see page 14) for national groups living within the European empires.

The mutiny at the Petrograd garrison during the Bolshevik Revolution in Russia in 1917

The Bolshevik Revolution inspired other revolutionary groups, including soldiers who were disillusioned by the effects of the First World War. They became determined to overthrow the capitalist system which – according to Marxist theories – was responsible for plunging the world into such a destructive conflict. There was a short-lived rebellion in Hungary, but perhaps most significant was the revolution in Germany, which led to the abdication of the German kaiser (emperor) and the emergence of a democratic government. The new German leaders were prepared to sign an armistice (ceasefire) in November 1918, thus ending the war. Later, a democratic constitution for Germany was drawn up in the town of Weimar; as a result, in the period 1919–33 the country was referred to as Weimar Germany.

Post-war problems

As well as causing the break-up of old empires, the war had serious economic consequences for both the victors and the defeated. Countries in Europe used up both human and material resources, gained massive debts, and lost trade to countries such as the USA and Japan. In addition, huge agricultural areas of Europe – in both the west and the east – were destroyed, along with railways, roads and bridges.

As you study the period 1919–39, it is important to remember that both statesmen and the ordinary people of Europe who lived through the First World War were determined to avoid any future conflict. When they met in Paris in 1919–20, therefore, the victorious nations attempted to create peace treaties that would ensure the First World War would be the 'war to end all wars'. Yet, in attempting to deal with so many issues, the peace treaties themselves actually created new problems. This is particularly true of the Treaty of Versailles, which was imposed on the new democratic government of Germany. Such a view of these treaties is not one simply proposed by historians with the benefit of hindsight. Many observers at the time recognised the problems – and warned of a future war.

PEACE AND FUTURE CANNON FODDER

The Tiger : "Curious! I seem to hear a child weeping!"

A British cartoon from 1919 showing the Allied leaders Clemenceau (France), Wilson (USA), Lloyd George (Britain) and Orlando (Italy) after the peace conferences; the cartoon is predicting a new war in 1940

The League of Nations

In order to uphold the terms of the peace treaties and avoid a future conflict, the victorious powers established the League of Nations, of which Britain and France were the most important members. Although the USA refused to become a member, and major European states such as Germany and Russia were not allowed to join at first, the League had a number of successes before 1929. Particularly important were the Locarno Treaty (1925) and the Kellogg–Briand Pact (1928). These agreements attempted to achieve collective security by guaranteeing the borders created by the peace treaties, and by encouraging countries to renounce aggression as a way of settling disagreements.

However, during this period the League faced several challenges. It was often bypassed by the Conference of Ambassadors, which was created to enforce the treaties and intervened directly in disputes. The League's attempts to achieve disarmament ultimately failed and, after the collapse of the US stock market in 1929 and the start of the Great Depression, many states began to adopt more aggressive foreign policies. As a result, the League increasingly failed to maintain collective security in the years 1929–39. Conflicts such as the Japanese invasion of Manchuria in 1931 and Italy's invasion of Abyssinia in 1935 highlighted the weaknesses of the League. By 1939, international diplomacy had collapsed, and the world was plunged into another war.

Terminology and definitions

In order to understand the history of the interwar years, you will need to be familiar with a few basic terms – both technical terms and those relating to political ideologies.

Appeasement

In the context of international diplomacy in the period 1919–39, appeasement refers in particular to the policy adopted by the British prime minister Neville Chamberlain. Using this strategy, Chamberlain hoped to avoid another war through peaceful negotiations with Nazi Germany over changes to parts of the Treaty of Versailles. Linked to appeasement is another term, 'revisionism', which in this context means a willingness to revise parts of the post-war peace treaties.

During the 1920s, politicians in several countries began to argue that the Treaty of Versailles had been too harsh on Germany. Many Germans also felt that the terms were unfair, referring to the treaty as a *diktat* (a 'dictated peace'), which had been imposed on them by the victorious powers. Chamberlain shared this attitude. A series of French governments were less sympathetic towards Germany and more determined to uphold the treaty terms. However, they supported Chamberlain's policy of appeasement, as they knew they could not fight another war without Britain's backing.

Collective security

Collective security refers to attempts by countries to act together in order to stop the use of military aggression as a way of solving problems. The League of Nations tried to ensure collective security through negotiation. If this failed, sanctions would be imposed on aggressor nations. Sanctions are actions taken to put pressure on a country (or individual) to force it to do – or to stop doing – something. For example, economic sanctions might include a trade ban or boycott, especially of vital products such as armaments or coal. In the last resort, there was the option to apply military force.

One aspect of collective security in the interwar years was the attempt to uphold the peace treaties of 1919–20. In particular, France was determined to enforce the demilitarisation of the Rhineland: the German territory to the west of the River Rhine, between France and Germany. The Treaty of Versailles stated that this region, along with a 50-km (30-mile) area of land to the east of the Rhine, should be demilitarised (that is, contain no German military units). Hitler's decision to break this agreement in 1936 – and the failure of Britain and France to take action against him – was, with hindsight, an important factor in the collapse of collective security.

In practice, the League's attempts to uphold collective security were undermined by the fact that several important countries regarded the organisation as a 'club of victors', whose main role was to enforce the unfair terms of the treaties.

Communism

Communism refers to the far-left political ideology associated with Karl Marx and Friedrich Engels, which aimed to overthrow capitalism and replace it with a classless communist society. The first attempt to apply these theories was made by the Bolsheviks in Russia. Under the leadership of Vladimir Ilyich Lenin, the Bolsheviks encouraged workers' uprisings in other parts of Europe and, in 1919, established the organisation Communist International (Comintern) in order to help spread revolution.

The Bolshevik regime was widely feared and hated and, in order to prevent the spread of revolution, other major European states tried to overthrow the Bolsheviks. When this failed, the European powers applied economic and trade embargoes in an attempt to isolate and weaken Russia (known as the Soviet Union, or USSR, after 1924). For many European politicians – even after the Nazis came to power in Germany in 1933 – the communist Soviet Union posed the most serious threat to stability in Europe.

Communism should not be confused with socialism. Although the two ideologies have some common aims, socialism focuses on achieving these aims by peaceful means, such as holding elections.

Fascism

This term is derived from the Italian word *fascio* (plural *fasci*), meaning a group, band, league or union. In 1919, Mussolini applied it to his Fascio di Combattimento ('Fighting' or 'Battle Group'), which was set up to oppose socialists and communists (see page 69). Mussolini later formed the far-right ultra-nationalist Fascist Party. After October 1922, he began to turn Italy into a one-party fascist dictatorship. Other far-right nationalist politicians in interwar Europe tried to follow his lead, including Hitler and the Nazi Party in Germany. The term fascist was then used to describe this political ideology, and all groups holding such views.

Fascism is opposed to liberalism, which is tolerant of different viewpoints and seeks non-violent and democratic solutions. Fascism is particularly opposed to left-wing political groups and tends to act in the interests of capitalist firms, especially the larger ones.

Left wing and right wing

The origin of these terms can be traced back to the French Revolution. In 1792, the most radical political groups (those wanting the most fundamental changes to the system) sat on the left side of the National Convention, while the most conservative groups (those opposed to change) sat on the right. In the centre were moderates, who wanted smaller-scale changes at a gradual pace. Since then, the term 'left wing' has been applied to socialist or communist groups, while 'right wing' has been applied to conservative or fascist groups; the moderate centre are referred to as liberals.

Self-determination

This refers to the idea – defended in particular by US president Woodrow Wilson at the 1919–20 peace negotiations – that national groups should be able to live in independent countries. However, although self-determination was applied to some ethnic and national groups from the former Austro-Hungarian and Russian empires, the claims of others were ignored. For example, German-speakers in Austria and some of the newly created states were not allowed *Anschluss* (union) with Weimar Germany. In some areas, the decision about where such populations should be placed was taken by plebiscites (public referendums on a single issue), organised by the League of Nations.

Successor states

This term refers to the new states in Central and Eastern Europe that were created – or, in Poland's case, re-created – by the post-war peace treaties. Poland had been divided between the pre-1914 German, Austro-Hungarian and Russian empires in the 18th century, and was re-formed after the First World War.

Two totally new states were created: Czechoslovakia (from land formerly part of the Austro-Hungarian Empire) and the Kingdom of Serbs, Croats and Slovenes – later called Yugoslavia. This was established by uniting parts of Austro-Hungarian land with the formerly independent Kingdom of Serbia. In addition, Austria and Hungary became two separate states, with reduced territory. Finland and the Baltic States (Estonia, Latvia and Lithuania) also gained their independence, having previously been part of Tsarist Russia.

Most of these new states were economically and militarily weak, and many had significant minority ethnic groups as part of their populations. These ethnic groups often wanted to be ruled by another country, or felt unfairly treated. Because of their general insecurity, some of these states formed alliances. For example, Czechoslovakia, Yugoslavia and Romania formed the Little Entente in 1920–21.

A map showing the successor states and the main ethnic groups

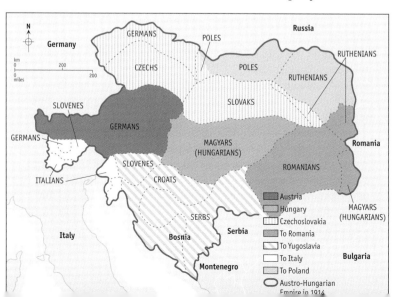

15

The Wall Street Crash

Wall Street was, and still is, the location of the US Stock Exchange, where shares in companies are bought and sold. In October 1929, share prices fell dramatically and investors lost large amounts of money. This collapse – known as the Wall Street Crash – caused a severe economic depression in the USA. As a result of this, the US was forced to end its loans to other countries. Germany was particularly affected by the Wall Street Crash (see Chapter 6), as it relied on US loans to pay the reparations (compensation) imposed on it by the Treaty of Versailles.

Most countries were soon plunged into what became known as the Great Depression. This was a global economic event, resulting in widespread distress – high unemployment, inflation, industrial decline in production and trade, and poverty – in most capitalist countries in the 1930s. (The economic crisis that began in 2008 is regarded as the worst since then.) One impact was to turn many of its victims towards supporting extremist political parties. Another was that during the 1930s, some countries – notably those with fascist or militaristic regimes – increasingly resorted to an aggressive foreign policy to solve their economic problems.

Summary

By the time you have worked through this book, you should be able to:

- understand the main decisions of the peacemakers in 1919–20, and explain the problems associated with the successor states
- understand and account for developments and policies in Weimar Germany between 1919 and 1933, including economic problems, the rise of political extremism, and aspects of foreign policy
- show an awareness of the significance of developments in Italy after 1919, and explain Mussolini's main domestic and foreign policies
- understand the impact of the Great Depression, with special reference to Germany
- understand and explain the significance of the Spanish Civil War of 1936–39, including how it contributed to the eventual outbreak of the Second World War
- understand and explain the main domestic and foreign policy decisions introduced by Hitler in Nazi Germany after 1933
- show a broad understanding of the main actions of the League of Nations in the period 1919–39, and the main diplomatic developments and disputes before the outbreak of the Second World War.

2 Weimar Germany 1919–23

Timeline

1918 **3 Oct:** Prince Max appointed chancellor and asks US for peace terms

3 Nov: Kiel Mutiny; sailors' and soldiers' soviets established

9 Nov: general strike in Berlin; Kaiser Wilhelm II abdicates; Prince Max hands power to SPD leader Friedrich Ebert; republic declared

11 Nov: armistice signed

30 Dec: German Communist Party (KPD) founded

1919 **8 Feb:** National Constituent Assembly meets in Weimar

11 Feb: Ebert becomes president of Weimar Republic

29 Jun: Treaty of Versailles signed

1920 **Mar:** right-wing Kapp *putsch* fails when Berlin workers call a general strike

1921 **Aug:** Centre Party leader Matthias Erzberger assassinated by right-wing extremists

1922 **Jun:** Jewish foreign minister Walther Rathenau assassinated by right-wing extremists

1923 **Jan:** French and Belgian troops invade Ruhr region

Aug: Gustav Stresemann becomes chancellor

Sep: hyperinflation

Nov: unsuccessful Munich *putsch* by Adolf Hitler and Nazi Party; Stresemann's government falls but he remains foreign minister

Key questions

- How did the new government of Germany address the political and constitutional problems it faced in 1918–19?
- To what extent was the country damaged by the Treaty of Versailles in 1919?
- In what ways did economic and financial issues cause problems for the new state?
- What were the political consequences of the economic situation?

In the autumn of 1918, after four years of war, a series of spontaneous revolutionary uprisings ended the rule of the German kaiser, Wilhelm II. He fled, and a new German republic – known from January 1919 as the Weimar Republic – was proclaimed. A strongly democratic constitution was drawn up the same month, with specific emphasis on the German people's rights and freedoms. It seemed that Germany was about to develop into a modern and progressive state.

However, the country's future was not yet assured. The Weimar Republic faced both communist and nationalist political risings and, in an attempt to keep order, the government made a deal with the army. The situation was further complicated by an economy severely weakened by the war, the terms of the Treaty of Versailles, and a French invasion of the Ruhr in 1923. All these factors contributed to a period of hyperinflation. Despite its promising beginnings in 1919, by the end of 1923 the future of the Weimar Republic did not look good.

Overview

- The Weimar Republic arose from the political turmoil that accompanied Germany's defeat in the First World War.
- The republic faced an immediate threat from the left-wing Spartacist movement, which forced moderate left-wing politicians into a dependence on the right-wing élites and the army.
- The Treaty of Versailles created huge problems for the new republic, causing anger and psychological trauma among the German people, as well as territorial losses.
- In the immediate post-war years, Germany suffered economically. The government responded to the economic difficulties by printing more money, but the value of the currency (the mark) declined dramatically.
- The issue of reparations was discussed at the Paris Peace Conferences and a final sum was agreed in April 1921. Having to make these payments to the victorious powers heightened Germany's economic problems.
- After Germany failed to meet its reparations payments, French and Belgian troops invaded the Ruhr in January 1923. Unable to respond militarily, Germany adopted a policy of passive resistance.
- The decline of industrial output in the Ruhr contributed further to Germany's economic difficulties. This led to hyperinflation, which had profound political and social consequences.
- A series of uprisings broke out in late 1923, including the failed Munich *putsch*, led by Adolf Hitler, leader of the National Socialist German Workers' Party (the Nazis).

Philipp Scheidemann proclaims the establishment of the Weimar Republic from the window of the Reichstag building in Berlin on 9 November 1918

How did the new government of Germany address the political and constitutional problems it faced in 1918–19?

The birth of the Weimar Republic

The abdication of Kaiser Wilhelm II, on 9 November 1918, marked the end of Imperial Germany. Although a relatively new European state – established in 1871 when 39 separate German states were united – pre-war Germany was a proud, militaristic empire. It had an elected parliament (the Reichstag), but power really lay with the kaiser and his chancellor. Imperial Germany enjoyed rapid economic growth in the period between 1890 and 1914, and this created an influential working class. This group favoured left-wing socialist policies and tended to vote for the Social Democratic Party (SPD). However, although the SPD had become the largest single political party represented in the Reichstag by 1912, the kaiser's ministers did everything they could to ignore or limit its influence. When war broke out in 1914, a wave of patriotism enabled the Army High Command to advance its own position, and by 1918 the military was running the government almost single-handedly.

The first German revolution

The war proved disastrous for Imperial Germany, and by autumn 1918 all hopes of victory had been abandoned. In an effort to win favourable peace terms and avoid the blame for what seemed like certain defeat, the Army High Command passed power to the civilian authorities on 2 October. Germany was transformed from a regime headed by the kaiser but dominated by the military 'warlords' (as they called themselves) **Paul von Hindenburg** and Erich von Ludendorff, into a parliamentary monarchy with Prince Max von Baden as chancellor.

Paul von Hindenburg (1847–1934) Hindenburg was an army general who was brought out of retirement to lead the German forces in the east in 1914. He was promoted to the rank of field marshal in 1914 and chief of staff of the armed forces in 1916. In this position, he and Ludendorff established a semi-military dictatorship in Germany in the last years of the war. Hindenburg returned to private life in 1918, but was called upon by the political right to run for president in the 1925 election, which he won. He was re-elected in 1932, and his consent was decisive in the appointment of Hitler as chancellor in January 1933. Hindenburg remained president until his death.

This is sometimes referred to as the 'first German revolution'. It was a revolution 'from above', designed to preserve the monarchy by creating a broad political base that allowed parliament to play a major role in government, as it did in other Western parliamentary democracies. However, this arrangement was unlikely to last long because the US president, Woodrow Wilson, refused to negotiate an armistice with a regime that was still headed by the kaiser.

Conditions in Germany were desperate, and the German people needed peace. The economic disruption caused by the war effort and the British blockade of German ports (in place since 1916) had reduced industrial production to around two-fifths and grain production to about half of their pre-war levels. The average German citizen existed on fewer than 1000 calories per day in the last months of 1918. Around 750,000 people died of starvation and malnutrition in the winter of 1918–19, when a flu epidemic added to the misery. Electricity supplies were cut off, public transport stopped operating and businesses were forced to close. The people felt demoralised. Around 2 million German soldiers had been killed and a further 5 million were left wounded or disabled – and it all seemed to have been for nothing.

The second German revolution

The worsening economic situation led to political upheaval. There was a naval mutiny in Kiel on 28 October 1918, when sailors refused to leave port for a final attack on the British navy. They took control of the harbour and raised the red (communist) flag on their ships.

This provoked what historian Geoff Layton has referred to as a 'genuinely revolutionary situation' in November 1918. Workers' and soldiers' councils (or soviets) were established in other ports and towns across Germany. These brought a series of strikes, mutinies and left-wing uprisings inspired by the recent Bolshevik Revolution in Russia (see page 10). In Dresden and Leipzig, these councils promised to arm the workers and establish a socialist society. In Bavaria, an independent socialist republic was proclaimed on 7 November, and in Berlin the Revolutionary Shop Stewards' movement encouraged disillusioned workers to challenge the authorities. This began Germany's second revolution – the 'revolution from below'.

It should be noted that few of the German revolutionaries genuinely wanted a communist-style workers' state. Most were not communists, they simply sought some form of democracy. Many of the councils were influenced by members of the Independent Socialist Democratic Party of Germany (USPD). This group had broken away from the mainstream socialists of the SPD in 1916 because they disapproved of the SPD's support for the war. For example, the leader of the Bavarian Republic, Kurt Eisner, was an independent socialist. According to William Carr, most councils were 'local ad hoc bodies formed by patriotic Germans aiming to maintain services in a time of national crisis'.

Nonetheless, Prince Max of Baden was unable to restore order. Afraid that the circumstances were being exploited by left-wing extremists, and that further uprisings would leave Germany vulnerable to invasion by its enemies, the SPD felt compelled to act. At first, its members tried to persuade Kaiser Wilhelm II (who had fled to Belgium) to abdicate in favour of one of his sons, but the kaiser refused. Therefore, on 9 November 1918, one of the SPD leaders, Philipp Scheidemann, simply went to a window of the Reichstag building and announced to the crowds gathered below that Germany had become a republic.

This decision was probably prompted by rumours that Karl Liebknecht, who led a group of extreme socialists known as Spartacists, was planning to proclaim a 'workers' republic' from a balcony at the Royal Palace in the centre of Berlin. Liebknecht actually did so two hours after Scheidemann's announcement, but – with few genuine revolutionaries among the masses – there was no Bolshevik-style uprising.

Prince Max announced Wilhelm's abdication (before the kaiser had agreed to it) and transferred his political authority to one of the most prominent members of the SPD, **Friedrich Ebert** (see page 22). This made the new political regime seem more formal and legitimate. The kaiser was angered by these events, but when the Army High Command agreed to support Ebert, he realised he was powerless to change the situation. Wilhelm formally abdicated and went into exile. At last the socialists had an opportunity to make a real difference in Germany.

Friedrich Ebert (1871–1925) Ebert was the son of a tailor and began his career as a left-wing journalist. He was elected to the Reichstag in 1912 and became president of the SPD in 1913. Ebert was briefly chancellor after Prince Max resigned in 1918, and was made president of the Council of People's Commissars during the November revolution that year. He negotiated the Ebert–Groener pact with the army to ensure the survival of the parliamentary government, and in doing so he marginalised the revolutionary left. Ebert was elected president of the Weimar Republic by the Reichstag in January 1919. He continued to defend parliamentary democracy until his death in 1925.

Discussion point

Is it always possible to discover the cause of an event? Is it ever possible to conclude that an event does not have a cause?

Activity

Create a spider diagram to show how Germany emerged from its defeat in the First World War. Colour code the political, economic, social and 'other' results of defeat.

The interim government

Ebert formed an interim government consisting of three SPD and three USPD members (the USPD members were led by Hugo Haase) in order to maintain control until elections could be held. This group was known as the Council of People's Commissars, to emphasise its left-wing beliefs and therefore win the support of the workers' and soldiers' councils. However, neither Ebert nor Scheidemann wanted to see a communist revolution in Germany, so Ebert reached an agreement with the right-wing army on 10 November 1918. By the terms of this pact, General Wilhelm Groener agreed to suppress the remaining revolutionary activity in return for a promise that the government would allow the army and its existing officers to maintain their authority.

Ebert has sometimes been accused of betraying his principles by signing a deal with the men who had ruled Germany under the kaiser. However, this move reflected his determination to protect the new republic from illegal protests. Ebert and his colleagues believed in parliamentary democracy, not direct action and campaigns like those of the Spartacists. Ebert probably overestimated the threat posed by extreme left-wing violence, but he seems to have acted in good faith.

In the evening of 10th November, I telephoned the Reich Chancellery and told Ebert that the army put itself at the disposal of the government and that in return for this the Field Marshal, Hindenburg, and the officer corps expected the support of the government in the maintenance of order and discipline in the army. The officer corps expected the government to fight against bolshevism and was ready for the struggle. Ebert accepted my offer of an alliance. From then on we discussed the measures which were necessary every evening on a secret telephone line between the Reich Chancellery and the high command. The alliance proved successful.

General Wilhelm Groener, recalling the pact between the German government and the army. Quoted in McKichan, F. 1992. Germany 1815–1939. Edinburgh, UK. Oliver and Boyd. p. 122.

How useful is Source A for historians studying the Ebert–Groener Pact? Consider its value and limitations.

While an armistice was being signed with the Allies on 11 November 1918, Ebert was negotiating with representatives of major industrial companies, led by Hugo Stinnes, and the trade unions under Carl Legien. On 15 November, they signed the Stinnes–Legien Agreement. By the terms of this agreement, the employers acknowledged that the unions were legal and agreed to introduce an eight-hour day. The unions promised to maintain production, end unofficial strikes and oppose the influence of the workers' councils, which were demanding the nationalisation of industry. An arbitration board was also set up to mediate in future conflicts.

Again, Ebert was accused by both by the Spartacists and members of the USPD of compromising his socialist principles and siding with the industrialists who had supported the kaiser's regime. However, Ebert feared that nationalising industries would only add to Germany's economic problems. He emphasised how significant it was that the employers now officially recognised the trade unions.

Ebert was also criticised for allowing several groups of people to keep their positions despite their often outspoken anti-republican views. These included many civil servants, military officers, judges, policemen, teachers and government officials. Some members of the USPD argued that the government needed to purge society completely before elections were held, but Ebert defended his policy decisions.

SOURCE B

We had to make sure, once we had taken over power, that the Reich machine did not break down. We had to make sure the machine continued to operate so as to be able to maintain our food supplies and the economy. And that was not an easy task. The six of us could not do that alone; we needed the experienced co-operation of the experts. Had we removed the experienced heads of the Reich offices, had we replaced them with people who did not possess the necessary knowledge and experience, then we should have faced failure in a few days.

Extract from a speech given by Friedrich Ebert, 25 November 1925. Quoted in McKichan, F. 1992. Germany 1815–1939. Edinburgh, UK. Oliver and Boyd. p. 125.

Do you agree with the view expressed in Source B? Give a reason for your decision.

Historian A. J. Nicholls has supported Ebert, stating: 'It is certainly clear that socialist experiments could have seriously worsened Germany's already difficult economic situation and might well have led to civil war.' However, Jürgen Tampke has argued against this: 'The SPD should have remembered – in the light of the Empire's pre-war and wartime policies, which aimed at establishing German leadership in Europe – that it would be necessary to crush, or at least severely curtail, the power of the reactionary army establishment and of sections of German industry.'

Keeping the support of the servants of the old empire was clearly more important to Ebert than retaining the loyalty of his USPD colleagues. On 23 December 1918, 1000 sailors broke into the government's headquarters, demanding overdue wages and a pay rise. They held Ebert captive until he gave in to their demands. This led to a fierce exchange between the USPD and SPD over the behaviour of the USPD police chief in Berlin, who had failed to stop the action. The USPD ministers resigned in protest.

 ## Theory of knowledge

History, individuals and determinism

To what extent do you think Ebert was the 'victim of circumstance'? Is this a helpful concept?

The Spartacist uprising

Elections to a new National Assembly were announced for 19 January 1919. However, before the elections could take place the government faced a violent challenge from the Spartacists, who had now renamed themselves the KPD, or German Communist Party. The Spartacists strongly opposed Ebert's moderate approach, and the Spartacist leaders Karl Liebknecht and Rosa Luxemburg wanted power to be given to the workers' councils (although some involved in the uprising, which included USPD members, were less extremist). The problems began when Ebert dismissed the USPD police chief. On 6 January, the Spartacists seized the SPD's newspaper office in Berlin in retaliation.

Fighting broke out on the streets of Berlin between the Spartacists and army units reinforced by the Freikorps, a group made up of recently demobilised soldiers of the former imperial army. These ex-soldiers were strongly opposed to communism, and Ebert called on them to put down the Spartacist rebels. On the orders of the new defence minister, General Noske, the Freikorps brutally crushed the uprising and killed Liebknecht and Luxemburg. By 15 January, the rebellion had ended.

Armed Spartacists in the streets of Berlin during the 1919 uprising; the violent suppression turned the communists into permanent opponents of the SPD, and prevented any future alliance between the two groups against the right-wing threats that later arose

The Spartacist uprising caused a serious division among the socialists. The USPD could not forgive the SPD for allowing some of its members to be killed by the Freikorps. Furthermore, the two men arrested for the murders of Liebknecht and Luxemburg were treated leniently due to a sympathetic right-wing judge – one escaped unpunished and the other served only a few months in prison. Unsurprisingly, the government was accused by some of its own left-wing supporters of condoning violence. However, the uprising also demonstrated the lengths to which the SPD would go to preserve the republic. The high level of support the SPD received in the January elections suggests that most Germans supported Ebert's actions.

The elections resulted in a decisive victory for supporters of the republic, headed by the SPD. However, the new government could not meet in troubled Berlin. Instead, it settled on Weimar, a cultural city with a very different image from that of Berlin. Ebert was elected as the first president of the new 'Weimar Republic' on 11 February 1919 (see election results in Source C on page 33).

In March 1919, the remaining German communists attempted another takeover in Berlin, which was again crushed by the Freikorps and the army. There were also troubles in Bavaria. Here, the USPD-led republic established in November 1918 came to a sudden end when its leader, Kurt Eisner, was shot by a right-wing student in February 1919. In the chaos that followed, the communists established a 'Republic of Workers' Councils', led by Eugen Leviné, including a guard of armed workers. In response, Ebert ordered the army to besiege the Bavarian capital of Munich. With its food supplies running out, and 700 people killed, the city surrendered on 1 May 1919.

A failed revolution?

There has been some historical debate about whether the events of October 1918 to May 1919 can really be referred to as a 'German revolution'. Marxists have suggested that Germany came very close to a true revolution, but others question whether the situation in Germany was really revolutionary, because the transfer of political power in October–November 1918 took place peacefully and the workers' uprisings came to nothing.

Sebastian Haffner has argued that there was no revolution because Ebert was prepared to co-operate with the traditional German élites. However, A. J. Ryder and Rudolf Cooper have suggested a different reason, blaming the workers for not being revolutionary enough in their aims. Modern historians tend not to emphasise the existence of a revolutionary situation, but Tampke condemns Ebert for his failure to seize the opportunity to break fully with the old regime, and claims this made it easier for the Nazis to come to power in the 1930s.

The new constitution

A committee of the Reichstag, led by the left-wing liberal and new secretary of state Hugo Preuss, drew up a new constitution for Germany. There was great debate over whether the country should have a strong central government, as it had in imperial times, or whether it should adopt a federal structure, which would mean power lay with the individual states (*Länder*) in Germany. Preuss preferred the centralised system, but a compromise was agreed. The *Länder* had control of their own police, schools and judges, but the central government controlled taxes and the military. Prussia and Bavaria also lost their monarchies.

The system of government in Weimar Germany

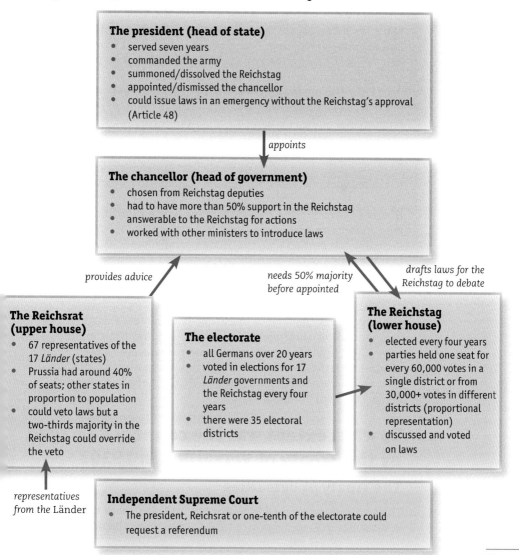

The president (head of state)
- served seven years
- commanded the army
- summoned/dissolved the Reichstag
- appointed/dismissed the chancellor
- could issue laws in an emergency without the Reichstag's approval (Article 48)

appoints

The chancellor (head of government)
- chosen from Reichstag deputies
- had to have more than 50% support in the Reichstag
- answerable to the Reichstag for actions
- worked with other ministers to introduce laws

provides advice

needs 50% majority before appointed

drafts laws for the Reichstag to debate

The Reichsrat (upper house)
- 67 representatives of the 17 *Länder* (states)
- Prussia had around 40% of seats; other states in proportion to population
- could veto laws but a two-thirds majority in the Reichstag could override the veto

The electorate
- all Germans over 20 years
- voted in elections for 17 *Länder* governments and the Reichstag every four years
- there were 35 electoral districts

The Reichstag (lower house)
- elected every four years
- parties held one seat for every 60,000 votes in a single district or from 30,000+ votes in different districts (proportional representation)
- discussed and voted on laws

representatives from the Länder

Independent Supreme Court
- The president, Reichsrat or one-tenth of the electorate could request a referendum

The constitution also laid down the 'fundamental rights and duties of German citizens', outlining individual freedoms (for example, of speech and the right to own property), and giving illegitimate children the same rights as legitimate ones. Other clauses promised the nationalisation of industry and the right of all Germans to 'earn a living through productive work' or to receive a state benefit.

Some historians regard this constitution as fundamentally flawed. Karl Bracher, for example, describes the presidential powers as 'a kind of substitute for the lost absolute monarchy'. Both Bracher and Gordon Craig also criticise proportional representation for several reasons, including the fact that it gave many different parties a place in the Reichstag, thus creating unstable coalition governments. Proportional representation also enhanced the power of the president and allowed extremist parties to win seats. Some historians claim that the division of power between president, chancellor, *Länder* and the centre weakened authority, while Michael Burleigh questions the use of referendums for allowing minority opinions to gain publicity.

However, while Bracher believes that the constitution did not go far enough because it 'preserved powerful elements of the absolutist state including the continuation of anti-democratic forces', Burleigh asserts that the 'spirit' of the constitution was sound – it was simply the way it was put into practice that caused problems. Hans Mommsen also disagrees that proportional representation was a main cause of instability in the new Weimar government, blaming instead the political parties' 'reluctance to assume political responsibility'. The constitution certainly worked reasonably effectively in the early years, when Ebert used his powers wisely, and perhaps even the continuity of administrative personnel was justified by the need for stability. It was a bold experiment and, as a result, Germany had the most democratic constitution in Europe.

To what extent was the country damaged by the Treaty of Versailles in 1919?

The Treaty of Versailles

The armistice was signed in November 1918, and peace talks began at Versailles in Paris in January 1919. Germany and the other defeated powers were not invited to attend the Paris Peace Conferences, and this led the Allies to draw up a treaty that appeared to show little concern for its effects on Germany.

The Fourteen Points

Germany was presented with a draft of the Treaty of Versailles on 7 May 1919, and was given 15 days to respond (actually extended to 21 days). The terms of the treaty came as a shock to the Germans; the armistice had been signed as an agreement between equals, and Germany had fully expected to be treated leniently.

In part, this expectation was based on US president Woodrow Wilson's 'Fourteen Points' – his vision for a new, democratic and peaceful post-war world, drawn up in January 1918. The Fourteen Points held a promise of just treatment for Germany after the war and, having broken with the past and created a new democratic state, the Germans felt they deserved a fair settlement. Instead, the Allies laid all responsibility for the war on Germany and used this to justify harsh terms.

Activity

Find out more about President Wilson's Fourteen Points. Why might they have given hope to the new German government?

Land and military losses

The treaty terms included the loss of German land, notably the regions of Alsace-Lorraine to France, North Schleswig to Denmark, Upper Silesia to Poland and Eupen-Malmédy to Belgium. Of even greater concern was the loss of the 'Polish Corridor', which cut Germany in two and left Eastern Prussia geographically isolated. (See map on page 30.) In addition, all Germany's overseas colonies were taken away.

The treaty also put severe restrictions on Germany's military (which became known as the *Reichswehr*). The army was limited to 100,000 troops and conscription was banned; only six battleships were permitted and Germany was allowed no submarines or air force. The Rhineland – an area of land along the border with France – had to be demilitarised. Germany also had to pay reparations (compensation) to the victorious powers for the cost of the war and post-war reconstruction.

The Germans demanded changes to the draft treaty, but only a few minor amendments were made. The final version was issued on 16 June. Germany was told to accept within seven days or face renewed military action.

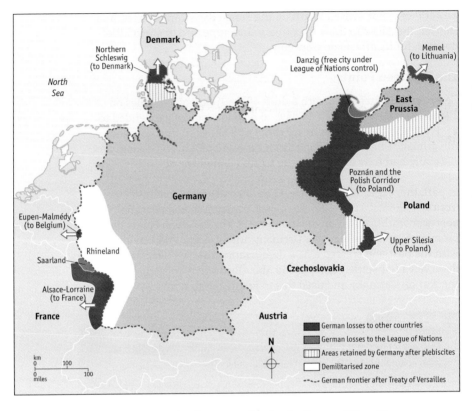

A map showing the land Germany lost by the Treaty of Versailles

Consequences of the treaty

German ministers debated the treaty for days, and the chancellor, Scheidemann, resigned in protest at the terms. However, there was little the government could do. After the German naval commanders at Scapa Flow scuttled (deliberately sank) the German fleet so they would not have to surrender it to the Allies, the attitude of the victorious powers hardened even more. There was little chance of further negotiation. Hindenburg (see page 20) urged the Germans to fight again, arguing that a heroic defeat was preferable to humiliation. However, this was not realistic – Germany could not afford to continue the war.

On 22 June, the day the ultimatum expired, the Reichstag voted to accept the terms by 237 to 138. The news sent shock waves through the country. It seemed that Wilson's Fourteen Points did not apply to Germany. Germany was to be disarmed whilst Britain, France and Italy could maintain whatever forces they wished.

Furthermore, Germany was not allowed to join the newly formed League of Nations (see page 12). 'National self-determination' (see page 14) was forbidden by the treaty. Germany was denied *Anschluss* (union) with Austria and, as the map of Europe was redrawn in the months after the war, many ethnic Germans – former citizens of the Austro-Hungarian Empire – found themselves living outside Germany's national boundaries, notably in the new state of Czechoslovakia and the re-formed country of Poland. The loss of Germany's overseas colonies also conflicted with Wilson's view that there should be 'impartial adjustment of all colonial claims' (Point 5 of the Fourteen Points).

German reactions to the treaty

In Germany, the treaty was regarded as a *diktat* (dictated peace) and it added to the Germans' sense of humiliation and isolation. According to Anthony Wood, 'the fundamental significance of Versailles was emotional rather than rational'. Hostility towards Article 231 of the treaty, the 'War Guilt' clause that blamed Germany for the war, united the enemies of the Weimar Republic.

Hindenburg's 'stab-in-the-back' myth – claiming that Germany had been betrayed by the socialist politicians who had first agreed to the armistice and then to the treaty – proved an effective slogan. Even moderates who had previously supported the republic began to take notice of nationalist and communist propaganda. In addition, the burden of reparations payments had a longer-term impact on Germany, leading to an economic crisis in 1923.

Although the Germans felt that the Treaty of Versailles was harsh, in fact its terms were more lenient than those Germany itself had imposed on Russia in the Treaty of Brest-Litovsk (the peace treaty between Germany and Russia agreed in March 1918). Indeed, German historian Eberhard Kolb has argued that the Treaty of Versailles was *too* lenient because it failed to destroy Germany as a great power. Despite its losses, Germany still had significant industrial assets. Its position in Europe was also potentially stronger in 1919 than it had been in 1914, because of the break-up of the Turkish, Austro-Hungarian and Russian empires. However, as Nicholls wrote: 'The one thing the new republic brought the Germans – peace – had been transformed by a settlement which their newspapers and political leaders all agreed was a form of prolonged slavery. It was not an encouraging start.'

Activity

Use the internet to find out the terms of the Treaty of Brest-Litovsk. Does this make you revise your opinion of the Treaty of Versailles?

The context of the elections of June 1920

The signing of the Treaty of Versailles led to the establishment of the Vaterländische Verbände, a group of right-wing patriotic organisations that used intimidation and violence to persecute public figures.

These groups had their own paramilitary forces made up of ex-soldiers, and they carried out 354 politically motivated assassinations between 1918 and 1922. One victim was USPD politician Hugo Haase, who was shot in front of the Reichstag building in October 1919.

A potentially dangerous right-wing rebellion occurred when the government started disbanding some Freikorps units – in accordance with the treaty – in January 1920. General Walther von Lüttwitz refused to co-operate, and he was supported by the right-wing civil servant, journalist and politician Wolfgang Kapp. On 12 March, they led 12,000 troops into Berlin and there declared a new government. The Weimar government was forced to withdraw to Dresden. When Ebert called on the army to crush the *putsch* (uprising), the army commander Hans von Seekt replied that 'troops do not fire on troops'.

The rising was not very co-ordinated. Bankers and civil servants, traditionally on the right in politics and who therefore might have been expected to support it, chose not to get involved, and some were even hostile towards the rebels. To restore order, the Weimar government called on the workers to begin a strike. This cut off transport, as well as power and water supplies in Berlin, bringing the city to a standstill. The *putsch* collapsed within four days, and the government returned to the capital. However, the episode highlighted the weakness of government authority. The rebels were treated leniently in court – almost all of them went unpunished, and General Lüttwitz was allowed to retire with a full pension.

Later that month, encouraged by the success of the workers' strike in Berlin, communists in the Ruhr region established a 'Red Army' of 50,000 workers. They fought the Freikorps for several weeks before order was restored. Other left-wing rebellions occurred in Halle, Dresden, Saxony and Thuringia.

The June 1920 elections

The first elections under the terms of the new constitution were held against the background of this political unrest. The German people were torn between fear of a communist revolution and hatred towards the politicians who had signed the Treaty of Versailles and who were associated with the violent actions of the Freikorps.

The results of the election showed a move away from the moderate centre-left parties that had dominated the first 18 months of the Weimar Republic. Extreme groups – both left- and right-wing – gained more support than they had previously. Although the pro-republican parties did not have a strong following among the powerful middle class (*Mittelstand*), they remained dominant. The results of the election meant that the SPD was forced to form a coalition government with the right-wing DVP. This showed acceptance of the republic by a centre-right party, but it also added to the political problems – making

SOURCE C

A table of statistics comparing the election results of June 1920 with those of January 1919. The old coalition parties of the SPD, DDP and Centre Party received only 43.5% of the vote (compared to 76.2% in 1919), while the right-wing DNVP increased its share of the vote to 14.9% and the left-wing USPD to 17.9%.

Party	January 1919 election			June 1920 election		
	Total votes	%	Seats	Total votes	%	Seats
SPD	11,509,100	37.9	165	6,104,400	21.6	102
USPD	2,317,300	7.6	22	5,046,800	17.9	84
KPD	–	–	–	589,500	2.1	4
Centre Party (Z)	5,980,200	19.7	91	3,845,000	13.6	64
BVP	–	–	–	1,238,600	4.4	21
DDP	5,641,800	18.6	75	2,333,700	8.3	39
DVP	1,345,600	4.4	19	3,919,400	13.9	65
Wirtschaftspartei	275,100	0.9	4	218,600	0.8	4
DNVP	3,121,500	10.3	44	4,249,100	14.9	71
Other parties	209,700	0.6	3	651,200	2.5	5

Adapted from McKichan, F. 1992. Germany 1815–1939. Edinburgh, UK. Oliver and Boyd. p. 128.

it difficult to reach decisions and provide the stability that Germany needed so badly. There were eight successive governments in the first four years of the republic. These constant changes made people lose confidence in the government, and left it vulnerable to attacks from the right and left extremes.

The main political parties in Germany in 1919–20

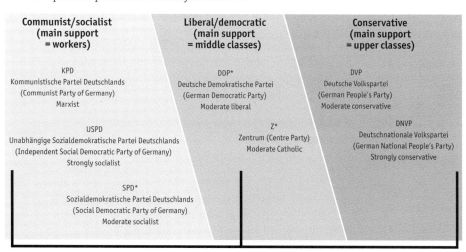

Communist/socialist (main support = workers)	Liberal/democratic (main support = middle classes)	Conservative (main support = upper classes)
KPD Kommunistische Partei Deutschlands (Communist Party of Germany) Marxist	DDP* Deutsche Demokratische Partei (German Democratic Party) Moderate liberal	DVP Deutsche Volkspartei (German People's Party) Moderate conservative
USPD Unabhängige Sozialdemokratische Partei Deutschlands (Independent Social Democratic Party of Germany) Strongly socialist	Z* Zentrum (Centre Party) Moderate Catholic	DNVP Deutschnationale Volkspartei (German National People's Party) Strongly conservative
SPD* Sozialdemokratische Partei Deutschlands (Social Democratic Party of Germany) Moderate socialist		

LEFT WING   CENTRE   RIGHT WING

* pro-republican parties of 1919

Political instability 1920–23

In December 1920, membership of the communist KPD increased dramatically when 400,000 former USPD supporters joined the party. This gave the KPD the confidence to start a new series of rebellions in the spring of 1921. Beginning in Merseburg in Saxony, these rebellions spread to Hamburg and the Ruhr. However, harsh action by the police and army in the Ruhr left 145 people dead.

There were 376 political assassinations between 1919 and 1923, 22 by the left wing and 354 by the right. The right-wing murders included that of the USPD leader, Karl Gareis, in September 1921. Philip Scheidemann narrowly escaped death after acid was thrown in his eyes. Matthias Erzberger, a former finance minister from the Centre Party (Zentrum, Z), who had led the German delegation that signed the armistice and had been present at the signing of the Treaty of Versailles, was assassinated (on the second attempt) by members of a right-wing nationalist league called Organisation Consul.

On 24 June 1922, the Jewish industrialist and DDP foreign minister Walter Rathenau was shot by Organisation Consul. He, too, had participated in the signing of the armistice. Rathenau had also just negotiated the Treaty of Rapallo (setting up trade and secret military links) with communist Russia, despite following a policy of co-operation with the West at the same time.

Fears for the future of the republic led to a new law, the Law for the Protection of the Republic, which increased the penalty for conspiracy to murder. However, many judges simply ignored it. Rathenau's four killers received an average of four years each in prison, and while 326 of the 354 right-wing assassins went unpunished, 10 of the 22 left-wing murderers were sentenced to death.

The last major series of political disturbances came in 1923. There were left-wing uprisings in Thuringia, Saxony and Hamburg in the autumn, and a right-wing *putsch* took place in northern Germany in October. In November, Adolf Hitler led another failed uprising in Munich, in Bavaria (see page 38). Despite this unrest, the Weimar Republic survived, largely by relying on the army. However, the people – particularly the middle classes – lacked faith in their government; it seemed all too often that their republican rulers were barely in control.

Look back through this section and make a two-column chart. On one side list (with dates) disturbances caused by the left wing and how they were addressed. On the other side, list disturbances caused by the right wing and how they were dealt with. What conclusions can you draw from your chart?

In what ways did economic and financial issues cause problems for the new state?

Economic instability 1919–21

Germany emerged from the war in considerable debt. The kaiser's government had financed the war effort by borrowing from other countries, assuming that it would be able to pay back its debts by seizing land and taking reparations from defeated nations after Germany won the war. Germany had also abandoned the link between paper money and its gold reserves in order to put more money into circulation.

The government did not want to raise taxes, so printing more money was simply a way of paying the army and armaments manufacturers. However, the more paper money there was in circulation, the more worthless it became, and this caused serious inflation. By 1919, there were 45,000 million paper marks in circulation compared with 2000 million in 1913. In the same period, the national debt rose from 5000 million to 144,000 million marks. There was no corresponding increase in productivity, so goods were in short supply and this raised prices. By 1919, the mark was worth less than 20% of its pre-war value.

The financial situation in Germany worsened as the terms of the Treaty of Versailles were carried out. Germany lost land in Europe and its colonies overseas, and with them the income this land generated. The coal mines of the Saar were passed to the League of Nations, to be run for the benefit of the French for 15 years, and Germany had to supply free coal to France, Belgium and Italy. In addition, 90% of the German merchant fleet was surrendered to the Allies, which severely limited trading opportunities. Russia had been paying Germany reparations since the Treaty of Brest-Litovsk in 1918, but these now ceased. Instead, in 1921 Germany itself was presented with a huge reparations bill.

Reparations

The issue of how much Germany should pay in reparations caused some disagreement among the Allies at the Paris Peace Conferences. Britain, France and Belgium were anxious to gain money to rebuild their own countries and repay their war loans to the USA.

Furthermore, under considerable pressure from their electorates, both Britain and France argued that Germany should be made to pay for starting the war. France was determined to ensure that Germany should not become a strong and threatening neighbour again. However, some delegates argued that a strong German economy could benefit Europe. Whilst the USA favoured some reparations, the attitude of the US and British representatives was less vengeful than that of the French. Initially, a sum of 20 billion gold marks was demanded. However, discussions continued and in April 1921 a final bill of 132 billion gold marks (£6.6 billion) was decided. Germany had to pay 2 billion marks a year and 26% of the value of any goods it exported.

Historians debate whether Germany's economic problems and the hyperinflation that developed in 1923 were mainly caused by unrealistic reparations demands. Historians such as Louis Snyder believe that reparations were a main reason for Germany's economic crisis. Others, including Geoffrey Layton, claim that the crisis was caused by long-term inefficiencies in the German economy, which were simply made worse by reparations. The British economist John Maynard Keynes referred to a 'policy of reducing Germany to servitude for a generation', while Detlev Peukert, writing in 1991, argued that the reparations – which represented only 2% of Germany's national output – were actually quite manageable.

Germany made its first reparations payment at the end of May 1921. However, by January 1922 the country was in such economic difficulties that the Reparations Commission – the organisation set up to oversee reparations payments – granted a moratorium (postponement) on the January and February instalments. In July, the German government asked for a further suspension of payments, and in November it requested a four-year non-payment period to allow the German currency to stabilise. The Weimar government also asked for a loan of 500 million gold marks. The French were very suspicious of this request, particularly as the Germans had just negotiated the Treaty of Rapallo with Russia, which outlined the basis of economic co-operation between the two countries.

Activity

Were the French right to be suspicious of Germany's request for a loan? Could Germany afford the reparations payments? Using books and the internet, find some more information and statistics on the state of the German economy in 1919–22. Then present a case putting forward your view.

The invasion of the Ruhr 1923

At a conference in Paris on 9 January 1923, the Reparations Commission concluded that Germany had deliberately defaulted on the coal deliveries it was required to make to France and Belgium.

Two days later, French and Belgian troops moved into the Ruhr to seize German coal, steel and manufactured goods as payment.

Historian Ruth Henig states that, as far as the French were concerned, 'if the invasion triggered off an economic crisis or fanned the flames of separatism in the Rhineland or in Bavaria, so much the better. Anything that weakened Germany and thereby contributed to French security in the future was seen as a positive outcome.' By the end of 1923, there were 100,000 French and Belgian troops in the Ruhr area – controlling mines, factories, steelworks and railways. They set up machine-gun posts in the streets and demanded food from local shopkeepers without paying for it.

With a greatly reduced army, Germany was in no position to fight back. Instead, the chancellor ordered a policy of passive resistance. The Germans refused to co-operate with the French authorities in the Ruhr. The Weimar government promised the workers strike payments if they stayed away from the mines, and paramilitaries (civilian soldiers) were sent to the area to blow up railways, sink barges and destroy bridges.

The French forces reacted harshly – shooting people, taking hostages and conducting aggressive house searches. Around 150,000 Germans were forced out of the Ruhr, and 132 were killed in clashes with the French police. The French brought in their own workers, but by May 1923 the mines were producing only one-third of their 1922 levels and overall industrial output in the Ruhr had fallen by 20%.

Hyperinflation

The loss of income from taxes and exports in the Ruhr added to the strain on the Weimar Republic's finances. Further shortages of goods pushed up prices, and the government met the demand for strike pay by printing more money. International confidence in the value of the mark collapsed, leaving Germany to pay for coal imports with its declining reserves of foreign currency.

In January 1922, one US dollar bought 80 marks; a year later, after the occupation of the Ruhr, a dollar was worth 18,000 marks. By the middle of 1923, 4420 billion marks were required in exchange for one dollar. A new chancellor, Gustav Stresemann (see page 47), was appointed in August 1923 and passive resistance in the Ruhr was called off the following month, but hyperinflation continued.

The printing presses could hardly keep up with demand for paper money, which was issued in increasingly large denominations. Workers had to be paid daily – or even twice daily – to keep pace with inflation. Due to the shortage of goods and the worthlessness of paper money, Germans began to trade by bartering (exchanging one type of product or service for another) rather than by using money.

They would get hold of any goods they could find, in the hope that they could exchange them for items that they needed. Some people from the towns and cities went to the countryside to get what they could from the fields. Many employers began to pay their workers 'in kind' (in goods rather than cash).

People who were in debt, had large mortgages or long-term fixed rents, or who were able to negotiate short-term loans, benefited from hyperinflation because they could pay back what they owed in worthless marks. Those with reserves of foreign currencies also did well, while farmers, some shopkeepers and skilled workers could benefit from the high demand for their goods.

However, people with savings, investments, fixed incomes or pensions, and those who relied on welfare benefits, suffered badly. Young people could not find jobs, while elderly pensioners and war widows struggled to survive financially. Those who had bought war bonds (fixed interest-rate loans to the government in wartime) and landlords who relied on rent from their tenants were also badly affected. Unskilled workers fared worst of all. Conditions varied around the country, but everywhere in Germany the economic crisis fuelled resentment and caused uncertainty about the future.

What were the political consequences of the economic situation?

Hyperinflation provoked further political uprisings. This led Ebert to use his emergency powers and issue laws without the approval of the Reichstag. In September 1923, he transferred power from local governments to regional military commanders. He also appointed a new Reich commissioner, forcing out the democratically elected SPD prime minister in Saxony.

The Munich *putsch*

The most notorious of the uprisings that occurred towards the end of 1923 was the attempted *putsch* in Munich, Bavaria, in November. Since the failure of the communist takeover in May 1919, Bavaria had been ruled by a right-wing government, and paramilitary groups with strong nationalist feelings continued to flourish in the region. These groups were outraged by the ending of passive resistance in the Ruhr in September 1923. The state governor, Gustav von Kahr, and commander-in-chief of the Bavarian army, Otto von Lossow, considered marching on Berlin to overthrow the federal government. The attitude of the Bavarian authorities and paramilitary groups encouraged **Adolf Hitler**, the leader of a small right-wing party, to plan a national uprising starting in Bavaria.

Adolf Hitler (1889–1945) Hitler was born in Branau, Austria, and was the son of a customs official. He left school in 1905 and moved to Vienna where, having twice failed to gain a place at the Academy of Arts, he lived as a vagrant. Hitler moved to Bavaria to avoid Austrian military service in 1913, but volunteered for the Bavarian regiment shortly before the outbreak of war in 1914. He was wounded twice during the war and was awarded the Iron Cross for bravery.

In 1919, Hitler was given a post in the army political department in Munich, and shortly afterwards he joined the right-wing German Workers' Party (DAP). The DAP disliked the wealth of the upper classes and was strongly anti-Semitic. It aimed to create a 'classless socialist organisation led only by German leaders'. Hitler helped to re-form the DAP as the National Socialist German Workers' Party (NSDAP, or Nazi Party) and became its chairman in July 1921. Hitler led the unsuccessful *putsch* in Munich in November 1923, but served only a brief term of imprisonment, during which he wrote his book *Mein Kampf* ('My Struggle'). After his release in 1924, he re-launched the Nazi Party.

Hitler tried to win the support of the middle classes, but despite large gains in the 1930 and 1932 elections it was not until January 1933 that he was appointed chancellor, at the head of a minority right-wing coalition. However, the Enabling Act of March 1933 gave his cabinet authority to act without approval of the Reichstag, and this effectively gave Hitler unlimited powers. After the death of Paul von Hindenburg in 1934, Hitler styled himself Führer (leader) of the German Reich and began his dictatorship. His invasion of Poland triggered the Second World War in 1939. Six years later, when it became clear that Germany would not win the war, Hitler committed suicide.

Hitler greets the crowds with a Nazi salute as he arrives at an NSDAP conference in Nuremberg in 1927

Background to the *putsch*

Hitler's single-mindedness and his skills as a public speaker had already helped him turn the small German Workers' Party, formed in September 1919 by Anton Drexler, into the more influential Nazi Party, which had 55,000 members by November 1923. Nazis were anti-democratic and authoritarian in their views, and were united by a sense of loyalty to Germany based on a belief in the superiority of the German race. The Nazis blamed communists and Jews for Germany's problems, and communists were regularly attacked by Nazi paramilitaries (the *Stürmabteilung*, Stormtroopers or SA).

The Nazis won support through carefully organised mass public meetings, with giant posters, banners, flags and the '*Heil Hitler*' salute. The Nazis' policies and beliefs were outlined in a 25-point programme in February 1920, which combined nationalist and socialist ideas. Key themes of the 25-point programme included:

- the abolition of the Treaty of Versailles and the union of Germany and Austria (which was forbidden by the treaty)
- German citizenship only to be granted to those of German blood (Jews were to be excluded)
- *Lebensraum* (more living space for Germans)
- a strong, central German government
- the nationalisation of large industries and businesses
- war profiteering to be made illegal
- large department stores to be divided up and leased to small traders
- a generous provision for old-age pensions.

This wide-ranging message appealed to many Bavarians. It was especially attractive to the lower middle class – merchants and low-ranking civil servants – and unskilled workers, as the Nazis promised to end unemployment.

> Which of the themes in the 25-point programme represent nationalist ideas, and which socialist? Why do you think the Nazis adopted a mix of left- and right-wing policies?

Events of the *putsch*

On 8 November 1923, Hitler and the SA broke into a meeting being held at a beer hall in Munich. The meeting was attended by 2000 right-wing sympathisers, and was being addressed by Lossow, von Kahr and Colonel Hans Ritter von Seisser, the head of the Bavarian state police. Hitler interrupted Kahr's speech and announced the start of a national revolution. He proclaimed the formation of a new government with General Ludendorff as the commander-in-chief. Hitler hoped that the three leaders at the meeting would take action, but he had to force them into a side room and hold them at gunpoint before they agreed to support his *putsch*.

On 9 November, 2000 members of the SA marched through Munich, copying Mussolini's fascist March on Rome the previous year (see page 71). By this time, Lossow (under orders from General von Seeckt) and von Kahr had publicly denounced Hitler's attempt to seize control. The march was halted by armed police. Fourteen Nazis were shot dead, Ludendorff was arrested and Hitler fled. He was captured and arrested two days later, and the army was sent from Berlin to re-establish control of Bavaria.

Hitler's *putsch* had been badly planned and executed. Afterwards, the Nazi Party was banned. Hitler was sentenced to five years in prison (although he only served nine months). The failed uprising ended the Nazis' hopes of bringing down the republic by force. However, it did bring Nazi ideology to national attention and, despite his time in prison, the episode did nothing to weaken Hitler's resolve.

SOURCE D

During his trial for high treason at Munich in April 1924, Hitler was allowed by nationally-minded Bavarian judges to launch a fierce attack on the whole Republican system. He did not attempt to excuse his role in the Munich putsch. On the contrary he glorified it. Hitler appeared as a fearless, honest leader willing to take the consequences for his actions. Hitler was incarcerated at Landsberg. His treatment was generous in the extreme. It was in prison that Hitler dictated *Mein Kampf*, a book which became one of Hitler's main sources of income in the lean years which followed the putsch. The right of the strong to dominate the weak, his violent racism, his fascination with the techniques of mass manipulation and his contempt for the masses themselves all found expression here.

Nicholls, A. J. 2000. *Weimar and the Rise of Hitler.* Basingstoke, UK. Palgrave Macmillan. pp. 144–45.

Conclusion

Hyperinflation severely damaged the Weimar government. The crisis was exploited by both the extreme left and right, and led the president to use his emergency powers. Furthermore, it lost the government the crucial support of the middle classes. Despite all this, there was never a full political collapse in Germany. The left and right wings were both divided within themselves and were therefore too weak to establish a real alternative to the Weimar government, and so it survived.

End of chapter activities

Paper 3 exam practice

Question

To what extent is it true to say that, by 1923, the weaknesses of the Weimar Republic vastly outweighed its strengths?
[20 marks]

Skill focus

Understanding the wording of a question

Examiner's tips

Although it seems almost too obvious to state, the first step in producing a high-scoring essay is to look **closely** at the wording of the question. Every year, students throw away marks by not paying sufficient attention to the demands of the question.

It is therefore important to start by identifying the argument that the question requires you to address, and the **key or 'command' words** in the question. Here, you are being asked to evaluate the strengths and weaknesses of the Weimar Republic by 1923. The argument centres on whether or not the republic would be able to survive. The key words are as follows:

- to what extent...?
- by 1923
- weaknesses
- vastly outweighed
- strengths.

Key words are intended to give you clear instructions about what you need to cover in your essay – hence they are sometimes called 'command' words. If you ignore them you will not score high marks, no matter how precise and accurate your knowledge of the period.

For this question, you will need to take a balanced look at the following aspects of the Weimar Republic:

- **its establishment:** did it have a strong foundation?
- **the constitution:** did this contain more strengths or weaknesses?
- **the attitude of the political parties, the position of the army and the old élites:** did these strengthen or weaken the republic?
- **the Treaty of Versailles:** how significant was this for the Weimar Republic?
- **the reparations issue and the 1923 economic crisis:** was this handled well and what was its legacy?

You will need to decide how each issue – or combination of issues – shows the republic's strengths and weaknesses. It is up to you to decide whether to address the strengths first and weaknesses afterwards in the final essay, or whether to look at themes, analysing the strengths and weaknesses of different aspects of the republic in turn.

Try to consider whether there were more strengths or more weaknesses, and decide whether it is fair to say that the weaknesses 'vastly outweighed' the strengths by 1923. This will form your 'thesis', or view, which you should maintain throughout your answer. However, your essay needs to be structured to show that you understand both sides of the question, and that you can introduce relevant evidence for a variety of possible interpretations, whilst still showing that your view is the most convincing.

Common mistakes

Under exam pressure, a particularly common mistake is to start at the beginning, describing the history of the Weimar Republic and perhaps making a few links to the question, but without explicitly addressing strengths and weaknesses or answering the question 'to what extent…?'

Another common mistake is to write a one-sided essay – for example, to put forward a strong case for the republic's weaknesses, but ignore any strengths it might have shown. You should pay particular attention to the dates in the question. Some candidates ignore these and include information that goes far beyond the end date given, which in this case is 1923.

Remember to refer to the simplified Paper 3 markscheme on page 225.

Activity

In this chapter, the focus is on understanding the question and producing a brief essay plan. Look again at the question, the tips and the simplified markscheme on page 225. Using the information from this chapter, and any other sources of information available to you, draw up an essay plan (perhaps in the form of a two-column chart, with one column for strengths and the other for weaknesses), which has all the necessary information for a well-focused and clearly structured response to the question.

Paper 3 practice questions

1   To what extent is it appropriate to refer to a 'revolution in German government' in the period 1919–23?

2   'It was not the Treaty of Versailles that weakened Germany in the years 1919 to 1923, but the attitude of its own politicians.' To what extent is this a fair representation of the early years of the Weimar Republic?

3   To what extent is it true to say that the Weimar Republic faced a greater challenge from the right than from the left in the years 1919 to 1923?

4   How valid is the view that in the years 1919 to 1923, the Weimar Republic's economic problems were greater than its political problems?

3 Weimar Germany 1924–29

Timeline

1924 Apr: Dawes Plan reorganises reparations

May: general election; 61% vote for republican parties

Dec: moderate parties gain at expense of extremists in general election

1925 Feb: Friedrich Ebert dies

Apr: Paul von Hindenburg elected president

Oct: Locarno conference; Germany accepts its western borders

1926 Apr: Treaty of Berlin with USSR extends Rapallo Treaty of 1922

Sep: Germany joins League of Nations

1927 agricultural prices start to fall

Jul: Unemployment Insurance Law introduced

1928 May: moderate parties make gains in elections

Oct–Dec: employers in the Ruhr lock out workers

1929 Jun: Young Plan eases reparations payments but is widely disliked in Germany

3 Oct: Gustav Stresemann dies

29 Oct: Wall Street crash

Dec: Anti-Young Plan referendum wins 5.8 million votes (14% of voters)

Key questions

- How and with what success did Gustav Stresemann address Germany's domestic problems in the years after 1924?
- What was Stresemann's contribution as foreign minister in this period?
- To what extent was the Weimar Republic politically stable in the years 1924 to 1929?

The years between 1924 and 1929 are sometimes referred to as the 'golden age' of Weimar Germany. The economic situation was eased by the reorganisation of reparations payments (in 1924 and 1929). In 1925, at Locarno in Switzerland, Germany took part in co-operative discussions with its former enemies. The following year, Germany was allowed to join the League of Nations. These factors, along with more stable (and longer-serving) governments and an economic revival that helped to make Berlin a vibrant cultural capital, all created a positive image.

However, beneath the surface very little had changed. Coalition governments still ruled, extremist parties had not gone away, and much of the success of the nation in international affairs depended on a single statesman – Gustav Stresemann – whose motives have been questioned. From April 1925, the republic had a right-wing, conservative president who openly expressed his dislike of democracy, while the revived economy was built on foreign and short-term loans. Stresemann himself commented that Germany was 'dancing on a volcano', and it remains a matter of debate whether the country really enjoyed a 'golden age' at this time.

Overview

- Gustav Stresemann's appointment as chancellor helped turn Germany's fortunes around.
- A new currency was introduced, and the Dawes and Young plans brought a reorganisation of reparations that helped Germany considerably.
- Foreign loans allowed the economy to improve and this resulted in a booming culture, particularly in the capital, Berlin. While many people enjoyed this new cultural lifestyle, there were some who objected to the Americanisation of society and condemned the 'un-German' behaviour of young people.
- The Locarno Pact, agreed in 1925, improved relations with other countries and led to Germany's admittance to the League of Nations in 1926.
- Between 1925 and 1929, there appeared to be greater political stability in Germany, despite continued government changes and the election of Paul von Hindenburg as president.
- However, beneath the surface political problems continued, as the fragile coalition governments experienced internal disagreements.
- Although extremist parties such as the Nazis and the communists lost popularity during this period, they remained a presence, and by 1929 the Nazi Party in particular was becoming a more influential force in Germany.
- Despite the positive developments, by 1929 there were signs of renewed economic, social and political instability. However, there was no suggestion that the Weimar Republic was about to fall.

A painting by Otto Dix, entitled The Big City, which shows some aspects of the freer atmosphere of post-war Berlin, although Dix's paintings usually depicted the brutality of war or satirised corruption in Weimar Germany

How and with what success did Gustav Stresemann address Germany's domestic problems in the years after 1924?

The impact of Stresemann's chancellorship

The appointment of **Gustav Stresemann** as chancellor on 13 August 1923 was a turning point in the development of the Weimar Republic, both politically and economically. Stresemann was the leader of the right-wing German People's Party (DVP) – a group that was bitterly opposed to the Treaty of Versailles and the payment of reparations.

Gustav Stresemann (1878–1929) Stresemann was born into a lower middle-class family in Berlin. He studied economics and became a successful businessman and industrial legal advisor. He was a member of the Liberal Party before and during the First World War, entering the Reichstag in 1907 as its youngest deputy. Stresemann became the leader of the Liberal Party in 1917, but he was also a member of the ultra-nationalist Pan-German League. When the liberals split, Stresemann became co-founder of the conservative DVP in 1918. He was made chancellor in August 1923, at the height of the inflation crisis, and left in November of that year. He was foreign minister of Germany from August 1923 until his death in 1929.

Alarmed by the hyperinflation crisis of 1923, Stresemann agreed to serve as chancellor, a position he held for just 100 days – until his coalition of the Centre Party, SPD and DVP collapsed in November. During this short time Stresemann not only set the Weimar Republic on the path to economic recovery, he also showed that middle-class parties such as the DVP could be more effective serving the republic than opposing it. This established greater political stability.

Stresemann called off the passive resistance in the Ruhr, reduced government expenditure – dismissing many civil servants – and promised to start making reparations payments again. He also appointed the banker-politician **Hjalmar Schacht** as currency commissioner and head of the Reichsbank, the German central bank. In November 1923, Schacht introduced the rentenmark (one rentenmark was worth a trillion old marks) as a temporary new currency. This currency was guaranteed by land and resources rather than by gold, and it was believed to be secure because its supply was limited.

Hjalmar Schacht (1877–1970) Schacht grew up in the USA, but returned to Germany to study economics before beginning a career in banking. From 1916, he was director of the German National Bank, and in 1923 he was appointed Reich currency commissioner. His introduction of the rentenmark halted hyperinflation. Schacht played an important part in the negotiations over the Dawes and Young plans. The Nazis appointed him head of the Reichsbank in 1933 and economics minister in 1934. However, the establishment of Göring's four-year plan in 1936 led to Schacht's removal as economics minister and president of the Reichsbank. He was imprisoned after the July Bomb Plot in 1944, but was cleared at the Nuremberg trials and resumed his banking career.

Schacht also controlled lending rates and introduced new taxes to keep inflation and the exchange rate at reasonable levels. The government stopped offering credit to industry, as this had encouraged speculation and inflation, and gradually stability was re-established. A number of companies went bankrupt in the process (233 in 1923 and more than 6000 in 1924), but this made the economy more efficient and resulted in greater confidence both within Germany and overseas.

The Dawes Plan and economic recovery

Stresemann also wanted to revise the reparations agreement. He was supported in this by the USA, which had a vested interest in Germany's ability to meet these payments. The US had made wartime loans to the Allies, and without reparations these countries – particularly France – were struggling to repay the debts. An American banker, Charles Dawes, led a committee that drew up the Dawes Plan in April 1924.

Although the original reparations sum of 132 billion gold marks (£6.6 billion) stayed the same, the Dawes Plan outlined a sliding scale of payments that Germany would find more manageable. The plan also stated that no action would be taken in the event of non-payment without joint consultation. In order to help Germany begin making payments again, the committee recommended a large US loan worth 800 million marks. In return, the Reichsbank was to be reorganised under Allied supervision and the rentenmark would be replaced by the reichsmark, which was backed by the German gold reserve.

The Dawes Plan was bitterly opposed by right-wing groups, including the DNVP and the Nazi Party, which wanted Germany to stop paying reparations altogether. However, the plan was formally agreed in July 1924, and in August the new reichsmark came into circulation. As a result of these steps, the French withdrew from the Ruhr in 1924–25, and better relations with France were established as Germany began payments once again.

Effects on industry

The plan contributed significantly to the recovery of the German economy. Industrial output had already reached its pre-war level by 1923 (despite the fact that the country was smaller), but from 1924 the economy grew rapidly and exports increased by 40% between 1925 and 1929. Germany received 25.5 billion marks in US loans and other substantial foreign investments between 1924 and 1930, and these were used to boost industry and improve the country's infrastructure.

German manufacturers replaced old machinery (some of which had been handed over as reparations) with new machines. This enabled them to adopt modern production methods and to increase efficiency. New management styles were introduced to German industry, and large manufacturers used American money to buy out smaller firms. Some of them merged assets to form cartels (unions of independent businesses) that could benefit from economies of scale. By 1925, there were around 3000 cartel arrangements, including one covering 90% of Germany's coal and steel production.

The old industrial giants – coal, iron and steel – flourished alongside newer industries such as electricals, chemicals and synthetic materials. The Leuna works near Merseburg began the large-scale production of artificial fertilisers, and the aircraft industry expanded. Although cars were still a luxury item, Daimler-Benz went into partnership in 1926, and two years later BMW began production.

As the inflation rate dropped almost to zero from 1924, and industrial disputes were resolved by a new system of arbitration introduced in October 1923, real wages began to increase and living standards rose. Roads, schools, hospitals and municipal buildings were built with the help of foreign capital, and the gas and electricity services were taken into public ownership and extended. There was also a massive house-building programme using state funds and self-build housing initiatives.

Social improvements

In keeping with the second part of the Weimar Constitution, new welfare schemes were developed and social benefits increased. A new National Insurance Code was launched in 1923, and a single agency was set up to administer social insurance for miners.

A Public Assistance Programme was introduced in 1924, and in 1925 the Accident Insurance Programme was reformed. This was followed by a National Unemployment Insurance Programme in 1927, which extended social insurance to provide relief payments to 17 million workers. Such measures helped raise the standard of living for many factory and industrial workers. The Weimar Republic finally seemed to be bringing prosperity to Germany.

Was there greater economic and social stability?

Although the German economy showed a strong recovery after 1924, its rate of growth was unsteady and by the late 1920s there were signs that the economy was slowing down. For example, in 1926, Germany's balance of trade moved into deficit (the country was importing more than it was exporting). Global economic conditions caused problems for Germany, which relied on exporting goods at a time when world trade was declining. Nonetheless, many other countries experienced greater economic growth rates than Germany (see Source A).

The German historian Kurt Borchhardt has suggested that Germany was living beyond its means. Social welfare benefits, pensions and attempts to compensate those who had lost savings through hyperinflation placed a severe burden on state finances and kept taxes high. The resulting lack of capital, made worse by the controls on the circulation of money, prevented the government from funding industry. Internal investment in the late 1920s was actually below that of the pre-war years, and wages – pushed upwards by powerful trade unions – rose considerably faster than productivity.

SOURCE A

A table of economic performance (where 1913 = 100), comparing Germany with the rest of the world.

	1920	1925
World	93	121
USA	122	148
Germany	59	95
UK	93	86
France	70	114
USSR	13	70
Italy	95	157
Japan	176	222
Sweden	97	113

From Waller, Sally. 2009. *The Development of Germany, 1871–1925.* Cheltenham, UK. Nelson Thornes. p. 139.

Borchhardt blames working-class greed for this 'sick economy'. However, Carl-Ludwig Holtfrerich believes that much of the responsibility lay with the industrialists, whose cartels reduced healthy competition and who relied on government subsidies rather than reinvesting their profits. Whatever the reason, this lack of internal capital made Germany over-dependent on its foreign loans and investments, many of which offered risky terms over a short-term period. Germany was therefore vulnerable to any recession in the world markets and, as Stresemann himself recognised, was living on 'borrowed prosperity'.

Furthermore, the new prosperity did not extend to everyone. The farming community only recovered slowly after 1918, and living standards in rural areas remained well below those of many towns. Although the Reich Resettlement Law of 1919 redistributed large estates among smaller farmers, by 1928 only 3% of small-scale farmers had benefited from the law. As landowners struggled to maintain their traditional lifestyle while prices fell due to worldwide overproduction, they put more pressure on their tenants. By 1927–28, farmers were seeing little return on the cost of running their farms, but they still faced high tax demands, rents or interest payments on mortgages.

The wealthy middle- and upper-class industrialists were also taxed heavily, as the Weimar government needed the income to support its extensive welfare system. These industrialists were angry at the state for favouring the workers. Some employers tried to get the working day increased from eight to ten hours. The cartels that they formed were used to monopolise production, limit competition and keep prices high. Some employers cut wages, and in 1928 employers in the Ruhr locked out 250,000 workers. Although the government resolved the dispute, the event highlighted the extent of the social divide.

Activity

What factors do you think should be taken into account when assessing a country's economic stability? Carry out some additional research and find some statistics to support your own judgement as to whether the Weimar Republic achieved economic stability in the period 1924–29.

A golden age of culture?

Throughout the 1920s, there was a wave of new cultural achievements in Germany. Cultural experimentation was not, of course, exclusive to Germany. Helped by improved methods of communication and a breaking-down of traditional controls, new forms of expression spread across Europe and the USA in the aftermath of the First World War. However, in Germany after 1924, 'modernism' became linked with 'liberty' and the new republican values.

The arts

New media such as radio, gramophones and film made the arts more accessible to the general population, and the government subsidised art exhibitions and sponsored cultural works that often reflected a strong left-wing bias. In the visual arts, George Grosz and Otto Dix used the Expressionist style to depict life in Weimar Germany. The writers Thomas Mann and Hermann Hesse conveyed blunt messages about the decadence of Western society. Readers and audiences were invited to challenge established ideas. Erich Maria Remarque's *All Quiet on the Western Front*, for example, questioned whether war was the heroic enterprise it had previously been depicted as.

Bertolt Brecht wrote plays such as *Mother Courage*, which encouraged sympathy for ordinary people. With the musician Kurt Weil, Brecht also produced the *Threepenny Opera* – a satirical look at contemporary Weimar society. Paul Hindemith introduced new musical forms, while Arnold Schoenberg and his pupils Anton von Webern and Alban Berg challenged musical convention. In architecture, the Bauhaus movement developed by Walter Gropius made use of ordinary geometric designs and emphasised the functionality of buildings.

Activity

Choose one area of Weimar culture – such as art, music, literature or architecture – and carry out some further research into it. How new was it and how did it reflect the republic's political values?

Popular culture

A new youth culture reflected the Americanisation of society, with its chewing gum, cigarettes, fashions and cropped hairstyles for women. Spectator sports, dance halls and Hollywood films, with stars such as Marlene Dietrich, became popular. Berlin was filled with nightclubs and cabarets with a more accepting climate for same-sex couples, naked dancing and women's boxing.

Reactions to the new society

For some, this tide of cultural experimentation was exciting and liberating. For others, it was a sign of the decline of a once-great nation. The Centre Party and right-wing nationalist groups campaigned against 'tides of filth', and in 1926 the Reichstag passed a law to 'protect youth from pulp fiction and pornography'. Grosz was fined for 'defaming the military' and state governments imposed their own forms of censorship.

Groups were formed to campaign against female emancipation, nudism, same-sex relations and Americanisation. The Nazis, exploiting Jewish involvement in the arts, argued against 'un-German' behaviour, and disrupted theatre performances and exhibitions. The views of the pessimists were reinforced by books such as Oswald Spengler's *Decline of the West* (first published in 1918 and reissued in 1923), which depicted democracy as the type of government of a declining civilisation. Spengler argued that only an 'élite of heroes' could save nations.

What was Stresemann's contribution as foreign minister in this period?

The Locarno Treaty 1925

One of Stresemann's greatest triumphs was persuading the Western European allies to meet with Germany at Locarno in Switzerland in October 1925, in an effort to improve relations. Stresemann wanted to prevent France and Britain from forming an anti-German alliance, since the French were beginning to feel threatened by Germany's industrial recovery. The USA also attended the Locarno conference, although the USSR did not. The outcome of the meeting was the Rhineland Pact and a number of arbitration treaties (often known collectively as the Locarno Treaty or Pact) which were finally signed in London on 1 December 1925.

THE CLASP OF FRIENDSHIP (FRENCH VERSION).

A cartoon commenting on the Locarno Treaty (or Pact), published in the British newspaper The Star *in 1925*

The Rhineland Pact confirmed Germany's acceptance of its western border, as agreed at Versailles, with the loss of Alsace-Lorraine to France and Eupen-Malmédy to Belgium. These borders were 'internationally guaranteed' by Britain, Italy, Belgium and France, which meant that Britain would come to France's aid if Germany attacked. It also meant that Germany would never face another Ruhr invasion. In addition, the French promised to withdraw troops from the Rhineland, which had been stationed there to enforce the Versailles treaty terms. (In fact, full withdrawal from the Rhineland was not completed for another five years.)

The arbitration treaties included Poland and Czechoslovakia, and gave some guarantees that any disputes in the east would be settled by committee. However, the eastern borders were not guaranteed in the same way as the western ones. The treaties were a triumph of diplomacy by Stresemann, but they left the new Eastern European states feeling very vulnerable.

At Locarno, Stresemann established Germany's position as an equal partner with France and Britain, with very little loss to Germany itself. He impressed the European allies with his emphasis on European co-operation, and his reputation soared.

SOURCE B

I should like to express my deep gratitude for what you said about the necessity of cooperation of all peoples – and especially of those peoples who have suffered so much in the past. This Europe of ours has made such vast sacrifices in the Great War, and yet it is faced with losing, through the effects of the Great War, the position to which it is entitled by tradition and development. We are bound to one another by a single and common fate. If we go down, we go down together; if we are to reach the heights, we do so, not by conflict, but by common effort. For this reason, if we believe at all in the future of our peoples, we ought not to live in disunity and enmity, we must join hands in common labour.

Gustav Stresemann to the French foreign minister, Pierre Laval. Quoted in McKichan, F. 1992. Germany 1815–1939. Edinburgh, UK. Oliver and Boyd. p. 140.

What are the value and limitations of Source B for a historian studying the influences on Stresemann's foreign policy?

Further diplomatic successes

In recognition of Stresemann's work towards international peace, Germany was admitted to the League of Nations and made a permanent member of the Council in September 1926. Stresemann himself was awarded the Nobel Peace Prize the same year for his contribution to the 'Spirit of Locarno'. However, Stresemann used the League of Nations as a platform from which to air Germany's grievances – for example, the ethnic Germans who were living under foreign rule and the failure of other nations to match German disarmament.

In 1926, Stresemann also renewed Germany's ties with USSR, first forged by Walther Rathenau in the 1922 Treaty of Rapallo (see page 34). The benefits of developing trade and military links with the USSR were obvious, and Stresemann did not want to risk losing these by making the Soviets feel that the Locarno Treaty was directed against them. In April 1926, therefore, he negotiated the Treaty of Berlin to reassure the USSR that Germany remained committed to good relations. This treaty also helped Stresemann win the trust of the German army, which had avoided the disarmament clauses of the Treaty of Versailles by conducting military training on Russian soil.

Under Stresemann, Germany took on a far more influential international role. A further example of this is the 1928 Kellogg–Briand Pact (see page 192), which condemned military action as a way of solving international disputes. Stresemann signed this pact on Germany's behalf, along with 64 other states.

The Young Plan

In February 1929, Stresemann achieved another success when he persuaded the USA to re-examine the reparations issue. The Young Plan – named after Owen Young, chairman of the committee that investigated the issue – of August 1929 reduced the total reparations sum from 132 billion marks to 37 billion. This meant much-reduced annual payments. The plan also included a 59-year payback period, the end of Allied supervision of German banking, and provision for any disputes to be settled at the International Court of Justice at The Hague.

The right wing objected to Germany paying any reparations at all, and opposed even the reduced sum agreed by the Young Plan. Nationalist groups led by Alfred Hugenburg of the DNVP forced a referendum on the issue, losing with only 14% of the votes. Hitler – whose Nazi Party had been re-formed and reorganised after his release from prison – made passionate speeches against the Young Plan, and became a household name.

Stresemann: an assessment

Stresemann died in October 1929, at the age of just 51. Almost immediately his achievements, strategies and plans began to be questioned. Although Stresemann encouraged European co-operation, his long-term aim was for the Treaty of Versailles to be revised. Even while he was negotiating the Locarno Treaty in September 1925, he wrote a letter to the ex-crown prince of Germany, in which he spoke of the 'three great tasks' that confronted the country: a solution to the reparations problem; the 'protection' of the 10–12 million Germans living under a 'foreign yoke'; and the 'readjustment' of Germany's eastern frontiers. Indeed, the aims Stresemann outlined in this letter are not very different from those that Hitler openly expressed.

Some historians, such as Jonathan Wright, regard Stresemann as a hypocrite who secured European trust, US money and protection from French invasion, in order to leave open the opportunity for a revision of Germany's eastern borders. However, not all historians see Stresemann's actions as hypocritical. A. J. Nicholls, for example, wrote: 'It is unlikely that the French or British politicians really imagined Stresemann had changed [from his nationalist views]. They knew the German foreign minister was a tough negotiator, well able to defend the interests of his country.'

Discussion point

Stresemann's motivation and actions are the subject of continuing historical debate. Is it possible for historians to discover the truth about individuals' motivation?

To what extent was the Weimar Republic politically stable in the years 1924 to 1929?

Political developments

There appeared to be much greater political stability in the period from 1924 to 1929. More than 50% of people voted for the republican parties (the SPD, DDP, DVP/BVP and Centre Party) in May 1924, and that percentage rose to nearly 60% in a second election in December 1924.

The extremist vote declined – in May, the Nazis polled 6.5% of the vote, but in December their vote fell to just 3%. The communist KPD saw their percentage of votes fall from 12.6% to 9% in the same few months.

Furthermore, from 1925 the nationalist DNVP chose to work with the republicans rather than against them, which meant that in the elections of May 1928 there was a 72.6% vote in favour of pro-republican parties. Although there continued to be a high turnover of governments, with six different coalitions between November 1923 and June 1928, the state appeared to be functioning as the authors of the constitution had hoped.

SOURCE C

A table of statistics comparing the election results of May and December 1924 and May 1928.

Party	May 1924 election			December 1924 election			May 1928 election		
	Total votes	%	Seats	Total votes	%	Seats	Total votes	%	Seats
SPD	6,008,900	20.5	100	7,881,000	26.0	131	9,153,000	29.8	153
KPD	3,693,300	12.6	62	2,709,100	9.0	45	3,264,800	10.6	54
Centre Party (Z)	3,914,400	13.4	65	4,118,900	13.6	69	3,712,200	12.1	62
BVP	946,700	3.2	16	1,134,000	3.7	19	945,600	3.0	16
DDP	1,655,100	5.7	28	1,919,800	6.3	32	1,505,700	4.9	25
DVP	2,964,400	9.2	45	3,049,100	10.1	51	2,679,700	8.7	45
Wirtschaftspartei	692,600	2.4	10	1,005,400	3.3	17	1,397,100	4.5	23
DNVP	5,696,500	19.5	95	6,205,800	20.5	103	4,381,600	14.2	73
NSDAP	1,918,300	6.5	32	907,300	3.0	14	810,100	2.6	12
Other parties	2,059,700	7.0	19	1,389,700	4.5	12	2,903,500	9.6	28

Adapted from Eddy, S. and Lancaster, T. 2004. Germany 1866–1945. London, UK. Causeway Press. p. 89.

Activity

Create a diagram to show the different ways in which the Weimar Republic recovered after 1923. Under each heading, give at least one reason why that recovery was not complete.

Further evidence of growing support for the republic came from the success of the Reichsbanner, a state defence force established in 1924. Its rallies honouring the flag and the constitution helped to spread a sense of national pride. Some of those from the old right-wing military associations joined, and within a year of its formation the Reichsbanner had over 1 million members.

Widespread revulsion at Rathenau's murder (see page 34), along with economic improvements, resulted in less political rioting. After 1924, there were no more attempted coups or assassinations and the number of right-wing paramilitaries declined. Prussia felt secure enough to lift the speaking ban that it had placed on Hitler in 1928, and the same year even the DNVP voted to renew a 1922 law that banned the former kaiser from ever returning to Germany.

Also in 1928, a 'grand coalition' was formed under the SPD leader **Hermann Müller**, bringing together the SPD, Centre Party, DVP, BVP and DDP. These parties seemed to have found something in common, and Müller's cabinet remained in office for nearly two years – longer than almost any other government in the Weimar period.

Hermann Müller (1876–1931) Müller joined the SPD in 1893. He was elected to the party leadership in 1906 and to the Reichstag in 1916. He was on the right of the party, and co-operated with the kaiser's government during the First World War. Müller was appointed foreign minister in 1919 and was one of the men who signed the Treaty of Versailles. He remained the chairman of the SPD throughout 1919–27 and was chancellor twice (March–June 1920 and 1928–30). Müller faced internal divisions in his later ministry, and his government eventually fell after disagreements about the unemployment benefit system during the economic crisis. This effectively marked the end of parliamentary government in Weimar Germany.

einen Beſſern findſt du nicht

Significantly, after Friedrich Ebert died in February 1925, there was a smooth transition to a new president. The constitution stated that unless a candidate received more than 50% of the vote in the first round of presidential elections then a second ballot had to be held. After the first vote, on 29 March, no clear winner emerged, so a second vote was taken on 26 April. At this point, Field Marshal Paul von Hindenburg chose to stand for the right. Wilhelm Marx (Centre Party) and Ernst Thälmann (KPD) stood against him, but because the left-wing vote was split between these two, Hindenburg won with 48.3% of the vote (Marx took 45.3% and Thälmann just 6.4%).

A poster for Paul von Hindenburg during the second round of the presidential election in 1925; it reads 'You won't find better'

Hindenburg was a widely respected conservative monarchist, and in many ways his election encouraged the political right to accept the republic. Hindenburg has been described as an *Ersatzkaiser* (kaiser substitute), who helped give the republic respectability and was, according to Geoff Layton, 'absolutely loyal to his constitutional responsibilities and carried out his presidential duties with absolute correctness'. However, Hindenburg had little understanding of economic matters, and he did not like the cultural innovation of the Weimar years. According to Sebastian Haffner, the right regarded Hindenburg's presidency 'not as the stabiliser of the republic, but as the transition to monarchy'.

In fact, the situation in Germany was not as politically stable as it appeared to be, and the coalitions of 1924–29 were fragile. This was partly caused by a drop in support for liberal/centre parties, such as the DDP and the DVP, and a rise in 'sectional interest' parties that split the moderate centre vote. An example of a sectional interest group was the Reich Party for People's Rights and Revaluation, which represented people who sought compensation after the hyperinflation crisis.

Without central support, the majority SPD remained in opposition until 1928. Gordon Craig believes that the SPD leadership acted foolishly and John Hiden considers their choice to remain out of government 'a serious mistake'. The result was a series of coalitions that struggled to work together. Those made up of the right-of-centre parties agreed on domestic issues but not on foreign affairs, while those of the centre-left shared a common foreign policy but had different domestic agenda. Detlev Peukert argues that this loss of a centre seriously weakened the republican administrations.

The Centre Party, which might have been a stabilising force, was weakened by a split between its left and right wings, while the DDP, DVP and DNVP all adopted a more right-wing position in the second half of the 1920s. According to William Carr, 'it was little short of tragic that precisely when the more moderate German nationalists [of the DNVP] were starting to play a constructive political role, the forces of reaction should have triumphed in the party'. Cabinets fell on quite minor issues, such as a heated debate over the new German flag. Few parties were willing to compromise, and even when the Grand Coalition was formed in 1928, there was still disagreement between the SPD and right-wing liberals.

Although extremist groups did not do well in the elections, they remained a presence on the political stage. The Nazi Party began to expand into a national organisation, with local branches, youth and other groups in addition to a well-trained SA (see page 40). Most importantly, the Nazis worked to increase support in the countryside, among farmers who had grown disillusioned with Weimar democracy.

The communists also kept a relatively strong following in working-class areas. Violence occasionally broke out between these extremist groups: the communist Red Fighting League was created in July 1924 and clashed in the streets with the Nazi SA.

The Nazi Party after the Munich *putsch*

The re-founding of the party, 1925	The *Führerprinzip*
• Although officially banned, the Nazi Party was unofficially led by Alfred Rosenberg while Hitler was in prison. • The Nazis fought their first elections in May 1924 and won 32 seats, but in the December elections they only took 14 seats. • When Hitler was released in December 1924, the party was in disarray. • Hitler was banned from political activity and not allowed to make public speeches (March 1925–March 1927). He could only speak at party gatherings. • The ban on the Nazi Party was lifted in January 1925. • On 26 February 1925, the NSDAP was officially re-founded.	• Hitler established his supreme power over the party – the *Führerprinzip*. • In 1924, the SA (stormtroopers led by Ernst Röhm) adopted the 'brownshirt' uniform with a swastika armband. They used passive aggression to provoke communist opponents and then posed as authority figures restoring order. Numbers grew steadily. • Hitler designed the Nazi flag (a swastika on red and white background) and insisted on the Nazi salute. • On 14 February 1926, Hitler called the Bamburg Conference to rewrite the Nazi programme and reassert his authority. He spoke for five hours, ending previous attempts to develop the party along socialist lines. **Joseph Goebbels** supported Hitler. • From November 1927, the party worked hard to win support from the lower middle class.
Reorganisation	Preparing for office
• A new party structure was established, controlled by Hitler from Munich. Germany was divided into *Gaue* (regions) – each *Gau* had a *Gauleiter*, or leader. • In 1928, the *Gaue* were reorganised to match the Reichstag electoral districts. These regions were divided into units. • Associated organisations for young people, women, students and different professions were established; a Welfare Organisation set up soup kitchens for the needy. • Activists were recruited to carry out door-to-door campaigns, issue pamphlets, posters and leaflets, and address meetings.	• Annual rallies (in Weimar in 1926 and in Nuremberg from 1927 onwards) were stage-managed to impress spectators. • Funds were gained from members through meetings and donations, and from some industrialists, notably the Thyssen family. • The Nazis had a disappointing result in the 1928 election (12 seats), while Hitler was still re-establishing his control. • In 1929, the Nazis backed Alfred Hugenberg's Anti-Young campaign, which enabled them to exploit his media empire for publicity. Goebbels was made responsible for Nazi propaganda. • **Heinrich Himmler** was given responsibility for developing an élite bodyguard for Hitler – the SS (*Schutzstaffel*).

Joseph Goebbels (1897–1945) After graduating from university with a doctorate in 1921, Goebbels joined the Nazis in 1924. He edited a Nazi newspaper and, at first, was part of the more radical wing of the party. He was appointed *Gauleiter* of Berlin in 1926, in return for his loyalty, and in 1929 he became director of Nazi propaganda. Goebbels was elected to the Reichstag in 1933 and was appointed minister for popular enlightenment and propaganda. He exercised huge control over Germany's mass media, which increased during the Second World War. Goebbels committed suicide in 1945.

Heinrich Himmler (1900–45) Himmler joined the Nazi Party in 1923 and took part in the Munich *putsch*. In 1929, Himmler was chosen to develop a unit to act as Hitler's personal bodyguard – the SS. He became a Reichstag deputy in 1930 and he built up the SS and his own political authority so that by the end of 1933, he was commander of the political police in all states except Prussia. Himmler helped organise the Night of the Long Knives in 1934 (see page 160), and later took control of the Gestapo and Prussian police. In 1936, he became Reichsführer SS, and his SS Death's Head Units ran the concentration and extermination camps. Himmler committed suicide at the end of the war.

Conclusion

The commitment to democracy in Weimar Germany was, in reality, not much greater after 1924 than it had been before. The right-wing élites continued to exert a dominant influence, and proposals for reform of the state came to nothing. There was little public sympathy for the politicians and their endless manoeuvrings. Hyperinflation caused great resentment among the middle classes, the industrialists complained about the taxes needed to pay for welfare, the army sought to maintain its independent status, and the aristocracy and élites did what they could to undermine the republic and retain their power and influence.

No one going to the polls in 1928 would have predicted that the Nazi Party, which received just 2.6% of the vote and gained 12 Reichstag seats, would become the ruling party of Germany in less than five years. Certainly all was not well within the republic, and large sections of the population were still not true supporters of democracy. However, it was not disillusionment and political disagreement that eventually destroyed the Weimar Republic – it was the worst economic crisis of the 20th century that brought down democracy in Germany.

 ## Theory of knowledge

History, causation and bias
When studying history, you are often asked your thoughts about the causes or consequences of an issue or event. Where do your thoughts come from? Can they ever be free from prejudice?

End of chapter activities

Paper 3 exam practice

Question

To what extent do the years between 1924 and 1929 deserve to be called the 'golden age' of the Weimar Republic?
[20 marks]

Skill focus

Planning an essay

Examiner's tips

As discussed in Chapter 2, the first stage of planning an answer to a question is to think carefully about the wording of the question, so that you know what is required and what you need to focus on. Once you have done this, you can move on to the other important considerations:

- Decide your **main argument/theme/approach before** you start to write. This will help you identify the key points you want to make. For example, this question clearly invites you to make a judgement about the so-called 'golden years' of 1924–29, weighing up positive and negative views. You will need to demonstrate your understanding of the 'golden age', and decide on an approach that helps you produce an argument that is clear, coherent and logical, showing whether the term is a good description of this period, whether it gives a false impression or whether you could offer a better description.

- Plan the **structure of your argument** – i.e. the introduction, the main body of the essay (in which you present precise evidence to support your arguments) and your concluding paragraph.

For this question, whatever overall view you have about the period 1924–29, you should try to make a **balanced** argument. You will need to look at the positives – the economic recovery, the revival of Weimar culture, Germany's improved international position and the greater political stability that seemed evident at this time. However, you will also need to consider the factors that made this period less 'golden' – the limitations to economic growth, the social division that arose from cultural experimentation, the risks of Stresemann's foreign policy and the weaknesses of the political structure. In order to assess the years 1924 to 1929 as a discrete period, you may also want to refer to how the situation compared with the republic before these years.

How much time you devote to each side will very much depend on your opinion, but you should plan to develop your ideas fully, while still allowing time to consider – even if only to dismiss – the alternatives. Although you could consider the positives first and limitations afterwards, a more sophisticated answer would adopt a thematic approach.

In any question, you should try to **link** the points you make in your paragraphs, both to the question and to the preceding paragraph, so that there is a clear thread that develops naturally, leading to your conclusion. Linking words and ideas help to ensure that your essay is not just a series of unconnected paragraphs.

You may well find that drawing up a spider diagram or mind map helps you with your essay planning. For this question, your spider diagram might look this:

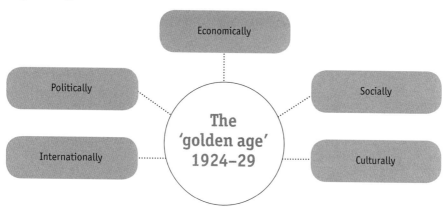

In each 'bubble' you will need to note the positive and negative signs in the relevant area.

When writing your essay, include **linking phrases** to ensure that each smaller 'bubble' paragraph is linked to the 'main bubble' (the question). For example:

Economically, the recovery experienced in these years was, at best, built on shaky foundations …

However, the economic situation was strong compared with the weaknesses in the political structure …

Similarly, Germany's position internationally looked impressive, but this hid a country still suffering from the impact of the Treaty of Versailles …

In addition, there were deep social divisions and resentments …

There are clearly many factors to consider, which will be difficult under the time constraints of the exam. Producing a plan with brief details (such as dates, views and main supporting evidence) under each heading will help you cover the main issues in the time available. Your plan should enable you to keep your essay balanced, so that you do not spend too long on any one aspect. It should also ensure you remain focused on the question and do not wander off into narrative description.

Common mistake

It is very easy to look at questions and adopt a one-sided view in response to them – 'yes, this was a golden age' or 'no it wasn't'. However, a more sophisticated answer might identify the term 'golden age' as appropriate to some areas but not to others. Linking different arguments can be difficult, but it is a good way of achieving the highest marks. Always consider the **full demands** of a question before you begin, and remember – your plan will help you to develop a convincing answer.

Activity

In this chapter, the focus is on planning answers. Using the information from this chapter and any other sources of information available to you, produce essay plans – using spider diagrams or mind maps – with all the necessary headings (and brief details) for well-focused and clearly structured responses to **at least two** of the following Paper 3 practice questions.

Remember to refer to the simplified Paper 3 markscheme on page 225.

Paper 3 practice questions

1 To what extent did the political and economic developments between 1924 and 1929 make the Weimar Republic more stable?

2 In the years 1924 to 1929, how successful was Gustav Stresemann in dealing with problems within Germany resulting from the Treaty of Versailles?

3 'An outstanding achievement' or 'a fundamental cause of weakness'? Which is the more convincing verdict on the welfare reforms in Weimar Germany between 1924 and 1929?

4 Analyse the reasons for the survival of the Weimar Republic in the years 1919 to 1929.

4 Italy and Mussolini

Key questions

- How did Mussolini establish his fascist dictatorship?
- What were Mussolini's main economic and social policies?
- How successful was Mussolini's foreign policy?

In October 1922, Mussolini became prime minister of Italy – and the first fascist ruler in Europe in the interwar years. He soon began to increase his powers and, after 1924, to create a fascist dictatorship. Despite promises to end class conflict and improve life for all Italians, his 'corporate state' mainly benefited the wealthier classes, while independent trade unions and strikes were banned. During the Great Depression of the 1930s, Mussolini's economic policies proved increasingly unsuccessful. He tried to widen support for fascism in a variety of ways – but, as with his economic policies, these measures had limited success. His foreign policy was based on the idea of recreating the old Roman Empire, and eventually brought about his downfall.

Overview

- In October 1922, following the fascist March on Rome, Mussolini was appointed prime minister of a coalition government in Italy. He immediately began moves to increase his power.
- After the 1924 general election and the murder of the socialist leader Giacomo Matteotti, Mussolini took steps towards establishing a fascist dictatorship. These included banning all opposition parties. In 1926, he began the creation of what he called the 'corporate state'.
- As well as launching a series of 'battles' to deal with some of Italy's economic and social problems, Mussolini increased support for fascism by making agreements with the Catholic Church in 1929.
- Before the onset of the Great Depression, Mussolini's foreign policy was mainly peaceful. He was initially concerned about Hitler's intentions when the Nazis came to power in Germany in the 1930s, and so Italy formed the Stresa Front with Britain and France.
- However, after Mussolini's invasion of Abyssinia, this agreement broke down. From then on, the Italian leader moved closer to Nazi Germany. In 1936, Italy and Germany formed the Rome–Berlin Axis; in 1939, they agreed the Pact of Steel.
- Despite this, Mussolini kept his country neutral when the Second World War began in September 1939. Italy only joined the war in 1940, when Mussolini became convinced that Germany would defeat Britain.

How did Mussolini establish his fascist dictatorship?

Benito Mussolini did not begin to form his Fascist Party until 1919, yet in October 1922 he became prime minister. The reasons for Mussolini's rapid rise to power – and for the policies he adopted after 1922 – can be found in the social and political situation in Italy during this three-year period.

Mussolini (centre) and his ministers meeting with Catholic leaders at the Vatican in 1932

What can you learn from this photograph about the attitude of Roman Catholic Church leaders towards fascism?

Benito Mussolini (1883–1945) At first a socialist, Mussolini abandoned his early beliefs during the First World War. He supported Italy's involvement in the war, and soon his political leanings moved towards a far-right ultra-nationalism that was violently opposed to socialism and communism. From 1919 to 1921, Mussolini formed Europe's first Fascist Party and was soon established as dictator of Italy. He remained in power until his execution in 1945, towards the end of the Second World War.

Mussolini's rise to power 1919–22

Before the First World War, Italy experienced many problems. These included a franchise (right to vote) that was still severely restricted: it was only in 1912 that all men were given the right to vote. In addition, the system known as *trasformismo*, by which liberal groups dominated the political system, undermined support for parliamentary politics. At the same time, economic and social divisions – especially between the more prosperous industrial north and the poorer agricultural south – resulted in significant disunity. One result of these problems was increasing opposition from a growing socialist movement.

By 1914, Italy was divided between nationalists who wanted an aggressive and expansionist foreign policy, and those who wanted their country to remain neutral. These problems were made worse by Italy's entry into the First World War in 1915. The high casualties resulting from the war, the subsequent inflation, and Italy's limited territorial gains from the peace settlements of 1919–20, led to increased tensions after 1919.

For these reasons, the post-war liberal government in Italy experienced several challenges. In addition to the increasingly dissatisfied nationalists, the liberals faced political opposition from other groups, including the Catholic Church. Previously, the papacy had banned any Catholic political party in Italy, but in January 1919 this ban was lifted, leading to the foundation of the Partito Popolare Italiano (Italian People's Party, PPI). More serious threats to the liberals came from both the political left and, especially, the right.

The socialist 'threat'

The economic problems resulting from the First World War caused great discontent among industrial and rural workers in Italy. The Partito Socialista Italiano (Italian Socialist Party, PSI) began moving towards an increasingly revolutionary position; in 1917, inspired by the Bolshevik Revolution in Russia, the PSI called for the overthrow of the liberal state and the establishment of a socialist republic. In 1914, the PSI had only 50,000 members; by 1919 this had increased to more than 200,000. However, in reality many socialist leaders were stronger on rhetoric than on action.

As unemployment in Italy rose to over 2 million in 1919, industrial workers began a wave of militant action that lasted from early 1919 to the end of 1920. This period became known as the *biennio rosso* (the 'two red years'). A series of strikes, factory occupations and land occupations – organised by trade unions and peasant leagues, and involving over 1 million workers – swept across Italy. By the end of 1919, socialist trade unions had over 2 million members, compared to about 250,000 at the beginning of the year.

In many areas, especially in the north, socialists seized control of local government. To many industrialists and landowners, and to the middle classes in general, it seemed that a communist revolution was about to begin. Yet the government did little to prevent this. It urged employers and landowners to make some concessions and, in response to riots against the high price of food, set up food committees to control distribution and prices. This lack of forceful action led many members of the middle and upper classes to view the government as dangerously incompetent.

The threat from the right

After the First World War, the various militant and disillusioned right-wing groups were joined by another force that was also in search of change. This was made up of demobilised and unemployed soldiers, who found it difficult to accept many aspects of post-war Italian society. One notable group was the Arditi ('Daring Ones'). The first Arditi Association was set up in Rome in January 1919, and from February

Arditi groups were established across Italy. As they grew in size, these groups increasingly used weapons to attack socialists and trade unionists, whom they regarded as the enemies of the Italian nation.

In March 1919, Mussolini – himself a member of the Arditi – tried to bring together all these separate right-wing groups by forming a Fascio di Combattimento ('Fighting' or 'Battle Group'). On 6 June, the *Fascist Programme* was published, which combined various left- and right-wing demands. However, the main feature that held these nationalists and ex-servicemen together was a strong hatred of the liberal state.

SOURCE A

In the Po valley, the towns were on the whole less red [communist] than the country, being full of landowners, garrison officers, university students, rentiers, professional men, and trades people. These were the classes from which Fascism drew its recruits and which offered the first armed squads.

Angelo Tasca, a member of the Italian Communist Party in the early 1920s, comments on the backgrounds of the fascist groups. Quoted in Macdonald, H. 1999. Mussolini and Italian Fascism. Cheltenham, UK. Nelson Thornes. p. 17.

Fasci di Combattimento soon existed in about 70 towns across Italy, yet the organisation was relatively weak. In the November 1919 elections (which, for the first time, used a system of proportional representation) not a single fascist candidate was elected. In all, there were probably only about 4000 committed fascist supporters throughout the entire country.

The economic élites and emerging fascism

However, the unrest of the *biennio rosso* gave a boost to Mussolini's organisation. In an attempt to end the factory and land occupations, he offered to send in *squadre d'azione* (action squads) to help the factory owners in the north and landowners in the Po Valley and Tuscany. These industrialists and landowners, frustrated and angered by the liberal government's concessions and inaction, were only too pleased to give money to Mussolini's groups in return for the *squadristi's* violent actions against the left's strikes and occupations. This growing alliance with industrialists, bankers and landowners began to finance the building of a mass base for Mussolini's Fasci di Combattimento among the middle and lower-middle classes, which feared socialist revolution.

The action squads were controlled by local fascist leaders, known as *ras*. As well as attacking strikers, the *squadristi* burnt down offices and newspaper printing works belonging to the socialists and trade unions in many parts of northern and central Italy. As time went by, the squadristi were mainly composed of disaffected and demobilised army officers and non-commissioned officers (NCOs), and middle-class students. These supporters were united by a hatred of socialists and a belief in violent action, rather than by any coherent political ideology.

The practical appeal of the fascist squadristi grew after September 1920, when a new wave of factory occupations hit the industrial areas of the north. At the same time, agrarian strikes and land occupations continued to spread in central Italy. Then, in the local elections, the socialists won control of 26 out of Italy's 69 provinces, mostly in northern and central parts of the country. All of this greatly increased the fears of the upper and middle classes, and encouraged the use of the action squads. As the squadristi proved effective in suppressing left-wing action, their numbers were swelled by recruits from the ranks of small farmers, estate managers and sharecroppers.

Mussolini's growing influence

Although the factory and land occupations began to decline by the end of 1920, squadristi violence did not. Mussolini soon realised the political and financial opportunities that could result from a more organised use of his fascist squads. Slowly – and facing a great deal of resistance at first – he began to assert central control, arguing that without his leadership the various groups would fall apart. In particular, Mussolini stressed the need to depict violence as a necessary measure to prevent a Bolshevik-style revolution in Italy.

While attacking the liberal state in public, Mussolini privately let liberal politicians know that talk of a fascist revolution was not to be taken seriously. As a result, some liberals offered the fascists an electoral alliance as an anti-socialist National Bloc for the elections due to be held in May 1921. During the election campaign, fascist squads continued their violence and about 100 socialists were killed. Nonetheless, the socialists remained the largest party with 123 seats; the PPI won 107 seats.

The liberals were disappointed by the election results, but Mussolini was pleased – his group had won 7% of the vote and obtained 35 seats. Mussolini himself was now a deputy and, significantly, all 35 fascist deputies were from the right of the movement. More importantly, having a place in parliament gave the fascists an image of respectability as well as some influence on national politics. Having achieved this success, Mussolini announced that the fascists would not support the new coalition after all.

Between May 1921 and October 1922, three weak coalition governments ruled Italy. Mussolini used this time to strengthen his control of the fascist movement. In October 1921, the Fasci di Combattimento were re-formed into the Partito Nazionale Fascista (National Fascist Party, PNF). Mussolini then set about dropping the more radical aspects of the 1919 *Fascist Programme*, which had angered the Roman Catholic Church and worried the upper and middle classes. By the end of 1921, the Fascist Party claimed to have over 200,000 members.

The March on Rome October 1922

From the spring of 1922, fascist violence – which was increasingly ignored by the police – resulted in a 'creeping insurrection' in northern and central Italy, which saw the fascists gaining control of many towns. When the socialists called a general strike at the end of July 1921 in protest against these actions, the fascists used violence to end the strike.

Having obtained increased local control, the *ras* now urged Mussolini to take national power. As a result, Mussolini agreed to co-ordinate the March on Rome, and fascist groups were organised into a 40,000-strong national militia. At first, the government declared a state of emergency and the fascists were halted by the army with little resistance. However, the king, Victor Emmanuel III, refused to authorise a state of martial law. The prime minister resigned in protest, and the king asked Mussolini to step into the post and form a new government.

Activity

Carry out some additional research on the different groups in Italy that supported Mussolini and the fascists before 1922.

The road to dictatorship 1922–24

Although Mussolini was now prime minister, Italy was not yet a fascist state. For that to happen, he needed to change the constitution and strengthen his own position – there were only four fascists in his cabinet, and the king still had the power to dismiss him as prime minister. To establish a one-party fascist state, with himself as dictator, Mussolini needed to win political allies and extend his powers. On 16 November 1922, Mussolini asked for emergency powers to allow him to deal with Italy's economic and political problems. These powers were granted to him for a one-year period.

The support of the élites

To increase his support amongst the conservative élites, Mussolini appointed the liberal Alberto de Stefani as his finance minister. Stefani's early economic policies (reducing government controls on industry and trade, and cutting taxation) pleased the industrialists. In March 1923, the small Nationalist Party – a member of the coalition with close links to big business and the army – merged with the fascists. This confirmed Mussolini's increasing shift towards the conservative élites, many of whom wanted an authoritarian government and a much-enlarged Italian empire.

Mussolini also worked to gain increased support from the Catholic hierarchy and to weaken the position of the Catholic PPI (see page 68), another member of the coalition government. Mussolini announced various measures, including making religious education compulsory and banning contraception. Pope Pius XI, already a fascist sympathiser, signalled his willingness to withdraw his support from the PPI. In April 1923, Mussolini sacked all PPI ministers from his government; in June, the pope forced the PPI leader to resign. By the summer of 1923, the PPI had lost most of its political importance.

The Acerbo Law and the Corfu Incident

Giacomo Acerbo, the under-secretary of state, outlined a new electoral law that would give two-thirds of the seats in parliament to the party (or alliance) that won at least 25% of the votes cast. To ensure that this law was passed, Mussolini threatened to abolish parliament, and used armed fascists to intimidate the deputies. Parliament passed the Acerbo Law by a large majority in July 1923. With this law in place, Mussolini now needed to make sure his party won the most votes in the next election. He was helped in this by an event that became known as the Corfu Incident.

In August 1923, an Italian general was murdered on Greek soil. Mussolini took advantage of this situation; he demanded that Greece pay 50 million lire as compensation and make a full apology. When the Greeks refused (as they had not been responsible), Mussolini ignored criticism from the League of Nations and ordered an invasion of the Greek island of Corfu. The Greek government paid the fine. Many Italians regarded Mussolini as a national hero after the Corfu Incident, and it increased his popularity for the election he planned to hold early the following year.

Why were the Acerbo Law and the Corfu Incident so important in helping to establish Mussolini's position?

The election of April 1924 and the Matteotti crisis

In January 1924, Mussolini set up a secret gang of thugs and gangsters, known as the Ceka. After Mussolini announced that the election would be held in April, the Ceka unleashed a wave of terror against anti-fascists, in which over 100 people were killed. During the election itself, fascists voted on behalf of dead people, and ballot boxes were stolen in regions where the fascists thought they might lose. As a result, the fascists (and the right-wing liberals, who had formed an electoral alliance with the fascists) won almost 65% of the vote.

When the new parliament met for the first time, on 30 May 1924, the socialist leader **Giacomo Matteotti** strongly condemned the fascist violence that had taken place during the election, and called the results a fraud. On 10 June, Matteotti was abducted in Rome and then murdered. Some newspapers began to suggest that Mussolini was involved in Matteotti's murder, and for a time it seemed as though the event might actually cause Mussolini's downfall. When he suspended parliament in order to prevent a debate about the murder, most of the opposition deputies (mainly socialists and communists) boycotted parliament in protest, in an attempt to force the king to dismiss Mussolini.

Giacomo Matteotti (1885–1924) Born into a wealthy family, Matteotti studied law at the University of Bologna. He soon became active in socialist politics, and opposed Italy's entry into the First World War. Matteotti was first elected to the Italian parliament in 1919, and eventually became leader of the United Socialist Party. He was an outspoken critic of fascist violence. He was abducted and murdered by fascist thugs in 1924.

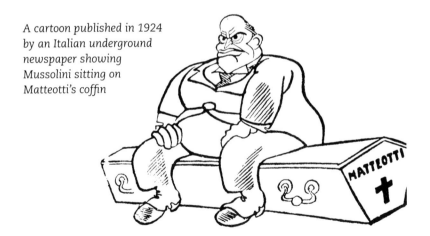

A cartoon published in 1924 by an Italian underground newspaper showing Mussolini sitting on Matteotti's coffin

However, instead of turning against Mussolini, the king accused the opposition deputies of 'unconstitutional behaviour'. The pope, and leading liberals and conservatives, supported Mussolini and backed him when he ordered press censorship in July and a ban on meetings by opposition parties in August. When further evidence of fascist violence emerged, however, Mussolini promised to remove the thugs in the Fascist Party, and sacked three fascist ministers from the government.

These actions provoked a revolt by leading *ras* in December 1924. They presented Mussolini with a clear choice: either he stop further investigations into fascist violence and become dictator of Italy, or they would replace him with a more hardline fascist leader.

SOURCE B

The unprecedented – and quite shameless – Fascist violence which had accompanied the [April 1924] election provoked bitter opposition protests when parliament, now with a crushing and exuberant Fascist majority, reopened. Both inside and outside parliament, the Fascists were now bent on making things unpleasant for their critics. One of the most outspoken was Giacomo Matteotti, a moderate socialist ... In June 1924 Matteotti was kidnapped by a gang of Fascist thugs and stabbed to death, his body remaining undiscovered until August. When Fascist guilt was exposed, Mussolini's moral if not actual complicity was inescapable ... The ensuing 'Matteotti crisis' proved crucial to the development of the Fascist regime. Amidst a wave of anti-Fascist sentiment, much of the ... opposition withdrew from parliament in protest: the so-called 'Aventine secession'. Mussolini panicked and would have resigned the premiership had the king required it. The king did no such thing, his inaction exemplifying the unwillingness even now of conservatives to abandon Mussolini.

Blinkhorn, M. 2006. Mussolini and Fascist Italy. London, UK. Routledge. pp. 33–34.

Building the fascist state 1925–45

After some hesitation, Mussolini decided to become dictator – but on his own terms. He was determined that this would be a personal dictatorship, and that he would be independent of the *ras*.

Suppressing the opposition

On 3 January 1925, Mussolini accepted ultimate responsibility for Matteotti's murder, but only because of his position as prime minister and leader of the PNF. Nonetheless, he made it clear that, instead of resigning, he would continue to rule Italy – by force 'if necessary'. However, in February Mussolini became seriously ill, and the newly appointed party secretary, Roberto Farinacci, launched a new campaign of violence against members of the Socialist and Communist parties and the PPI. Farinacci also supervised a purge of PNF members and local leaders who were believed to be insufficiently loyal to Mussolini.

In July 1925, Mussolini, now recovered from his illness, took the first step towards establishing a fascist dictatorship by imposing a series of laws to control the press. Anti-fascist newspapers were closed down and other newspapers were only allowed to print articles that were approved by the government. From December 1925, all journalists had to be on a register drawn up by the Fascist Party.

However, Mussolini's position was still not secure – the king and the Chamber of Deputies still existed, as did the opposition parties. Thus, in October 1926, all parties other than the PNF were banned and their deputies were expelled from the Chamber; trade unions were also outlawed. In 1927, Mussolini formed the OVRA, a secret police force (under state, not party, control) to suppress all political opponents.

Activity

Carry out some further research on the OVRA and make notes on its methods and activities. When you have read Chapter 8 of this book, compare and contrast these methods and activities with those of the Gestapo in Nazi Germany. To what extent were they similar?

For the May 1928 elections, Mussolini changed the electoral system so that only men aged 21 or over who belonged to fascist syndicates (see page 76) could vote. The Fascist Grand Council (the supreme decision-making body within the Fascist Party, which had been formed in 1922) drew up a list of 400 candidates from lists approved by confederations of employers and employees. Voters only had the choice of voting either for or against this list. Fear of fascist violence meant most Italians voted 'yes', as fascist officials in the polling stations were able to identify those who voted 'no' (the voting slips were different colours).

Having secured a clear electoral victory, Mussolini was established as dictator of Italy. The Chamber contained only fascist deputies, and the king's power was drastically reduced.

Controlling the state

Mussolini also increased his personal power by controlling central and local government. On 24 December 1925, the Legge Fascistissime law made him head of government, and in January 1926 he assumed new powers that allowed him to issue decrees without parliamentary approval. This effectively meant that Mussolini was responsible only to the king. Soon, Mussolini insisted on being called Il Duce ('The Leader'). By 1929, he held eight ministerial posts, excluding many fascist leaders from these key positions.

At the local government level, in August 1925 Mussolini replaced elected mayors and councils with fascist officials known as podesta. Although the podesta were members of the Fascist Party, they were mainly conservative and were drawn from landowners and the military. This helped Mussolini further secure control of the Fascist Party.

The Fascist Party

This authoritarian regime was not a Fascist *Party* dictatorship – instead, Mussolini deliberately made a series of decisions that increasingly restricted the influence of the party. Despite the existence of the Fascist Grand Council, Mussolini insisted on having sole power over appointments. In January 1923, the regional fascist squads were formed into a national fascist militia, the MVSN, which was funded by government money. This paramilitary organisation swore an oath of loyalty to Mussolini, not the king, and its existence considerably reduced the power of the *ras*.

However, Mussolini made no serious attempt to 'fascistise' the system of government. Instead of appointing leading fascists, he used members of the traditional conservative élites. After October 1926, the party was purged of the more militant fascists; these purges increased in the 1930s. By 1943, the PNF was a mass party, with almost 5 million (mainly inactive) members, which acted as a loyal basis of support for Mussolini. At the same time, party posts were filled by appointment from above, not through election by party members. Party influence was further reduced in 1928, when the Fascist Grand Council was made part of the state machinery of government.

The corporate state

The corporate, or corporative, state was supposed to replace the traditional parliamentary democracy with corporations representing the nation's various economic sectors. These corporations, each with equal representation for employers and employees, would give prime consideration to the interests of the nation.

The fascist syndicates

During their rise to power, the fascists closed down traditional labour-movement trade unions in the areas they controlled. They replaced these with fascist-controlled syndicates, which were still supposed to represent workers' interests. By 1922, a Confederation of Fascist Syndicates had been set up, which aimed to create corporations that would force industrialists to make some concessions to the workers. However, the confederation was opposed by the Confindustria, the organisation that represented the main industrialists.

In December 1923, the Chigi Palace Pact was signed. By the terms of this agreement, the industrialists promised to co-operate with the Confederation of Fascist Syndicates, although they insisted on maintaining their own independent organisations. Despite the pact, many employers refused to make any significant concessions to workers, and this led to a series of strikes in 1925. The resulting Vidoni Palace Pact confirmed that the Confindustria and the Confederation of Fascist Syndicates were the only organisations that were allowed to represent employers and employees respectively. It was also made clear that workers were not to challenge the authority of employers and managers. All non-fascist trade unions were abolished, and in 1926 strikes were made illegal.

The corporations

In July 1926, Mussolini decided to establish corporations for each major economic sector, such as mining. Each corporation was made up of representatives of employers and workers of the same economic or industrial sector, with the state's representatives acting as referees and final adjudicators. Mussolini then created a Ministry of Corporations, with himself as minister. In practice, this was mainly run by Giuseppe Bottai, the under-secretary of corporations.

The corporations weakened the fascist syndicates, and in 1928 the Confederation of Fascist Syndicates was abolished. In 1929, Bottai took over as minister of corporations and, in March 1930, he set up the National Council of Corporations (NCC), which represented the seven largest corporations. By 1934, there were 22 corporations represented by the National Council. These sent delegates to the General Assembly of Corporations (also headed by Mussolini), which was supposed to make important decisions about economic policy, including setting wage and price levels. In fact, Mussolini usually ignored the General Assembly and made the important decisions himself. At the same time, employers had much more influence within the corporations than employees did.

In 1938, in a belated attempt to give the corporate state greater credibility, Mussolini decided to abolish the Chamber of Deputies and instead to put in its place the Chamber of Fasci and Corporations. Mussolini hoped to establish a new form of politics, in which people were given a voice according to their economic function rather than their territorial location. In reality, this had little substance or power as it was dominated by fascists appointed from above.

Activity

Using the information in this chapter, and any other resources available to you, construct a timeline to show the main steps Mussolini took in establishing his dictatorship in the years 1922–38.

What were Mussolini's main economic and social policies?

One of Mussolini's main concerns was to make Italy a rich and great power, by achieving autarchy (self-sufficiency) in food and in raw materials. To achieve this, Mussolini wanted to modernise industry and agriculture, and conquer a large empire. The effects of the

Great Depression led Mussolini to increase this push for autarchy –
especially after 1935, when the League of Nations imposed economic
sanctions on Italy following its invasion of Abyssinia (see page 87).

The economy

To achieve the economic greatness he desired, Mussolini decided to
launch a series of initiatives he called 'battles'.

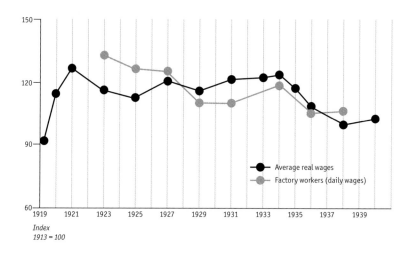

*A graph showing the impact of Mussolini's policies on real wages and those of
factory workers*

Mussolini's 'battles'

In 1924, Mussolini launched the Battle over the Southern Problem,
which aimed to overcome the long-term poverty of southern Italy.
This was to be achieved by building thousands of new villages in Sicily
and the south. In 1925, the Battle for Grain began: Italian farmers were
encouraged to grow more cereals in order to reduce foreign imports.
As well as introducing import controls, more land was made available
for growing grain, by ploughing up pasture land, orchards and
vineyards. In the more prosperous north, farmers shifted from growing
maize to wheat, and adopted more mechanised farming methods.

The Battle for Land – to further increase the amount of available
farmland – began in 1926 with the draining of marshes and swamps.
This created many small farms, while the work – financed from public
funds – created jobs for the unemployed. Attempts were also made to
farm on cleared woodland sites and on hillsides. Also in 1926, the Battle
for the Lira began when the value of the Italian currency dropped.
To restore its value abroad, the lire was re-valued. This allowed Italy
to continue importing coal and iron for armaments and shipbuilding.

Dealing with the Great Depression

Once the Depression began in 1929, unemployment rose in Italy. By 1933, there were 2 million unemployed, and millions more suffered from underemployment. Mussolini initially resorted to limited state intervention, encouraging job-sharing schemes and forcing many women to give up their jobs so that the positions could be filled by unemployed men.

In 1931, public money was used to help prevent the collapse of banks and industries that were hit by the Depression. Then, in 1933, the Istituto per la Ricostruzione Industriale (Institute of Industrial Reconstruction, IRI) was established. This took over various unprofitable industries and by 1939 the IRI was a massive state company controlling many industries, including most of the iron and steel industries, the electrical industry and even the telephone system. However, these industries were not nationalised, and parts of them were regularly sold to larger private organisations.

Success and failure

Mussolini's economic policies achieved some moderate successes. By 1940, industrial production had increased by 9%, and industry overtook agriculture as the largest proportion of Gross National Product (GNP) for the first time in Italy's history. Also, between 1928 and 1939, imports of raw materials and industrial goods dropped significantly. In fact, A. J. Gregor is one historian who claims that Mussolini's regime was a relatively successful 'modernising dictatorship'.

> **Activity**
>
> Try to find some more information on the historical debates surrounding Gregor's ideas of 'modernising dictatorships'. Do you think Mussolini succeeded in modernising Italy?

However, many of Mussolini's economic policies, especially his 'battles', were less successful. None of the new villages promised by the Battle over the Southern Problem was built. Although the Battle for Grain succeeded in almost doubling cereal production by 1939, it also resulted in Italy having to import olive oil. Fruit and wine exports dropped, as did the numbers of cattle and sheep.

During the Battle for Land, only one area – the Pontine Marshes near Rome – was effectively reclaimed. The Battle for the Lira caused a decline in exports and therefore a rise in unemployment. The re-valuation of the currency also undermined the economic policies of 1922–25, and began a recession in Italy. In short, most of Mussolini's 'battles' caused as many problems as they solved.

Overall, the result of fascist economic policy was not a significant modernisation of the economy, or even increased levels of productivity. As a result, it took Italy much longer than most other European states to recover from the effects of Great Depression.

SOURCE C

Mussolini's economic policies had never been designed simply to increase the wealth of the country ... and this became very apparent by the mid 1930s. As the Dictator became increasingly pre-occupied with foreign affairs, living standards and the general welfare of the economy suffered. He believed that war, either in Europe or to further his African Empire, was almost inevitable and that Italy must be prepared. The armaments industry must be promoted, and Italy's economy must become self-sufficient. Italy should be an autarky – able to support itself with all the food and material needed to fight a modern war ... Despite [his] efforts the Italian economy was still far from self-sufficient when the Duce declared war in 1940, and indeed it had run into major difficulties.

Robson, M. 1992. Italy: Liberalism and Fascism 1870–1945. London, UK. Hodder & Stoughton. p. 100.

L'inquadramento: the social impact of fascism

One of Mussolini's great aims was to unite the Italian people and integrate them into the fascist 'project'. This process of 'co-ordination' was known as l'inquadramento.

Fascism and class

Mussolini claimed he would replace class conflict with class harmony, and bring equal benefits to employers and employees as they worked in partnership for the good of the nation. The actual results were quite different, though.

During 1922–25, male industrial workers benefited from a drop in unemployment, and an improvement in living standards (although this was mainly the result of the general economic revival in Europe in the early 1920s). Throughout 1925–26, however, workers lost their independent trade unions and their right to strike (see page 77). Instead of ending class conflict, Mussolini's fascist state merely suppressed the ability of workers to defend their interests. As the economy began to decline in the second half of the 1920s, employers were able to end the eight-hour day and extend the working week. At the same time, the government cut wages; between 1925 and

1938, the level of real wages dropped by over 10%. As a result, by 1939, working-class standards of living had declined significantly. Some social welfare legislation was passed, including old-age pensions, and unemployment and health insurance, but this 'social wage' did not make up for the decline in real wages and working conditions.

The lower-middle classes, who formed the backbone of the Fascist Party, were affected in different ways. Many small businesses were hit quite hard by the Depression as well as by Mussolini's economic policies. However, those who became part of the state bureaucracy or the Fascist Party experienced relative prosperity, with good wages and considerable extra benefits.

The people who gained most from the fascist corporate state were the industrialists and landowners. Even during the Depression, large firms benefited in many ways – either from government contracts or through the IRI (see page 79), which gave financial assistance and also helped in the creation of huge monopolies. Large landowners also benefited: during the Depression, government restrictions on migration kept unemployment high in rural areas, and this meant that landowners could cut wages. Agricultural wages were reduced by over 30% during the 1930s. There was also no attempt to redistribute land, as had been intended by a law passed in 1922. By 1930, 0.5% of the population owned 42% of land, while 87% of the rural population (mainly small landowners) owned only 13%.

Women

Women particularly suffered under fascism. The Battle for Births, for example, stressed the importance of a woman's traditional role as housewife and mother. Launched by Mussolini in 1927, this campaign aimed to increase the Italian population from 40 million to 60 million by 1950. From this, Mussolini planned to create a large army that would help expand Italy's empire.

The fascist state offered maternity benefits and awarded prizes to women who had the most children during their lives. Taxation policy was also used to encourage large families – couples with six or more children paid no taxes at all. In 1931, laws were imposed against abortion and divorce, and same-sex relations were outlawed. The state also tried to exclude women from paid employment. In 1933, the government announced that only 10% of state jobs should be held by women; in 1938, this rule was extended to many private firms.

For all Mussolini's grand plans, though, these government policies largely failed. The number of births actually dropped throughout the 1930s, while nearly one-third of Italy's paid workforce continued to be female.

SOURCE D

The demographic program, the ruralisation of the peninsular, and the effort to revive the traditional female virtues ... all appear to have been unsuccessful ... Fascism may have been instrumental in removing women from the job market, but the statistics are [inconclusive] ... Fascist anti-feminism was not particularly successful and/or may not have been pursued with any special application. In any event, Fascist anti-feminism was, at best, a subsidiary concern of Fascist social policy, and made its appearance largely as a consequence of concerns with a declining birth rate and rising unemployment.

Gregor, A. J. 1979. Italian Fascism and Developmental Dictatorship. Princeton, USA. Princeton University Press. p. 290.

Discussion point

'Fascism – and most other right-wing ideologies – are hostile to equality for women.' Why do you think Mussolini's fascist movement was so hostile to women's rights? Do statements such as this apply to all far-right groups?

The Church

Mussolini was more successful in gaining support for fascism from the Roman Catholic Church. By the 1929 Lateran Treaty, the pope officially recognised the fascist state; in return, the state accepted papal sovereignty over Vatican City. In separate agreements, the state gave the pope 1750 million lire (£30 million) in cash and government bonds as compensation for the loss of Rome, while Mussolini agreed that Roman Catholicism should be Italy's official state religion, with compulsory Catholic religious education in all state schools. In exchange, the papacy agreed that the clergy should not join political parties. The pope (and thus the Catholic Church) gave official backing to Il Duce.

However, rivalry between Catholic and fascist youth movements continued even after the Lateran Treaty. In addition, although the Church agreed with several specific fascist policies – such as the invasion of Abyssinia and involvement in the Spanish Civil War, as well as Mussolini's opposition to contraception and abortion – several other disagreements emerged. Thus it was clear that Mussolini never fully controlled the Church.

Why did the Roman Catholic hierarchy give so much support to fascism during the 1920s and 1930s?

Young people

Mussolini believed that young people held the key to a great future for Italy, and he particularly targeted them in his efforts to unite all Italians under fascism. Various methods were used to 'fascistise' the young, including indoctrination. In infant schools, the day started with a prayer that began, 'I believe in the genius of Mussolini'. In primary schools, children were taught that Mussolini and the fascists had 'saved' Italy from communist revolution. All school textbooks were inspected by the state, and many were banned and replaced with new ones, which emphasised the role and importance of Mussolini and the fascists.

Attempts to indoctrinate older schoolchildren were less successful. The focus on traditional academic subjects, and the difficult exams they were required to take, prevented many young people from going to secondary school or university. The School Charter of 1939, which promised to improve the status of vocational training in schools and colleges, came too late to widen the fascists' base of support.

Mussolini also tried to indoctrinate young people by setting up youth organisations. In 1926, all fascist youth groups were made part of the Opera Nazionale Balilla (ONB). Within the organisation were different sections for boys and girls, according to age. There was also the Fascist Levy (Young Fascists) for older boys aged 18–21. In 1937, the ONB was merged with the Young Fascists to form the Gioventù Italiana del Littorio (GIL), and membership was made compulsory for all young people aged 8 to 21. All members of the GIL – and of the GUF (the Fascist University Groups) – had to swear loyalty to Mussolini.

However, the impact on schoolchildren was not as great as Mussolini had intended. Around 40% of 4–18 year-olds managed to avoid membership. In particular, private and Catholic schools tended not to enforce ONB membership. Also, because of the entrance exams required for secondary school, many children left school at the age of 11. Contempt for – and even resistance to – fascist ideals was not uncommon in the universities.

Dopolavoro

It was also important to Mussolini to influence the minds of adults. To achieve this, he set up organisations intended to control after-work activities. The Opera Nazionale Dopolavoro (OND) – *dopolavoro* is Italian for 'after work' – was established in 1925, and soon comprised a vast network of clubs, libraries and sports grounds. It also organised concerts, dancing and summer-holiday activities in most towns and villages. The main function of the OND was to spread fascist ideology, and although its activities did lead to some popular support, many local organisers ignored the indoctrination aspects.

To further increase fascist influence amongst ordinary Italians, concerted efforts were made to expand membership of the Fascist Party and its associated organisations between 1931 and 1939. From 1931 to 1937, during the worst of the Depression, the party established its own welfare agencies to provide extra relief. Although this led to increased party contact, party membership did not rise dramatically. According to some sources, by 1939 only about 6% of the population belonged to the party.

Race and the *Romanità* movement

While overt racism had not been a feature of the early fascist movement, a general racist attitude existed within the Fascist Party's plans for imperial expansion. Until the signing of the Rome–Berlin Axis in 1936 (see page 89), however, anti-Semitism did not play a part in fascist politics. In Italy, this began significantly only in July 1938, when Mussolini issued the Charter of Race, which ruled that Jewish people did not belong to the Italian race.

Further racial laws and decrees were issued between September and November. These excluded Jewish teachers and children from all state schools, banned Jewish people from marrying non-Jews, and prevented them from owning large companies or estates.

An element of racism also existed within the *Romanità* ('Romanness') movement, which was another of Mussolini's methods of broadening the appeal of fascism. As part of the *Romanità* movement, fascist writers and artists portrayed fascism as a revival of, and a return to, the greatness of ancient Rome. As part of this link, much emphasis was placed on 'the resurrection of the empire'.

What is meant by the term *l'inquadramento*?

How successful was Mussolini's foreign policy?

Mussolini wanted to make Italy a great power – based in the Mediterranean but with a large African empire – to gain what was called *spazio vitale* ('living space') for the Italian people. His foreign policy is generally regarded as having three distinct periods: 1922–35, when policy was mainly peaceful; 1935–39, when it became more aggressive and Italy was increasingly allied to Nazi Germany; and 1940–45, when Mussolini took Italy into Second World War. The results of Mussolini's foreign policy eventually brought disaster to Italy – and are generally regarded as the main factor in his downfall.

Fascist diplomacy 1922–35

Initially, Mussolini was not in a position to achieve his aim of a great new empire by force. The new state of Yugoslavia (see page 15) seemed a potential obstacle to Italian ambitions along the Adriatic Sea. More importantly, Britain and France controlled strategically important areas in the Mediterranean and in Africa.

While Mussolini's use of force in the Corfu Incident (see page 72) increased his support within Italy, it also showed the relative weakness of the country in the face of French and British opposition. An organisation linked to the League of Nations, the Conference of Ambassadors, forced the Italians to withdraw from Corfu and, although Mussolini received the compensation he wanted from the Greeks, they made no official apology.

Italy and Europe

As a result of this, Mussolini adopted a largely peaceful form of diplomacy for the next 11 years. In 1924, he persuaded Yugoslavia to sign the Pact of Rome, which accepted Italian occupation of Fiume – a valuable port city that Italy had originally hoped to gain by the peace treaties of 1919–20. In 1925, Mussolini signed the Locarno Treaty (see page 53). The following year, talks with Britain and France resulted in parts of Kenya and Egypt being given to the Italian colonies of Somaliland and Libya respectively.

A map showing the Italian Empire in 1939

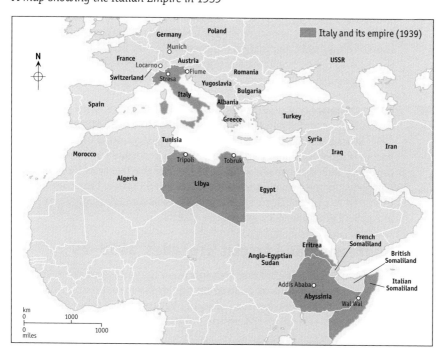

However, Mussolini was also using non-diplomatic methods to increase Italy's influence in Europe. He gave financial backing to an Albanian chieftain who seized power and proclaimed himself King Zog in 1929. A Treaty of Friendship quickly followed. Mussolini also increased secret support of extreme nationalists in Germany, Bulgaria, Austria and Yugoslavia. Nonetheless, in 1928 he signed the Kellogg–Briand Pact, which outlawed war – despite his disapproval of France's alliance with Yugoslavia, Czechoslovakia and Romania in 1927, known as the Little Entente. The Little Entente threatened to block future Italian expansion in the Balkans, and France's position in North Africa also raised problems for expansion there.

From 1929, Mussolini's foreign policy began to change. He called for the 1919–20 peace treaties to be revised, and plotted with Hungary to overthrow the king of Yugoslavia. In 1931, he noted the ineffectiveness of the League of Nations over Japanese aggression in Manchuria. Then, in 1933, details emerged of Italian arms deliveries to a right-wing paramilitary group in Austria and to the Ustase (a Hungary-based Croat terrorist group, which wanted independence from Yugoslavia). This information caused great concern in Britain and France.

Nazi Germany and the Stresa Front

In 1933, Hitler became chancellor of Germany. However, although Hitler was a fellow fascist, Mussolini distrusted the German leader's plans for expansion. He was concerned about the Alto Adige area in northern Italy (which contained many German-speakers), and believed that Austria fell within the Italian sphere of influence. To alleviate his concerns about German expansion, Mussolini proposed a Four Power Pact between Italy, Germany, Britain and France. This agreement, signed in July 1933, reaffirmed the Locarno Treaty and sought to settle the differences between the four nations. In September 1933, Mussolini also signed a non-aggression pact with the USSR.

In 1934, Mussolini worked to establish closer relations with Austria and Hungary, and when Hitler attempted to take over Austria in July 1934, Mussolini prevented this by placing Italian troops on the Austro–Italian border. In January 1935, he made an accord with France. When Germany defied the disarmament clauses of the Treaty of Versailles, Mussolini formed an alliance with Britain and France. This coalition – intended to prevent German expansion – was agreed at Stresa in Italy in April 1935 and was known as the Stresa Front.

Aggression and fascist 'crusades' 1935–39

Mussolini's first imperial war was intended to create a modern version of the old Roman Empire, centred on the Mediterranean and Adriatic seas and Africa. The campaign officially began on 2 October 1935, when 500,000 Italian troops invaded Abyssinia (modern Ethiopia).

The invasion of Abyssinia

Abyssinia lay between Italy's two existing colonies in East Africa – Eritrea and Somaliland – and Mussolini had been making plans to invade the country since 1932. When the invading forces moved in, they met little serious resistance: the Abyssinians were often only armed with spears, while the Italians had tanks, bombers and poison gas. Mussolini's calculations that Britain and France would not seriously object to his invasion seemed confirmed when they drew up the Hoare–Laval Pact, which offered Italy two-thirds of Abyssinia. However, a public outcry against the deal caused it to fall through, and instead the League of Nations imposed sanctions against Italy as the 'aggressor nation'.

A cartoon published in the British newspaper The Evening Standard *in 1935, commenting on Italy's brutal invasion of Abyssinia*

BARBARISM.   CIVILIZATION. *(Copyright in All Countrie*

 ## Theory of knowledge

History, empathy and emotion

The historian James Joll (1918–94) wrote: 'The aim of the historian, like that of the artist, is to ... give us a new way of looking at things.' But is it possible for historians to empathise with violent and racist regimes such as Mussolini's Fascist Italy, without making moral or value judgements? If historians' personal views affect what they write, does this make history less valid as an academic discipline than, for example, the natural sciences?

Until this time, Hitler had backed Abyssinia in its war against the Italian invaders. However, he changed this policy when Britain and France began to oppose Italy's invasion. Hitler also took advantage of this crisis to move German troops into the Rhineland (see page 212), in direct defiance of the Treaty of Versailles. This put Austria under great pressure, and the Austrians expected support from Italy. However, a rift had developed between Italy and its former allies Britain and France, and Italy was now less able to prevent any takeover. These tensions soon led to the collapse of the Stresa Front.

The League of Nations' weak protests about the Italian invasion had little effect, especially as the limited sanctions imposed specifically excluded vital war supplies. In addition, Britain did not close the Suez Canal to Italian ships and Germany ignored all sanctions. Consequently, by May 1936 Italian forces had captured the Abyssinian capital, Addis Ababa. Abyssinia was then merged with the other Italian colonies to form Italian East Africa. Thus, Mussolini's first steps in carving out a new Roman Empire had been successful. Despite this, the conquest brought Italy little benefit – Abyssinia had poor agricultural land and very few raw materials. Furthermore, the invasion alienated Britain and France, and made Italy increasingly dependent on Nazi Germany.

SOURCE E

Ethiopia proved a troublesome colony ... Most of the western zones had not been conquered and guerrilla war continued there for years. In July Mussolini authorised ... a terror policy of reprisals against rebels ... But the cost was huge. Ethiopia provided no loot, indeed swallowed up Italian resources. By 1937-8 about 12.5 per cent of the total state budget was being spent in East Africa alone ... Ethiopia bled Italy dry ... The other consequences were diplomatic ... and even more serious. When the Hoare-Laval scheme collapsed in December 1935, the 'Stresa front' against Germany collapsed with it.

Clark, M. 2005. Mussolini. Harlow, UK. Pearson. pp. 198–200.

The Spanish Civil War

In January 1936, Mussolini informed Hitler that he would not object to a German *Anschluss* (union) with Austria, and hinted that he would not support any action the League of Nations might take against the German reoccupation of the Rhineland. On 6 March, Italy withdrew from the League. This shift to a pro-German policy was confirmed in July 1936, when Mussolini agreed to join Hitler in intervening in the Spanish Civil War, to help General Francisco Franco overthrow the democratically elected Popular Front government. As with Abyssinia, this military adventure brought very few tangible results, although Italy did gain the islands of Mallorca and Menorca. Mussolini and Hitler also confirmed their joint opposition to communism, and agreed to divide Europe into spheres of influence. The Mediterranean and the Balkans fell within Italy's sphere.

The Rome–Berlin Axis

Neither Britain nor France was willing to risk war over Italy's and Germany's interference in the Spanish Civil War, but Mussolini's actions widened the gap between the former Stresa Front allies. At the same time, Hitler offered Mussolini the opportunity of an alliance with Nazi Germany. The Rome–Berlin Axis, signed in October 1936, marked a significant turning point in Italy's foreign policy, establishing co-operation and support between Italy and Germany. The two fascist dictators moved even closer in December 1937, when Mussolini joined Germany and Japan in their Anti-Comintern Pact.

The road to war

In March 1938, Hitler completed his *Anschluss* with Austria. Italy took no action to prevent the takeover. Despite this, in April 1938 Mussolini signed a pact of friendship with Britain, and throughout that year he resisted strong pressure from Hitler to sign a firm military alliance. In September 1938, Mussolini attended the Munich Conference, where European leaders attempted to avert war. Mussolini played the role of peacemaker between Germany and Britain and France at the conference, but he also ordered the Italian navy to prepare for war against Britain in the Mediterranean. Mussolini's belief that Britain and France would never take any firm action against German expansion seemed to be confirmed when these nations made no response to Hitler's invasion of Czechoslovakia in March 1939.

In April 1939, Mussolini attempted to annex Albania and turn it into an Italian protectorate. Ominously, Italian troops had difficulty in conquering even this small state. In May 1939, Mussolini and Hitler finally signed a formal military alliance – the Pact of Steel. This committed Italy to fight on Germany's side in the event of war. However, Mussolini warned that he needed three years to prepare for war. He was shocked, therefore, when Hitler invaded Poland on 1 September 1939.

Mussolini and the Second World War

Mussolini did not join Hitler in his attack on Poland. When Germany failed to supply Italy with the strategic resources it needed, Mussolini stated that Italy could not participate in the war, although he said he would send agricultural and industrial labourers to Germany.

Italy finally entered the war on 10 June 1940. The poor performance of the Italian army played a large part in Mussolini's overthrow on 24 July 1943. At Hitler's urging, Mussolini later set up a new fascist state in north-eastern Italy. However, this Italian Social Republic was little more than a German puppet state. When the Germans withdrew from Italy in April 1945, Mussolini tried to flee with them, but he was arrested on 27 April by a group of Italian partisans. The following day, he was executed alongside 15 other fascist leaders.

End of chapter activities

Summary activity

Copy the spider diagram below to show the main aspects of domestic and foreign policy developments in Mussolini's Italy during the period 1922–39. Then, using the information in this chapter and any other sources available to you, complete the diagram. Make sure you include, where relevant, brief comments about different historical debates/interpretations.

Paper 3 practice questions

1 Analyse the results of Mussolini's economic policies in the period 1922–39.

2 How far did Mussolini's social policies succeed in widening the basis of support for fascism?

3 Mussolini said: 'Higher education for women should just cover what the female brain can cope with, i.e. household management.' In what ways, and with what results, did Mussolini try to impose fascist values on women?

4 To what extent was Mussolini's foreign policy in the period 1922–39 successful?

5 Evaluate the impact of Mussolini's foreign policy on Italy between 1935 and 1939.

5 The impact of the Great Depression: Europe and the world

Timeline

1929 Oct: Wall Street Crash

1930 Jun: Hawley–Smoot Tariff Act passed

1931 May: collapse of Austria's largest bank

Jul: banking crisis in London

Aug: formation of National Government in Britain under Ramsay MacDonald

Sep: Britain leaves gold standard

1932 Mar: Import Duties Act (Britain abandons free trade)

1934 Jan: right-wing demonstrations in Paris

1936 Feb: Japanese government comes under military dominance

May: Popular Front government of Léon Blum comes to power in France

1939 Sep: Second World War begins

Key questions

- How did the Great Depression spread from the United States to the rest of the world?
- What was the impact of the Great Depression on Europe?
- What was the impact of the Great Depression on other parts of the world?

The origins of the Great Depression that affected the world economy in the 1930s lay in the collapse of the New York stock market in October 1929. This began a global economic decline characterised by high unemployment, falling production, the almost total collapse of international trade, and a profound loss of confidence in the capitalist system itself and in the ability of governments to cope with the crisis. The industrial economies of Europe, which had close trade and financial links with the USA, were affected immediately, as investments were withdrawn, banks collapsed and factories closed. Countries and colonies in other parts of the world were affected too, as demand and prices for their agricultural and mineral exports fell on the global markets.

This economic crisis also had significant social and political effects, as European governments struggled to solve the problems within a democratic framework. Not all of them succeeded. The Depression created political upheavals in other parts of the world, increasing anti-colonial activities and strengthening nationalist opposition to colonialism.

Overview

- The Wall Street Crash and the start of the Great Depression in the USA spread to Europe, which was already affected by the problems of reparations, war debts, overproduction and the post-war weakness of Britain as a financial leader.
- US measures to protect its own economy led to a dramatic drop in world trade. The withdrawal of American loans to other countries led to a financial crisis in Europe.
- Governments applied different economic measures in order to solve the economic crisis. These included deflation, devaluation, protective tariffs and exchange controls. None of these measures was successful, and critics called for radical political and economic changes.
- Massive unemployment led to considerable social and political problems, and the insecurity and uncertainty of the times significantly influenced art and literature.
- Scandinavian governments had some success in solving the economic problems by applying socialist economic measures.
- Britain and France formed coalition governments to cope with the crisis. Political moderation remained a feature of British politics, but in France there was a bitter polarisation between left-wing and right-wing parties.
- The Depression also caused economic problems, social unrest and political instability in other parts of the world. In Japan, it led to the rise of a military dictatorship. In colonies in Asia, Africa and the Caribbean, it strengthened opposition to colonial rule.

How did the Great Depression spread from the United States to the rest of the world?

To understand how the collapse of share prices on the New York Stock Exchange created an international economic crisis, it is necessary to know how the world economy functioned at the time (in the 1920s and 1930s) and to understand the economic links between the United States and the rest of the world – especially Europe.

Hungry people wait outside a soup kitchen in Paris in the winter of 1931–32

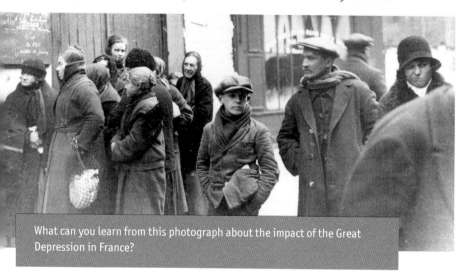

What can you learn from this photograph about the impact of the Great Depression in France?

The world economy after the First World War

The period before the First World War is sometimes referred to as the 'golden age' of capitalism. Although there had been periods of economic decline at various times during the 19th century – causing unemployment and hardship for workers when businesses failed and factories closed – the economies had recovered each time. People had come to accept that cycles of 'boom and bust' were an inevitable feature of capitalism.

However, faith in the capitalist system was shaken by the First World War and the communist revolution in Russia. After the war, governments hoped that there would be a return to the prosperity of the pre-war period. Politicians spoke about a return to 'normalcy' (a word first used by US president Warren Harding). They set about restoring the financial systems and structures that had been in place before the war. For example, most countries returned to the 'gold standard', establishing a fixed link between their currencies and gold.

Activity

Carry out some research to find out how the gold standard operated and what the advantages and disadvantages of the system were.

However, there were problematic factors that had not been features of the pre-war situation:

- Germany was expected to pay large sums of money to Britain, France and Belgium as compensation for damages caused during the war. It was anticipated that Germany would continue to pay these until the end of the 20th century. From 1924 onwards, Germany made these payments by borrowing from the USA. Most of the loans took the form of investments in or loans to German industries, or the purchase of German government and municipal bonds by financial institutions in the United States.
- Britain, France and Belgium owed vast sums in war debts to the USA for materials supplied and loans made during the war. They relied on reparations payments from Germany in order to pay these war debts. The US rejected any suggestions that the war debts should be cancelled.
- Wartime demand had expanded agricultural and industrial production, but there was not enough demand for these products after the war. By the late 1920s, prices were falling and unsold goods were piling up.
- The war seriously weakened the British economy. Britain lost many of its overseas markets for manufactured goods, and was forced to sell off assets to buy arms. When the British government made the controversial decision to return to the gold standard in 1926, it meant that the British pound was overvalued, making British exports too expensive for many countries to buy. The US had the strongest economy in the post-war world, but it was unwilling to take the lead in the global system of banking and finance that Britain had dominated before the war.

How and why did the success of the European economy after the First World War depend on the stability of the US economy?

The Wall Street Crash and the start of the Great Depression

The 1920s were a period of economic boom in the United States – a time of extraordinary economic growth – but this ended with the collapse of the New York Stock Exchange on Wall Street. During the boom years, share prices rose steadily and speculators, bankers and brokers assumed that this pattern would continue.

During October 1929, however, during the presidency of **Herbert Hoover**, doubts led to a loss of confidence and the value of shares dropped by 47% as anxious investors tried desperately to sell their shares. The boom came to a sudden and dramatic end.

Herbert Hoover (1874–1964) Hoover was a Republican and a multi-millionaire businessman. He won the 1928 presidential election, and was president from 1929 to 1933. He was thus in power when the Wall Street Crash occurred. In foreign affairs, Hoover (like many Republicans) tended to be an isolationist, although this policy applied more to European diplomacy than to developments in Central and Latin America or in the Pacific. However, Hoover did involve the US in various economic and disarmament conferences.

The collapse of the stock market had a devastating effect on the entire US economy. Shares became worthless, so investors were unable to repay loans to the banks. People lost confidence, so they were unwilling to invest money or leave it in banks.

When banks began to fail, other investors lost their life savings. As people lost their money, they could no longer afford many goods, so demand dropped. As a result, factories began to close and workers lost their jobs. In this downward spiral of economic collapse, prices, employment, wages, investment, production and international trade all declined. After 1929 they remained at seriously low levels, and the economic crisis became known as the Great Depression.

The Depression spreads

The United States was not the only country affected by the Great Depression. The economies of the industrialised world were so dependent on each other that a collapse in one of them quickly affected the others. After the Wall Street Crash, the Depression spread first to countries that relied on US loans and investments (mainly Germany), and to those with investments or trading interests in the USA, such as Britain and France. Soon, however, virtually the whole world was affected, as the demand for exports declined and prices for products on world markets collapsed.

As the economic crisis in the USA deepened, the US Congress adopted drastic measures, introducing protective tariffs in an attempt to prevent further industrial collapse. The 1930 Hawley–Smoot Tariff Act imposed the highest import duties in US history (an average of 59%), despite objections from over 30 countries. This effectively closed off American markets to foreign products. However, this move proved to be counter-productive, as many countries retaliated by imposing their own protective tariffs, closing their own markets to US imports.

By 1931, tariff rates in Europe had increased by 64% from the 1927 level. The direct result of these protectionist policies was a downward spiral in world trade, as the graph below shows.

The contracting spiral of world trade, January 1929 to March 1933, showing the downward trend in the total imports of 75 countries (measured in US dollars)

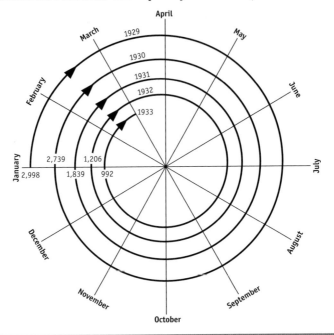

According to the trade figures for January on this spiral graph, in which year was the decline in international trade the most severe? In what ways is a graph like this useful for understanding the impact of the Depression?

Historians disagree about exactly why the Depression spread to the rest of the world. Carter Vaughan Findley and John Rothney suggest that the policies of the US government were partly responsible, blaming the USA's refusal to cancel the war debts, its protective tariffs, and its unwillingness to assume Britain's former role as financial leader during the banking crisis that hit Europe in 1931. These historians believe that by these actions the USA signalled that 'in a world Depression, it was every nation for itself'.

Charles Kindleberger, a leading American economic historian of the Great Depression, is also critical of the USA's role. He suggests that the Depression was so severe and so long-lasting because of Britain's 'inability and the United States' unwillingness to assume responsibility' for stabilising the world economic system at a crucial time.

However, John McKay, Bennett Hill and John Buckler believe that the problem was made worse by poor economic planning in most European countries. In these states, governments tried to cut their budgets and reduce spending, instead of borrowing and spending money to stimulate their economies.

What was the impact of the Great Depression on Europe?

Even before the Wall Street Crash, European economies were facing difficulties. Prices for agricultural products had dropped, largely as a result of over-supply arising from the expansion of agriculture in places such as Canada, the USA, Argentina and Australia during the First World War. During the 1920s, countries in Central and Eastern Europe introduced tariffs to shut out this foreign competition. Coal-producing regions were also experiencing problems. The demand for coal never regained its pre-war levels, partly due to the availability of new sources of energy such as oil and hydro-electricity. This caused particular problems for coal-mining areas in Britain and Belgium.

Historian Eric Hobsbawm points out that unemployment remained surprisingly high in most of Western Europe during the 1920s. Even in the boom years of the mid to late 1920s, unemployment averaged 10–12% in Britain, Germany and Sweden, and 17–18% in Norway and Denmark.

The financial crisis in Europe

Almost immediately after the Wall Street Crash, US banks withdrew their loans to European countries. These nations desperately needed the funds to address the growing economic crisis, and Germany was particularly badly affected as it also had to meet its reparations payments. Banks became far more cautious about lending money. As a result, gold reserves began to flow out of Europe and, in panic, people started to withdraw their savings from banks. In May 1931, this led to the collapse of Austria's largest commercial bank, the Credit-Anstalt, followed by banks in Hungary and Germany. The financial crisis spread, as other banks fell in quick succession. When they tried to save themselves by cancelling loans and calling in credits, many businesses became bankrupt.

The banking crisis was accompanied by a fall in production, and between 1929 and 1933 the world production of goods dropped by an estimated 38%. As the extent of the economic crisis became apparent, European leaders sought solutions to problems that they had never encountered before.

Responses to the economic crisis

In an attempt to solve the economic crisis, the League of Nations arranged a World Economic Conference in London in 1933. Although the United States sent representatives to the conference, they made it clear that the US did not want to be part of an international attempt to solve the crisis. European countries were therefore forced to seek national solutions to their problems.

Economic liberalism

The economic policies that had dominated the world economy since the Industrial Revolution of the 18th and 19th centuries were based on certain accepted principles. These included balanced budgets, free trade and a stable system of financing international trade. This was referred to as 'economic liberalism'. In the crisis now facing Europe, the immediate response of most governments was to apply this orthodox (traditional) liberal economic thinking. They tried to balance their budgets by reducing spending and cutting wages. They hoped in this way to keep the price of exports competitive by lowering costs. This economic strategy, known as 'deflation', was not popular and led to social unrest.

Socialist economics

Socialists argued that the only way to halt the Depression was to end the capitalist system. If workers owned the factories and farms, and shared in the wealth that was created, they could afford to buy more, which would solve the problem of overproduction. However, there were no socialist parties in power at the time that had sufficient support to apply these principles. Some, like the British Labour Party government in office at the time of the Wall Street Crash, applied orthodox liberal economic strategies.

New economic solutions

Some economists argued for a 'middle way' between liberalism and socialism. They wanted to preserve the basic function of capitalism by reforming it. The most famous 'middle-way' thinker was **John Maynard Keynes**. His most important book, *The General Theory of Employment, Interest and Money*, published in 1936, revolutionised economic theory and he is regarded as one of the most influential economists of the 20th century. The 2008 world economic crisis sparked a revival of interest in Keynesian economic theories.

John Maynard Keynes (1883–1946) Keynes was a British economist who argued that the solution to the unemployment caused by the Depression was for governments to spend money on public works programmes to stimulate the economy and provide jobs. This would raise the incomes of lower social groups, thereby creating a bigger market for goods. Keynes' proposal that governments should borrow money to finance this was a highly controversial idea at the time.

The gold standard issue

As the crisis deepened, each country turned inwards in an effort to protect its own economy. In doing so, nations abandoned the principles of economic liberalism. During the 1920s, most European countries had returned to the pre-war gold standard, believing this was the best way to ensure stable international trade. However, in a desperate attempt to retain an advantage, some countries turned to 'devaluation'. This meant leaving the gold standard to devalue the currency, thus making exports more competitive.

In 1931, after a run on the reserves of the Bank of England, Britain abandoned the gold standard, refusing to convert pounds into gold, thus reducing the value of the pound. The aim was to make British exports cheaper and gain an advantage on world markets. However, as more than 20 other countries, including the USA, also went off the gold standard, none of them gained any lasting advantage.

Protective tariffs and exchange controls

Governments used other methods to protect their own economies. One of these was protective tariffs. In 1932, Britain abandoned its traditional support for free trade by passing the Import Duties Act, introducing protective tariffs on a variety of imported items. Free trade had been a key feature of British economic policy since the 1840s, and Hobsbawm sees this move as symbolising the 'rush into self-protectionism at the time'.

Other governments used exchange controls. This meant strict government control of the import and export of currency, which had the effect of limiting foreign trade. By the end of 1931, 12 European countries had introduced exchange controls to prevent the transfer of capital abroad.

 Theory of knowledge

The role of the historian

In commenting on the fact that economists and politicians do not seem to have learnt from the mistakes that caused and prolonged the Great Depression, historian Eric Hobsbawm suggests that this 'provides a vivid illustration of society's need for historians, who are the professional remembrancers of what their fellow citizens wish to forget'. Critically examine this view of the role of historians. What other functions do historians fulfil?

The economic, social and cultural impact of the Depression

The financial crisis in Europe led to the same downward spiral that had hit the United States: cuts in production, factory closures and rising unemployment. Soon, millions were out of work.

Most countries had little or no social security for the unemployed. Even in Britain, which had the best system of unemployment insurance schemes at the time, less than 60% of the workforce was covered by it, and benefits were usually paid for only two weeks of unemployment. In other parts of Europe, unemployment relief ranged from none at all to 25% of the workforce who could claim. The effects of unemployment had wide social and political implications.

SOURCE A

Along with its economic effects, mass unemployment posed a great social problem that mere numbers cannot adequately express. Millions of people lost their spirit and dignity in an apparently hopeless search for work. Homes and ways of life were disrupted in millions of personal tragedies. Young people postponed marriages they could not afford, and birthrates fell sharply. There was an increase in suicide and mental illness. Poverty or the threat of poverty became a grinding reality. In 1932 the workers of Manchester, England, appealed to their city officials – a typical appeal echoed throughout the Western world:

'We tell you that thousands of people ... are in desperate straits. We tell you that men, women and children are going hungry ... We tell you that great numbers are being rendered distraught through the stress and worry of trying to exist without work ... If you do not do this – if you do not provide useful work for the unemployed – what we ask is your alternative? Do not imagine that this colossal tragedy of unemployment is going on endlessly without some fateful catastrophe. Hungry men are angry men.'

Mass unemployment was a terrible time bomb waiting to explode.

McKay, J. P., Hill, B. D. and Buckler, J. 1988. A History of World Societies. Boston, USA. Houghton Mifflin Company. p. 1088. Petition from Manchester workers quoted in Clough S. B. et al (eds). 1968. Economic History of Europe: Twentieth Century. New York, USA. Harper and Row. pp. 243–45.

Activity

Explain how unemployment posed economic, social and political problems. Which of these categories do you think would have been of greatest concern to governments at the time?

The Great Depression also meant that most of the world was living in psychological depression because politicians, economists and business leaders admitted that they could not find solutions.

It was a time of pessimism and insecurity. In the face of this uncertainty, many people began to look for new ideas, and showed an interest in alternative economic and political systems. They also expressed their despair and anger through art.

It was not only the working class that felt the effects of the Depression; here an unemployed English office worker in the 1930s shows that the middle class was also affected

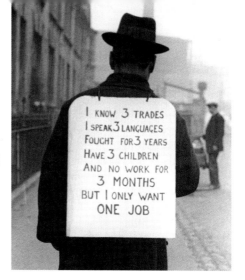

I KNOW 3 TRADES
I SPEAK 3 LANGUAGES
FOUGHT FOR 3 YEARS
HAVE 3 CHILDREN
AND NO WORK FOR
3 MONTHS
BUT I ONLY WANT
ONE JOB

SOURCE B

The 1930s were a brilliant period for mordant social criticism in novels, essays, and the theater (painting, among the visual arts, had largely relinquished the role of social criticism to photography and film). There was a notable shift of emphasis away from the private self-expression of the 1920s toward expression of social concerns. The fiction, essays and drama of the 1930s often speak with the authentic voices of the angry and bewildered during the depression. For the wounds of the depression were not merely physical want. They were the psychic wounds of humiliating helplessness among willing workers unable to provide for their families; there were sharpened and polarized social antagonisms and the search for a savior. All these concerns permeate the art of the 1930s.

Paxton, R. O. 1997. *Europe in the Twentieth Century (3rd Edition)*. Fort Worth, USA. *Harcourt Brace College Publishers. p. 315.*

The political impact of the Depression

The Great Depression had a dramatic impact on politics and public opinion, and led to changes of government in several countries. Many Western governments, trying desperately to find solutions to the widespread unemployment, were acutely aware that the one country that had escaped the effects of the Depression was the Soviet Union, which had rejected the capitalist system. While the industrialised West struggled in the 1930s, the USSR tripled its industrial production and had full employment. However, although radicals and some intellectuals expressed an interest in adopting a more communist system, there was no real move towards the left in the rest of Europe.

By the mid 1930s, few states remained unaffected by the Depression. However, as Hobsbawm explains, the political effects differed from country to country. Sweden and Norway applied democratic socialist policies and coped more successfully with the impact of the Depression than other Western democracies, but in most of Europe there was a move to the right. One significant example of this was in Germany (which you will read about in Chapter 6). In the countries that remained democratic, there were varied political responses to the Depression.

The policies of the National Government in Britain

The Labour Party was voted into power in Britain in 1929, and the government of **Ramsay MacDonald** faced the deepening economic crisis. By 1931, nearly a quarter of the British workforce was unemployed. At first, the government tried to address the problems by increasing public works and unemployment benefits. However, when the banking crisis hit London in July 1931, US investors refused to help the Bank of England by providing loans unless the British government reduced spending. When MacDonald agreed to cut unemployment benefits, the majority of the Labour cabinet resigned in protest against what they saw as a betrayal of their party's principles. MacDonald then formed a coalition National Government in August 1931, in which all three major parties (Labour, Conservative and Liberal) were represented. Although most of the government were members of the Conservative Party, MacDonald stayed on as prime minister.

Ramsay MacDonald (1866–1937) MacDonald was Britain's first Labour prime minister. He began his career as a teacher, but then moved to London and worked as a clerk and journalist before going into politics. He became leader of the Labour Party, which took office briefly in 1924 and then again in 1929. As leader of the Conservative-dominated National Government after 1931, MacDonald was not a popular figure. He was rejected as a traitor by his former Labour colleagues and regarded with contempt by many Conservatives. As a result, his physical and mental health deteriorated. He died of a heart attack on board a ship on his way to the USA in a quest to restore his health.

Under MacDonald and his Conservative successor, Stanley Baldwin, the National Government took further steps to alleviate the crisis: in 1931, Britain moved off the gold standard and the following year, protective tariffs were introduced (see page 95). The economy began to improve after this, and industrial production increased. However, unemployment persisted, and in 1937 there were still 1.5 million unemployed in Britain.

Some areas of the country were particularly badly affected by the collapse of world trade. One such area was the north-east of England, where shipbuilding was a major industry along the River Tyne.

When the shipyards were closed, whole communities were affected. In the town of Jarrow, for example, unemployment rose to 75%. In October 1936, 200 men from Jarrow made a 480-km (300-mile) march to London to present a petition to parliament to highlight their situation.

The Jarrow Crusade of October 1936; the dignity and sense of purpose of the marchers increased awareness of the human suffering caused by the economic collapse

Discussion point

Why do you think the Jarrow marchers called their campaign a 'crusade'? What sort of historical analogies were they trying to suggest?

Although the National Government's cautious efforts to solve the economic problems were criticised by some, most people were confident in the government, and there was little support for radical political ideas. The British Union of Fascists, founded by Oswald Mosley in 1931, proposed some of the measures adopted in Fascist Italy and Nazi Germany as a solution to Britain's problems, but it failed to win a single seat in parliament. The British Communist Party only won two. Source C (on page 104) explains how the 'hunger marches' in Britain helped to limit class conflict and political radicalism during the Depression.

SOURCE C

In England, "hunger marches" emerged as an effective means of social protest and political mobilization. Groups of men, and occasionally women and children, participated in demonstrations to call attention to unemployment and the inequities of the Means Test. While the leadership of such movements often included political radicals, the marchers themselves frequently generated considerable sympathy among lower- and even middle-class observers. Despite the persistence of economic problems, marchers served to mediate the apparent conflict between the classes. In contrast to the situation prior to the Depression, the British public was far more aware of the relative deprivation suffered by those in situations of economic distress. At the same time, even those in oppressed conditions – excepting the most radical of political activists – seemed to accept the legitimacy of the current political situation and sought to influence, rather than overthrow, their elected leaders at the local and national levels.

From www.dhr.history.vt.edu/modules/eu/mod04_depression/conclusion.html

Why do you think the Great Depression did not result in deep divisions and radical political protests in Britain?

Polarisation between right and left in France

The effects of the Depression reached France later than they did many other countries. This was partly because France was less industrialised than other countries, and also because it remained on the gold standard longer and so attracted international investors. However, when the Depression did hit it was more severe and more long-lasting, and was aggravated by political instability. There were a large number of political parties in France, and they could not reach agreement on how to solve the problem; in 1933, a series of five coalition governments formed and fell within a few months.

Right-wing groups formed fascist-type organisations and campaigned for policies similar to those introduced by Mussolini in Italy and Hitler in Germany. In 1934, these groups rioted and threatened to overthrow the government; 14 people were killed and many more injured in a demonstration in Paris. The government seemed unable to solve the economic problems or to suppress the social unrest.

Alarmed by the growth of right-wing groups, the communists, socialists and the Radical Party formed the Popular Front in 1935 to unite their efforts. When the Popular Front won the 1936 general election it was hailed as a victory by the French working classes, who hoped that the new government would provide a socialist alternative to the collapsing capitalist system. The number of communists elected to parliament rose dramatically from 10 to 72, and the Socialist Party, led by **Léon Blum**, emerged as the strongest party with 146 seats. Historians McKay, Hill and Buckner suggest that the results of the 1936 election reflected the growing polarisation in French politics. On the left, the moderate radicals lost support to the communists and socialists, while on the right, the conservatives lost support to the far right.

Léon Blum (1872–1950) Blum was the first socialist leader of France. He was also France's first Jewish prime minister and was almost beaten to death in a brutal anti-Semitic attack shortly before the Popular Front came to power. During the Second World War, Blum was imprisoned by the pro-Nazi Vichy French government and sent to Buchenwald concentration camp in Germany. After the war, he successfully negotiated loans from the US for post-war reconstruction in France, and served briefly as prime minister of a coalition government.

The Popular Front government introduced some progressive labour reforms: a 40-hour working week, paid holidays for workers, and the right of trade unions to work together on wage claims and other social reforms. In this way, Blum hoped to stimulate recovery by raising productivity and workers' spending power. The government also nationalised the Bank of France, the railways and the arms industry. These moves were welcomed by workers and the lower-middle class, but they alienated business and banking leaders and conservative middle-class voters. Wealthy people sent their money out of the country and right-wing critics accused the government of promoting dangerous revolutionary policies. Growing labour unrest and a mounting financial crisis forced Blum to resign in 1937.

Activity

Use the internet to carry out some additional research to find out how the Spanish Civil War created bitter political divisions in France and was a factor in forcing Léon Blum to resign.

French industrial production did not regain 1929 levels until 1939. The Depression years caused deep divisions in French society, and many people lost faith in the French republic and democratic principles.

What was the impact of the Great Depression on other parts of the world?

By 1929, many countries and colonies in other parts of the world relied on the export of agricultural or mineral products to the USA or Europe. This was especially true for many Latin American, African and Southeast Asian countries, and for India. The Great Depression caused particularly severe economic problems in Japan, and this had significant implications for later foreign policy and the outbreak of the Second World War.

In the boom years after the First World War, the Japanese silk industry tripled its output to meet the American demand for silk stockings – 90% of Japan's silk exports went to the USA. After 1929, the collapse of world markets for silk and rice, Japan's other main export crop, hit

peasant farmers hard and created areas of extreme poverty and starvation. Junior army officers from rural areas saw the suffering and blamed the government for failing to help those who were worst affected by the economic crisis. Political unrest increased and several moderate politicians were assassinated. More and more conservative Japanese looked to the army to maintain stability. The army grew increasingly powerful until eventually it dominated the government and the economy. By 1936, Japan was a military dictatorship.

In fact, Japan's industry recovered surprisingly quickly, and exports doubled between 1930 and 1936 despite the measures taken by other countries to protect their own economies. Japan's recovery was due partly to the devaluation of its currency, the yen, and also to increased government spending on public works and armaments after 1936.

Unemployed Japanese men queue to find work in 1931, at the height of the Depression in Japan

Activity

Carry out some additional research to find out whether it was only economic factors that were responsible for the emergence of militarism in Japan in the 1930s.

The impact on colonial empires

The Great Depression created political upheavals in many parts of the world, and increased anti-colonial resistance. This was due in part to the collapse of commodity prices – on which colonial economies depended – and also because during the Depression the colonial powers looked inwards and sought to protect their own economies, often at the expense of their colonies. In the colonies in West Africa and the Caribbean, there was social unrest and increasing discontent with colonial rule, caused directly by the collapse of prices for cocoa and sugar respectively.

In other colonies, such as Egypt and India, the Depression strengthened nationalist opposition to colonialism. In Egypt (affected by the collapse of prices for cotton) there was increasing support for the conservative Muslim Brotherhood, and in India support increased for the nationalist movement led by Mohandas Gandhi.

SOURCE D

Gravely eroded by World War I, the foundations of the European global pattern were further undermined by the Depression. The dependent peoples of the world had already seen their European masters locked in a death-struggle that left none unscathed. After 1929, Asians, Africans and Latin Americans saw that the technological dynamism of Western civilization had not averted an economic calamity that engulfed them, too. The Depression of the 1930s cruelly drove home to the dependent peoples the extent of their economic subordination, and further discredited the Western claim to rule the globe by right of cultural superiority. Though most colonial peoples would win political independence only after the second 'European civil war' (World War II), 1929 like 1914 was a fateful date on the way to the post-1945 'end of empire'.

Findley, C. V. and Rothney, J. A. M. 1986. Twentieth Century World. Boston, USA. Houghton Mifflin Company. p. 112.

What are the links between the Great Depression and the post-Second World War 'end of empire' referred to in Source D?

Conclusion

After the First World War, politicians hoped to build a lasting peace and restore pre-war prosperity. For a while during the 1920s, it seemed as if this had happened. Then the fragile stability was shattered by the Wall Street Crash and the Great Depression. International trade and industrial production collapsed, causing unemployment, poverty and misery on a global scale. The Depression also affected foreign policy, as countries focused on domestic issues, or resorted to aggression to solve economic problems (as in the cases of Italy, Germany and Japan).

It was only the outbreak of the Second World War in 1939, which brought full employment in armaments industries and the armed forces, that finally ended the Depression. During the 1930s, the old liberal ideas of individual rights, elected governments and economic freedom proved to be ineffective, which caused people to consider political and economic alternatives.

SOURCE E

It [the Great Depression] was a catastrophe which destroyed all hope of restoring the economy, and the society, of the long nineteenth century. The period 1929–33 was a canyon which henceforth made a return to 1913 not merely impossible, but unthinkable. Old fashioned liberalism was dead or seemed doomed. Three options now competed for intellectual-political hegemony [dominance or control]. Marxist communism was one … A capitalism shorn of its belief in the optimality of free markets and reformed by a sort of unofficial marriage or permanent liaison with the moderate social-democracy of non-communist labour movements was the second, and, after World War, proved to be the most effective …

The third option was fascism, which the slump transformed into a world movement, and, more to the point, a world danger … as the tide of fascism rose with the Great Slump, it became increasingly clear that in the Age of Catastrophe not only peace, social stability and the economy, but also the political institutions and intellectual values of nineteenth century liberal bourgeois society, were in retreat or collapse.

Hobsbawm, E. 1994. Age of Extremes. *London, UK. Abacus. pp. 107–8.*

How appropriate is the analogy of a 'canyon' to describe the period 1929–33? Which three options does Source E suggest were now competing to replace liberalism as the dominant ideology? Why were the intellectual values of the 19th century 'in retreat or collapse'?

End of chapter activities

Paper 3 exam practice

Question

To what extent did the policies adopted by European governments during the Great Depression threaten orthodox economic liberal theories?
[20 marks]

Skill focus

Writing an introductory paragraph

Examiner's tips

Once you have planned your answer to a question (as described in Chapter 3), you should be able to begin writing a clear introductory paragraph. This needs to set out your main line of argument and to outline **briefly** the key points you intend to make (and support with relevant and precise own knowledge) in the main body of your essay. Remember: 'To what extent ...?' and 'How far...?' questions clearly require analysis of opposing arguments – and a judgement. If, after writing your plan, you think you will be able to make a clear final judgement, it's a good idea to state in your introductory paragraph what overall line of argument/judgement you intend to make.

Depending on the wording of the question, you may also find it useful to define in your introductory paragraph what you understand by key terms – such as 'economic liberalism'.

For this question, you should:

- establish what is meant by orthodox economic liberalism
- consider how these economic theories were threatened by the Depression and the policies put in place to cope with it
- write a concluding paragraph that sets out your judgement.

You need to cover the following aspects of economic policies:

- the basic principles of economic liberalism: balanced budgets, free trade, stable international monetary system
- attempts to apply them: deflation/balancing budgets/reducing wages and benefits
- protectionist measures: countries sought to protect their own economies
- protective tariffs: to raise the cost of imports
- devaluation and the gold standard issue: to make exports competitive
- exchange controls: to stop runs on currencies.

Setting out this approach in your introductory paragraph will help you focus on the demands of the question. Remember to refer back to your introduction after every couple of paragraphs in your main answer.

Common mistake

A common mistake (which might suggest to an examiner that the candidate has not thought deeply about what is required) is to fail to write an introductory paragraph at all. This is often done by students who rush into writing **before** analysing the question and doing a plan. The result may well be that they focus on explaining the economic policies that were applied by different governments without measuring them up to the theories of economic liberalism. Even if the answer is full of detailed and accurate own knowledge, this will **not** answer the question, and so will not score highly.

Sample student introductory paragraph

During the Great Depression, European governments were forced to adopt new policies to cope with the economic crisis. At first, they had tried to balance their budgets by reducing government spending, but this was very unpopular because it meant that wages were cut. So governments decided to take measures to protect their own economies, and by doing so they abandoned the principles of economic liberalism. They abandoned free trade by introducing protective tariffs to make imports more expensive. They tried to make their own exports more competitive by devaluing their currencies and going off the gold standard. They stopped the free flow of money by introducing exchange controls. Instead of balancing their budgets, some countries borrowed money to spend on public works programmes to create jobs. These policies threatened the liberal economic principles that had dominated the world economy before the Great Depression, such as balanced budgets, free trade and an international monetary system based on gold.

This is a good introduction, which focuses on the essay question and demonstrates a good understanding of the topic. It sets out a clear and logical plan, and shows how the candidate intends to structure the answer. It suggests that the candidate has an understanding of complex economic issues, although it needs to demonstrate that he/she properly understands key terms such as 'gold standard' and 'protective tariffs'. However, a strong point about this introduction is that it shows a sound appreciation of the fact that the answer needs to compare the measures that were taken with the principles of economic liberalism, and assess whether the latter were threatened by them. This indicates that the answer – if it remains analytical and is well-supported – is likely to be a high-scoring one.

Activity

In this chapter, the focus is on writing a useful introductory paragraph. Using the information from this chapter and any other sources of information available to you, write introductory paragraphs for **at least two** of the following Paper 3 practice questions.

Remember to refer to the simplified Paper 3 markscheme on page 225.

Paper 3 practice questions

1   To what extent was the spread and severity of the Great Depression in Europe a direct result of the responses of the US to its own domestic crisis between 1929 and 1931?

2   Evaluate the success of Britain and France in coping with the economic and social problems caused by the Great Depression.

3   Compare and contrast the impact of the Great Depression on domestic politics in Britain and France during the early 1930s.

4   How do the effects of the Great Depression illustrate the interdependence of the world economy in the 1930s?

6 Case study: Germany and the Great Depression 1929–33

Key questions

- What was the immediate impact of the Depression on Germany?
- How did a succession of governments address the economic and political crises?
- Did the Great Depression cause the collapse of the Weimar Republic?
- How did the Great Depression affect the Nazis?

The Great Depression had a considerable impact on Germany, and the repercussions of this were felt in Europe and beyond. The most crippling economic and social effect was widespread unemployment, which affected one-third of the global workforce by 1932. The Depression also created political instability, resulting in a succession of coalition governments that struggled – and failed – to tackle the economic crisis. This undermined confidence in democratic institutions and fuelled the growth of conservative opposition to the Weimar Constitution. Hitler and the Nazi Party used the opportunities presented by the Depression to increase their support, using a combination of effective propaganda and aggressive intimidation. Hitler's appointment as chancellor of Germany in January 1933 symbolised the end of the democratic Weimar Republic.

Overview

- The withdrawal of US loans from Germany following the Wall Street Crash led to the closure of factories and businesses, a drastic decline in industrial output, large-scale unemployment and the collapse of the banking system.
- A succession of weak coalition governments failed to provide effective solutions to the economic problems, resulting in a loss of confidence in democracy, and growing support for authoritarian measures to solve the crisis.
- There is thus a direct link between the Great Depression and the collapse of the Weimar Republic. It caused severe economic problems and political instability, and undermined the process of parliamentary democracy, making it easier for the Nazis to come to power in 1933.
- This situation provided Hitler and the Nazi Party with the opportunity to increase their support and present themselves as the only viable solution to Germany's problems.

By 1932, over 6 million Germans were unemployed; this Nazi election poster proclaims 'Our Last Hope: Hitler'

Analyse the appeal of this Nazi poster.

What was the immediate impact of the Depression on Germany?

Germany was extremely vulnerable to the world economic crisis that developed after the Wall Street Crash. Its industry and banking system depended on foreign investment and short-term loans – 40% of the total amount of US capital invested abroad was in Germany.

Even before the 1929 crash, American investors, attracted by the high profits to be made on Wall Street, had started to withdraw their loans. This trend escalated after October 1929, when investors withdrew even larger amounts of capital from German and other European investments. This was partly because they needed the funds to meet obligations at home, and partly because they were losing confidence in the stability of the German economy and the safety of their investments. By 1931, German banks had been seriously weakened by the loss of funds.

Industry and agriculture

Industry in Germany was heavily dependent on foreign capital and, with the withdrawal of this funding, industrial production was cut back. At the same time, exports to the United States declined, partly as a result of lower demand but also because of the protective tariffs that the US government placed on imports.

The decline of overseas markets, together with the withdrawal of loans, led to a dramatic rise in the number of bankruptcies. Factories closed and industrial production fell by nearly 50% between 1929 and 1932. Agriculture was also affected. Even before 1929, farmers had been hit by falling prices for their crops. With the collapse of agricultural prices on world markets, their position became much worse and, by 1932, many were bankrupt.

Unemployment

Unemployment soared from 2 million in 1929 to 4.5 million in 1931. With the sharp rise in unemployment, the government fund for unemployment benefits soon ran out. By the end of 1932, over 6 million people – more than one-third of the labour force – was unemployed, according to official statistics. However, historians such as Eric Weitz suggest that the real number was even higher, as the official figures did not include women, who were usually the first to be fired and rarely received unemployment benefits. Unable to pay their rents or mortgages, many unemployed people were forced out of their homes to live in makeshift housing in shanty towns.

The banking crisis

A banking collapse in 1931 heightened the crisis. After the collapse of the Credit-Anstalt bank in Austria in May 1931, the banking crisis quickly spread to Germany. When Germany's second-largest bank, the Danat Bank, fell in July 1931, it triggered a loss of confidence in the whole German banking system, and four other major banks were forced to close.

Fears about declining foreign exchange and decreasing gold reserves in Germany led to a run on the German currency. Investors – both foreign and German – tried to sell off their marks for gold or other currencies before it was too late. In August, the German government was forced to 'freeze' foreign credits, refusing to transfer German marks held by foreigners into foreign currencies.

In response to the banking collapse – and after an appeal from the German president Paul von Hindenburg – the US president Herbert Hoover proposed a one-year moratorium (postponement) on debt repayments, in order to give Germany time to solve its financial crisis. This would cover both reparations and war debts. The following year, at a meeting in Lausanne, Switzerland, the European powers agreed to cancel reparations and suspend the repayment of war debts. However, these measures failed to solve the economic crisis in Germany.

> Why did the impact of the Depression on the German economy gain momentum?

How did a succession of governments address the economic and political crises?

The main economic problem facing governments in Germany after 1929 was unemployment – not hyperinflation as in the financial crisis of 1923 (see page 37). However, the government, as well as most Germans, had bitter memories of the 1923 crisis, and this influenced government policies and voting patterns during the Depression years.

The Depression led to parliamentary instability, as governments failed to agree on economic policies or to find effective solutions to the problems. As a result, people lost faith not only in individual politicians and specific parties, but in the whole democratic system itself. Between October 1929 and January 1933, there were frequent elections and changes of government as a succession of chancellors sought solutions to the economic and political crises.

Hermann Müller (June 1928–March 1930)

Hermann Müller (see page 58) had led Germany since 1928 as chancellor of the centre-left Grand Coalition. With the onset of the Depression, however, the five political parties in the coalition could not agree on measures to deal with the crisis. Like most governments at the time, the Weimar Republic had to choose between cutting expenditure (notably unemployment benefits) in order to balance the budget, or maintaining benefits to increase spending power and stimulate the economy. However, there were fears that spending their way out of the crisis might result in disastrous inflation, as it had in 1923.

Unable to agree whether to reduce unemployment benefits or to risk unpopularity by raising taxes, the government asked the New York banks for a loan to cover immediate government expenditure. However, the banks refused to consider a loan to a government that would not balance its budget. Anxious to maintain the confidence of remaining US investors, Müller's government reluctantly decided to cut unemployment benefits. This decision had important political repercussions: the trade unions forced the Social Democrats to withdraw support for the coalition, and the Grand Coalition collapsed on 27 March 1930. Historian Robert Paxton suggests that the Weimar Republic's parliamentary system ceased to function at this point. For the next three years, Paul von Hindenburg used the authority granted by Article 48 of the Weimar Constitution, which allowed the government to rule without the approval of parliament (see page 27).

Heinrich Brüning (March 1930–May 1932)

To replace Müller, Hindenburg appointed **Heinrich Brüning**, the conservative Centre Party leader, as chancellor. Brüning was a firm believer in economic liberalism (see page 98), and he tried to solve the economic crisis by deflation. This meant cutting prices, wages and state spending, to reduce the cost of exports and also to encourage foreign investors to keep their money in Germany. Unable to win parliamentary support for these measures, Brüning persuaded Hindenburg to allow him to rule by decree to enforce them.

Heinrich Brüning (1885–1970) Brüning was a teacher who served in the German army during the First World War. He entered politics and became leader of the Centre Party in 1929. As chancellor, the austerity measures he adopted to meet the economic crisis made him very unpopular with voters, and resulted in a rise in support for more extreme parties. Brüning left Germany in 1934 and settled in the United States.

Brüning cut civil servants' salaries by 12–16%, twice reduced unemployment benefits and other social welfare payments, and ordered that wages be reduced to their January 1927 levels. He tried to compensate for these austerity measures by lowering rents and the cost of goods. However, the government could not enforce these two decrees, and so workers and the unemployed suffered accordingly. Brüning became known as the 'Hunger Chancellor'. Historians McKay, Hill and Buckler suggest that Brüning's policies not only hastened the economic collapse in Germany, they also convinced the lower-middle classes that its leaders were 'stupid and corrupt'.

Chancellor Brüning gives a speech to the Reichstag in 1932 about the three key issues facing Germany – disarmament, reparations and how to overcome the economic crisis

The strict measures failed to stop the economic downturn, and unemployment soared. Brüning's unpopular policies made him increasingly dependent on presidential decree. Mistakenly believing that he could gain a parliamentary majority of centre-right parties, he dissolved the Reichstag in September and called for new elections. However, German voters demonstrated their anger and frustration at the government's unsuccessful and unpopular attempts to solve the economic crisis. They turned towards the more extreme parties – the Communists and the Nazis – both of which were hostile to the democratic parliamentary system. The Nazis made the most significant gains, jumping from 12 to 107 seats in the Reichstag.

This made them the second-largest party after the Social Democrats. The success of the extremist parties in the election scared foreign investors, and increasing numbers of them withdrew their loans.

Brüning remained as chancellor, but without parliamentary support he was forced to continue issuing unpopular decrees. However, in May 1932 he lost the support of Hindenburg and his most influential advisor, General Kurt von Schleicher. Schleicher was opposed to Brüning's decision to ban marches of the SA stormtroopers (see page 40), and Hindenburg withdrew his support over a proposal to cut government subsidies to estate owners in Prussia. Brüning was forced to resign as chancellor.

Discussion point

Explain how democracy was undermined during the chancellorship of Heinrich Brüning.

Franz von Papen (June–November 1932)

Hindenburg's next choice as chancellor was **Franz von Papen**, a conservative Catholic aristocrat and a former member of the Centre Party. Papen tried to ease the financial crisis by imposing exchange controls, which gave the government strict control over the import and export of currency. However, the controls had a negative effect on foreign trade.

Franz von Papen (1879–1969) Papen was a right-wing politician and friend of Hindenburg who served briefly as chancellor despite limited political experience. He negotiated the Nazi–Conservative alliance that brought Hitler to power in January 1933. Under the Nazi regime, Papen served as German ambassador to Austria and then Turkey. Although he was tried and acquitted at the war-crimes trials at Nuremberg, he was later imprisoned for three years by a German court.

In an unsuccessful bid to increase his support, Papen called for new elections in July 1932. The results showed a dramatic increase in support for the Nazi Party. With 230 seats, and 37.3% of the vote, it was now the largest party in Germany, making its support critical for any government to succeed. However, when Papen offered Hitler a position in his government, Hitler declined and instead demanded to be made chancellor. Hindenburg refused. Papen hoped to strengthen his own position by holding further elections in November 1932. This time the Nazis lost support – winning 196 seats and 33.1% of the votes. Despite this, Papen failed to gain enough support to govern effectively; Hindenburg lost confidence in him, and replaced him with Schleicher.

SOURCE A

A table of statistics showing the election results in Germany from 1928 to 1933.

Party	Seats				
	September 1928	July 1930	July 1932	November 1932	March 1933
KPD	54	77	89	100	81
SPD	153	143	133	121	120
BVP	78	87	97	90	93
DVNP	73	41	37	52	52
NSDAP	12	107	230	196	288
Other parties	121	122	22	35	23

Adapted from www.atschool.eduweb.co.uk/.../Germany%201919.../

Activity

Between them, the two left-wing parties – the Communists (KPD) and the Social Democrats (SPD) – won nearly 40% of the seats in the Reichstag between 1928 and 1932. Carry out some research to find out why they failed to co-operate to form a united front against Hitler.

Kurt von Schleicher (December 1932–January 1933)

Kurt von Schleicher did not survive long as chancellor. He tried to keep his government in power by asking for further emergency powers, which Hindenburg was not prepared to grant. Schleicher was appointed because he convinced Hindenburg that he could divide the Nazi Party by winning over some of its leaders, but this plan failed. The main result of his political manoeuvring was to antagonise Papen. In a bid to increase his own power, Papen finally persuaded Hindenburg to appoint Hitler as chancellor of a coalition government, whose 11 members included only three Nazis and in which Papen would be deputy chancellor.

Kurt von Schleicher (1892–1934) Schleicher was an army officer who held various posts linking the army and the government between 1919 and 1932. As a close and influential advisor to Hindenburg, he was responsible for the appointments of Brüning and Papen as chancellor, and reluctantly accepted the post himself. Schleicher was concerned about the growing power of the Nazis, and hoped to control their influence by including them in government. He was murdered by the Nazis during the Night of the Long Knives in 1934.

The conservative advisors surrounding Hindenburg believed that Nazi extremism would be held in check by the conservative majority in the government. They were also influenced by evidence of growing support for the Communist Party in the November 1932 election. As a result, on 30 January 1933, Hitler was appointed chancellor. Historians John Hite and Chris Hinton suggest that the conservatives were trying to use Hitler's popular appeal to enhance their own power, which turned out to be a 'fatal, though understandable, miscalculation'. Over the next three months, Hitler proceeded to destroy the Weimar Republic, and Germany became a totalitarian dictatorship under Nazi control.

It is ironic that by late 1932 the German economy was actually starting to improve. This was due in part to some public works programmes set up by Brüning and the allocation of some unused land to dispossessed farmers and workers by Papen. However, the improvements were too limited to influence the voters. It was the Nazis who later won credit for Germany's economic recovery.

Discussion point

Discuss the validity of the following statement by historian Robert Paxton:

'Parliamentary government in Germany was destroyed by its inability to deal with the Depression several years before Hitler came to power.'

 ## Theory of knowledge

History and economics

How do events in Weimar Germany between 1929 and 1933 demonstrate that historians need to examine the link between economics and politics in order to understand historical events?

Did the Great Depression cause the collapse of the Weimar Republic?

Some historians consider that there were fundamental flaws in the Weimar Republic and that it was doomed to failure anyway. Others argue that the Depression caused the collapse of a system that might otherwise have survived. Historians also debate whether it was the appeal of the Nazis that brought them to power, or the growth of conservative and authoritarian forces working against the democratic system. There is general agreement, though, that the Great Depression reduced the Weimar Republic's chances of survival. Sources B and C reflect some of these debates.

SOURCE B

The Nazis were extremely successful in presenting themselves as a dynamic party that would resolve the Depression, re-establish morality, and restore German grandeur. In Hitler they had an enticing and clever figure in whom so many Germans chose to place their hopes. But Hitler would have been just another Weimar crank, the Nazi Party just another tiny grouping on the radical fringe, had not Weimar's succession of crises given them an opening. The toll of the war and the Versailles Treaty, hyperinflation, and, finally, the Depression had left a battered population that, by the winter of 1932–33, was desperate for some sort of solution. Moreover, the longstanding 'democratic deficit' in Germany, the persistence of authoritarian structures and mentalities going back to the founding of the state in 1871, provided a strong basis for right-wing politics of all sorts in the post World War I era.

Without the established conservatives, without the support of elite officers, businessmen, civil servants, and nobles, the Nazis would never have come to power.

Weitz, E. D. 2007. Weimar Germany: Promise and Tragedy. Princeton, USA. Princeton University Press. p. 358.

SOURCE C

From 1929 the Depression radicalised sections of the population which inflation had already rendered unstable, turning them either to the extreme right or the far left. It also destroyed any possibility of political consensus and, as we have seen, returned Germany to the practice of authoritarian government.

There is a final irony. Hitler came to power as the impact of the Depression was beginning to lessen and as support for the Nazis was beginning to ebb. The reason for this seems to be that conservative and authoritarian politicians were determined that the parliamentary democracy destroyed by the Depression should never be reintroduced. It seemed preferable to hand over power to Hitler, especially now that an impending improvement in the economy seemed likely to reduce his appeal and therefore his power. Even Hindenburg, who initially disliked Hitler, was won round to the argument that Hitler could be controlled, even manipulated, within the context of a carefully constructed coalition. The authoritarian regime, in other words, would continue to function as it had done since 1931.

Lee, S. J. 1987. The European Dictatorships, 1918–1945. London, UK. Routledge. pp. 150–51.

Activity

Compare and contrast the views expressed in Sources B and C (on page 121) about the links between the Depression, the decline of democracy in Germany and the Nazis' rise to power.

How did the Great Depression affect the Nazis?

From the outset, the Nazis took full advantages of the economic crisis and the breakdown of parliamentary democracy. Although their economic policies were not well developed, they promised solutions to unemployment at mass rallies and through a constant flood of propaganda. The Nazis focused their appeal on the middle and lower-middle class – the *Mittelstand* of small businessmen, independent artisans, small shopkeepers, office workers and farmers.

They played on the memories these groups had of the economic catastrophe of 1923, and on their panic as bankruptcies increased and unemployment levels soared. Many voters deserted the moderate and conservative parties to vote for the Nazis. Young people also flocked to join the Nazis. In 1931, nearly 40% of Nazi membership was made up of young people between the ages of 18 and 30. Source D explains the appeal of the Nazis to many German voters.

SOURCE D

Disgusted with the floundering of the Weimar government, which could not restore sanity to an economy gone crazy for the second time in ten years, these voters saw a striking contrast in Nazi dynamism. They also expected Nazi force to restore law and order to a turbulent political scene. Eighty-two people had been killed and hundreds wounded in six weeks of street fighting in one German state alone. If the price of an end to chaos was the establishment of a dictatorship, many were prepared to pay it – indeed looked forward to it.

Findley, C. V. and Rothney, J. A. M. 1986. Twentieth Century World. Boston, USA. Houghton Mifflin Company. p. 143.

Violence on the streets, co-ordinated by the SA, as well as intimidation of voters, also played a role in the dramatic increase in support for the Nazis in 1930, when they increased their representation from 12 to 107 seats in the Reichstag. Encouraged by this success, they made a huge effort over the next two years, using posters, public meetings and eight Nazi-owned newspapers. The surge in support for the Nazis in the July 1932 elections was a direct result of this campaign.

SA stormtroopers on the streets of Berlin in 1932

However, 1932 also brought two electoral setbacks for the Nazis. In April, when Hitler felt confident enough to stand against Hindenburg in the presidential election, the results were a disappointment for them: Hitler gained only 26.8% of the vote, and Hindenburg was re-elected by a convincing 53%. Then, in yet another Reichstag election in November, Nazi support declined from 230 to 196 seats. It was as a result of these failures, according to Lee, that Hitler turned to 'the back-door methods of diplomacy and intrigue' to gain power.

What other factors contributed to Hitler's rise to power?

Apart from the fundamental weaknesses in the Weimar Republic and the direct results of the Depression, other factors played a role in Hitler's rise to power.

- **The rise of extremism:** During the Depression, the German electorate turned to parties that offered extreme solutions. The communists blamed the economic collapse on the failure of the capitalist system and pointed to the apparent stability of Stalin's Soviet Union as evidence of a workable alternative. The Nazis blamed the Weimar system, the Treaty of Versailles, the communists and the Jews for Germany's problems, and promised strong, decisive leadership as a solution.

- **Fears of communism:** As support for the communists grew, the Nazis used propaganda to play on middle-class fears of the 'communist threat'. Increased support for the Communist Party in the elections frightened the conservative élite into backing the Nazis. One of the Nazis' aims was to win the support of leading industrialists, who willingly financed them to prevent a communist takeover. This was partly due to the efforts of a powerful ally, Alfred Hugenberg – a nationalist leader and owner of a chain of right-wing newspapers. In October 1930, Hugenberg and other influential business leaders joined the Nazis to form the Harzburg Front, an alliance that was determined to keep the communists out of power.
- **The use of propaganda and technology:** The Nazis made skilful, cynical and extremely effective use of propaganda to undermine their opponents and spread the appeal of Nazism. Above all, they promised work to the unemployed, stability to the middle classes, and a revival of pride to German nationalists. They were the first party to demonstrate the effectiveness of the new medium of radio as a means of mass political communication. In the presidential election of 1932, the Nazis chartered planes to fly Hitler all over Germany to speak at Nazi rallies. In this way, even though Hitler did not succeed in defeating Hindenburg, the Nazi message was spread. Mass rallies, parades, uniforms and marches reinforced the message that the Nazis were a party of action, organisation and teamwork.
- **Divisions among the opposition:** As we have seen, the system of proportional representation in the Weimar Constitution gave rise to numerous parties, none of which could gain a workable majority in the Reichstag. There were too many divisions between the parties for them to unite to oppose the threat posed by the Nazis. The main left-wing parties, the Social Democrats and the Communists, refused to work together. Some of the conservative parties saw the Nazis as a preferable alternative to the left-wing parties. All of them underestimated the Nazis (see the table of election results on page 119).
- **The collapse of democracy and political intrigue:** The use of presidential decree in place of parliamentary rule, which had started under Brüning, hastened the collapse of democracy. By 1932, Germany had effectively become an authoritarian state in which a handful of individuals held political power. Their intrigues, largely motivated by self-interest, provided Hitler with the opportunity he wanted. He did not need to risk seizing power in an unpredictable *putsch* (which the SA had been urging); he was offered it by short-sighted and self-serving politicians. The 'backstairs intrigue' between Papen and Hindenburg allowed Hitler to come to power legally. They mistakenly believed that, while the Nazis were strong enough to keep the communists out of power, they were too weak to threaten the position of the traditional political élite, which they thought could retain control in Germany. Their error soon became clear.

End of chapter activities

Paper 3 exam practice

Question

Analyse the impact of the Great Depression on the rise of the Nazi Party between 1929 and 1933.
[20 marks]

Skill focus

Avoiding irrelevance

Examiner's tips

Do not waste valuable writing time on irrelevant material. If it's irrelevant, it won't gain you **any** marks. This problem can arise because:

- the candidate does not look carefully enough at the wording of the question (see page 42)
- the candidate ignores the fact that the question requires selection of facts, an analytical approach and a final judgement; instead the candidate just writes down all that they know about a topic (relevant or not), and hopes that the examiner will do the analysis and make the judgement
- the candidate has unwisely restricted their revision, and tries to turn the question into a topic they were expecting instead of answering the question that has been asked; whatever the reason, such responses rarely address any of the demands of the question.

For this question, you will need to:

- cover the economic problems caused by the Great Depression and how these affected the Nazis
- explain the political impact of the Depression and how this also played into the hands of the Nazis
- analyse the significance of these two factors.

Common mistakes

One common error with this type of question is for candidates to write about material they know well, rather than material directly related to the question.

Another mistake is to present too much general information, instead of material specific to the person, period and command terms.

Finally, candidates often elaborate too much on events outside the dates given in the question.

Sample paragraphs of irrelevant focus/material

The Great Depression played a significant role in the rise of the Nazi Party between 1929 and 1933. In 1928, before the Depression started, the Nazis had only 12 seats in the Reichstag, but by 1932 they were the largest party in Germany. This was due to the Depression.

Hitler was born in Austria and fought in the German army during the First World War. After the war, he joined the Nazi Party, which was small and poorly organised and had only 50 members. He soon became one of its leaders. The party adopted the swastika as its emblem and created a force of armed stormtroopers, the SA. By 1923, the party had 50,000 members. When the German economy collapsed in 1923, the Nazis tried to seize power in the Munich Putsch. The coup failed and Hitler was imprisoned. While he was in prison he wrote 'Mein Kampf', which was an outline of his political ideas.

Hitler wanted to restore German pride by rejecting the Treaty of Versailles and uniting all German-speaking people. The Nazis believed in leadership by a small group, and placed a great emphasis on action. The Nazi Party was also strongly anti-Semitic and believed in a hierarchy of races in which the Germans were the superior master race. Hitler blamed the Jews for Germany's economic and political problems ...

This is an example of a **weak** answer. Although a brief comment on the position of the Nazi Party before 1929 would be relevant and helpful, there is certainly no need to go into detail about the period 1919–29. The question also requires an analytical answer, not a narrative account. Thus, virtually all of the material underlined is irrelevant, and will not score any marks. In addition, the candidate is using up valuable writing time, which should have been spent on providing relevant points and supporting own knowledge.

[There then follow several paragraphs on the policies of the Nazis and Hitler's attempts to build up the party during the economic recovery under Stresemann, when there was little support for the Nazis.]

Activity

In this chapter, the focus is on avoiding writing answers that contain irrelevant material. Using the information from this chapter, and any other sources of information available to you, write an answer to **one** of the following Paper 3 practice questions, keeping your answer fully focused on the question asked. Remember – doing a plan **first** can help you maintain this focus.

Remember to refer to the simplified Paper 3 markscheme on page 225.

Paper 3 practice questions

1   Critically examine the impact of the US economic collapse on Germany between 1929 and 1933.

2   How, and with what success, did successive Weimar governments seek to solve the economic problems caused by the Great Depression?

3   To what extent is it accurate to say that democracy had disappeared in Weimar Germany even before Hitler came to power in 1933?

4   Analyse why the Weimar government had less success in handling the problems caused by the Great Depression than the British and French governments did.

5   To what extent can Hitler's rise to power in 1933 be attributed to factors other than the economic problems caused by the Great Depression?

7 The Spanish Civil War 1936–39

Key questions

- What were the causes of the Spanish Civil War?
- How important was foreign intervention in deciding the outcome of the war?
- What were the main consequences of the Spanish Civil War?

Throughout the 20th century, Spain was a deeply divided society. Because of the bitter political divisions between left and right, and the fact that the Spanish Civil War was followed within a few months by the start of the Second World War, several historians – notably Ernst Nolte – have argued that the whole period 1936–45 can be seen as a European Civil War. The majority of historians, however, consider the Spanish Civil War to be a separate entity, although it clearly had an impact on European diplomacy and thus contributed to the outbreak of the Second World War in 1939.

Overview

- By 1900, Spain was divided by economic inequalities, conflict between reformers and conservatives, regional differences and political instability.
- The First World War was followed by several years of unrest, which ended in 1923 when a military dictatorship was established under Miguel Primo de Rivera. This lasted until 1930.
- In 1931, Spain became a republic once again. From 1931 to 1933, a left-wing government introduced a number of changes, but between 1934 and 1936 a new right-wing government reversed all these reforms and began suppressing left-wing uprisings.
- Leftist parties united to form the Popular Front, which won a narrow victory in the February 1936 elections. However, civil war broke out after an attempted army coup in July 1936.
- The Spanish Civil War – between republicans (supporters of the elected government) and nationalists (opponents of reform) – soon attracted foreign intervention from countries such as Germany and Italy. However, Britain and France followed a policy of non-intervention.
- Many individuals from different countries also volunteered to fight in what they believed to be a struggle against the growing threat of fascism.
- The war was characterised by bombings and atrocities against civilians and political opponents, and was a sign of the changing nature of warfare – which became fully evident in the Second World War.
- By April 1939 the nationalists, led by Francisco Franco, had won the war. Franco established an authoritarian, reactionary and often brutal regime that lasted until 1975.

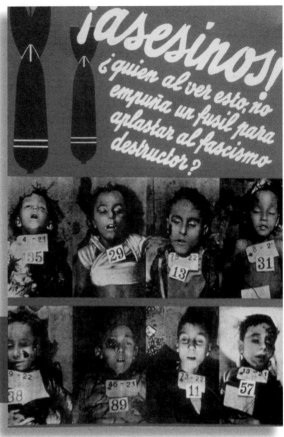

This 1937 republican poster shows eight children killed during a nationalist air raid on Madrid; it says: 'Murderers! Who, on seeing this, won't seize a gun to crush the fascist destroyers?'

What makes this such an effective propaganda poster?

What were the causes of the Spanish Civil War?

There were several reasons that civil war broke out in Spain in 1936. Some of these were short-term, but others can be traced back to the 19th century and beyond.

Spain before 1931

The Spanish élites

By 1900, the political system in Spain was based on an alliance between the monarchy, the army, the landowning aristocracy and the Catholic Church. These élites opposed any modernisation or reform that undermined their privileged position, influence and interests. However, after 1917, many workers and farm labourers in Spain were encouraged to challenge these élites by the success of the Bolshevik Revolution in Russia.

After several years of unrest, in September 1923 a military coup led by **Miguel Primo de Rivera** overthrew the parliamentary government in Spain, and Rivera established himself as dictator. The Spanish élites supported Rivera's dictatorship, believing that a strong leader was needed to suppress the working classes and restore order. The king, **Alfonso XIII**, did not approve of a constitutional monarchy, and had frequently come into conflict with the parliamentary government of Spain. As a result, the king gave the new dictatorship legitimacy by officially making Rivera prime minister.

Miguel Primo de Rivera (1870–1930) Rivera was an aristocrat and military officer who seized power in a military coup after years of political protests, strikes, revolts and economic decline. He promised to eliminate corruption and to suppress the left-wing unrest. To achieve this, he suspended the constitution, established martial law and imposed a strict system of censorship. The Great Depression affected Spain badly and, in January 1930, Rivera resigned.

Alfonso XIII (1886–1941) Alfonso became king of Spain the day he was born, as his father had died a few months earlier. He supported Rivera's coup in 1923, and appointed him prime minister. When Rivera resigned in 1930, Alfonso established another military government. Although he left Spain in April 1931, after the declaration of the Second Republic, Alfonso never formally renounced the throne. He supported the nationalists in the civil war, but after Franco won he would not permit Alfonso to return as king.

The Catholic Church in Spain was a strong supporter of the monarchy. Much more conservative than in other European countries, the Church was closely identified with the privileged and wealthy classes. It also had almost total control over education, but it paid little attention to literacy, and secondary education was limited in Spain. These factors contributed to the rise in discontent among the Spanish people, and affected the Church's influence over the masses. In the south in particular, landless peasants turned away from the Church and towards atheism and anarchism (see page 133). At the same time, industrial workers grew increasingly attracted to socialism and even communism.

The army, dominated by the conservative and aristocratic élites, upheld the monarchy and the political system. After Rivera's coup, the army ruthlessly suppressed any protests or uprisings and, like the Church, it came to be widely despised by Spaniards. While the lower classes faced a range of social and economic problems such as poverty and poor standards of education, the Spanish élites flourished under Rivera's dictatorship and regarded this period as a 'golden age'.

Economic and social conditions

Even before the Wall Street Crash of 1929 and the resulting Great Depression, the Spanish economy was underdeveloped compared to the economies of most European countries. Modern industry only began to appear in Spain in the late 19th and early 20th centuries, and even then it tended to be limited to the north and north-east of the country. There was an important coal-mining industry in Asturias, and a steel industry in the Basque region in the north, while Catalonia had a significant textile industry. However, wages and working conditions were poor, as were living conditions. There was no welfare system for the unemployed, injured or sick.

By 1929, more than half the population of Spain still worked on the land – often in terrible poverty. This was especially true in regions such as Andalusia in the south, where farming was controlled by the owners of large estates known as *latifundia*. These landowners employed landless labourers on a daily basis, and many of these workers lived in conditions of near-starvation.

Political developments

These issues led to significant political divisions and bitter struggles in Spain, and as a result there were frequent civil conflicts. Spain was (and still is) a country that is greatly divided, geographically and linguistically. Two regions in particular had strong nationalist aspirations: the Basque country in the north and Catalonia in the north-east. Basque nationalism developed considerably in the early 20th century, but was largely repressed before 1931. In Catalonia, too, there began to be separatist demands for autonomy (self-rule) in the early 20th century.

Activity

Carry out some additional research on the different regions of Spain. Then write a couple of paragraphs to explain why separatist movements were particularly strong in the Basque region and in Catalonia.

Revolutionary political movements that challenged the élites and the old order had existed in Spain for some time. The Spanish Socialist Workers' Party (PSOE) was formed in 1879, and in 1888 it founded a national trade union, the Union General de Trabajadores (General Workers' Union, UGT). Support for socialism grew after the Bolshevik Revolution in 1917, and in 1920 the Spanish Communist Party (PCE) was formed, although this was much smaller than the PSOE.

The rise of anarchism – in particular a revolutionary left-wing type of anarchism known as anarcho-syndicalism – was also significant. In 1910, anarchists set up their own national trade union, the Confederación Nacional del Trabajo (National Confederation of Workers, CNT), which became a powerful rival to the socialist-dominated UGT. Rivera banned anarchist organisations in the 1920s, but in 1927 the more militant anarchists formed the Federación Anarquista Ibérica (Spanish Anarchist Federation, FAI). The FAI gained increasing influence within the CNT and, after 1931, anarchist groups strongly re-emerged.

A map showing the regional and political divisions in Spain in 1931

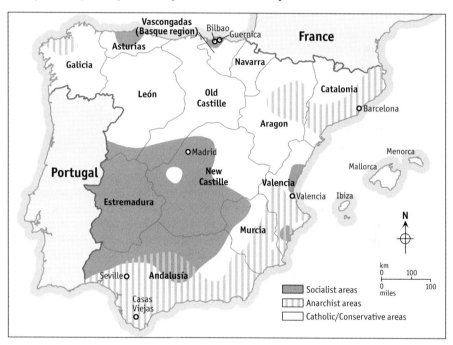

The Second Republic 1931–35

The short-term causes of the Spanish Civil War arose between 1931 and 1936. Rivera resigned in 1930 and in his place Alfonso XIII appointed another military dictator. However, in the troubled economic climate the king himself was losing support, and calls for a republic grew louder. Local elections were held in April 1931, in which republican and socialist parties made sweeping gains. A Second Republic was declared to replace the monarchy, and Alfonso fled the country. A provisional government was established to maintain control until a new constitution could be drawn up.

The left and reform 1931–33

The new Spanish republic was formed by a coalition of four parties that spanned the political spectrum: the PSOE (see page 132), the Partido Acción Republicana (Republican Action Party), the Partido Republicano Radical (Radical Republican Party) and the conservatives. In the national elections held in June 1931, these parties won a large majority and the conservative Niceto Alcalá Zamora was made prime minister. However, it soon became clear that there were serious differences of opinion over policy between the various members of the coalition, and Zamora resigned in October 1931. He was replaced by **Manuel Azaña**.

Manuel Azaña (1880–1940) Azaña was a wealthy lawyer. In 1926, he and José Giral founded the Partido Acción Republicana, a group largely made up of middle-class progressives. Azaña became prime minister of the new Spanish republic after Zamora resigned, and continued in that post after the new constitution was approved in December 1931, thus becoming the first prime minister of the Second Republic. In 1934, Azaña founded the Izquierda Republicana (Republican Left), and became president in May 1936, just before the civil war broke out. After Franco's victory, Azaña fled to France.

The new constitution was finally agreed in December 1931. Right from the start, though, several of its provisions worried conservative members of government, in particular its call for a 'democratic republic of workers'. By the new constitution, women were allowed to vote for the first time, and new laws on marriage and divorce were introduced that were the most advanced in Europe at the time. However, the main areas targeted for reform at the start of the Second Republic were the army, the Church, the treatment of workers and regional autonomy:

- The number of army officers and Spain's military budget were both reduced. These steps angered many in the military, who believed that the army was Spain's main defence against internal 'enemies'.
- Church and state were separated, and plans were made to close all religious schools. Such reforms, and unofficial anti-clerical actions in some regions, alienated most Catholics.
- During April–July 1931, decrees established the eight-hour working day and overtime pay. Small tenant farmers were protected against unfair evictions.
- In the 1931 local elections, Catalonian separatists won a sweeping victory and proclaimed a totally independent Catalan Republic. In September 1932, the Catalan Statute officially restored a large measure of autonomy for Catalonia.

Before 1931, social, economic and political power in Spain had all been in the hands of the same groups, the components of the reactionary coalition of landowners, industrialists and bankers …

However, the establishment of the Republic meant that for the first time political power had passed from the oligarchy to the moderate left … Together, they saw themselves using state power to create a new Spain. However, to do so required a vast programme of reform which would involve destroying the reactionary influence of the Church and the army, more equitable industrial relations, breaking the near feudal powers of the *latifundio* estate-owners and meeting the autonomy demands of Basque and Catalan regionalists …

Ultimately, then, the Spanish Civil War was to grow out of the efforts of the progressive leaders of the Republic to carry out reform against the wishes of the most powerful sections of society.

Preston, P. 2006. *The Spanish Civil War: Reaction, Revolution and Revenge.* London, UK. Harper Perennial. pp. 38–40.

Unrest and repression

It was not long before the Second Republic faced opposition from both left and right. Those on the political right strongly opposed rights for women and workers as well as the introduction of secular education and regional autonomy.

Anarchists and socialists were angered by the government's failure to enforce its reforms against the old élites – the landowners, industrialists, the army and the Church – in any meaningful way. Left-wing groups organised strikes and called for revolution, but the government responded harshly, using the army and the Civil Guard (a paramilitary police force) to suppress these rebellions.

In January 1933, farmers in Cadiz province – angry at the slow pace of reform and inspired by anarchist actions elsewhere – killed some Civil Guards and began an uprising in the town of Casas Viejas. The authorities sent in reinforcements, including the Assault Guards, which had been formed in 1931 to deal with urban unrest. The Guards set houses on fire, and many people were burned alive; 20 of the rebels were eventually shot – some after prolonged torture. Such acts of repression disillusioned many workers and landless peasants.

The aftermath of the massacre at Casas Viejas in January 1933

In February 1933, the growing unrest led to the formation of the Confederación Española de Derechas Autónomas (Spanish Confederation of the Autonomous Right, CEDA). CEDA was a coalition of right-wing parties, under the leadership of **José María Gil Robles**. Its purpose was to defend religion, property rights and national unity, and the group gained considerable financial backing from landowners and industrialists, who hoped that CEDA would win the elections and reverse Azaña's reforms. Another significant development in right-wing extremism in 1933 was the formation of the fascist group the Falange Española (Spanish Falange) by Rivera's son, José Antonio.

José María Gil Robles (1898–1980) Gil Robles was the leader of Acción Nacional, which was later renamed Acción Popular. He later formed CEDA, which won the elections in 1933. However, Zamora chose Alejandro Lerroux as prime minister of the new government instead of Gil Robles, although he later served as minister of war. When the civil war began, Robles authorised the donation of CEDA funds to the nationalists. He dissolved the organisation in 1937.

By autumn 1933, disagreements within the coalition caused the socialists to stop all efforts at co-operation with the republicans. As a result, Zamora dismissed the government, and ordered an election to be held in November.

The reaction of the right 1934–35

Although CEDA won a sweeping victory in the November 1933 elections, Zamora overlooked its leader Gil Robles and instead asked **Alejandro Lerroux**, the leader of the Radical Republicans, to form a government.

Alejandro Lerroux (1864–1949) The strongly anti-clerical Lerroux formed the Radical Republican Party in 1908. During the period of Rivera's dictatorship, Lerroux's party was weakened when many members left to form the Radical Socialist Republican Party in 1929. Lerroux was prime minister of Spain three times between 1933 and 1935 – once as part of the centre-left coalition, and twice following the electoral victory of the right in November 1933.

Over the next two years – known to the left as the *bienio negro* ('two black years') – the Radical Republicans and their CEDA allies reversed most of Azaña's reforms. Lerroux allowed religious schools to continue; he also repealed several laws granting rights and protection to industrial and agricultural workers, and he cut wages significantly. The UGT (see page 132) called a general strike in protest, but this was crushed by the Civil Guard. In October 1934, Gil Robles forced Lerroux to form a coalition government that contained three CEDA ministers.

During this period of growing political polarisation, the Socialist Party began to adopt a more revolutionary position, believing that Gil Robles favoured an authoritarian, even fascist, government in Spain. The socialist **Largo Caballero** called for an armed uprising to oppose the increasing power of the right. An even stronger right-wing backlash triggered violent left-wing action in Catalonia and Asturias.

Largo Caballero (1869–1946) From 1925, Caballero was leader of the Spanish Socialist Workers' Party (PSOE) and of the UGT. From 1931–33, he was minister of labour relations under Zamora and Azaña. After the CEDA victory in November 1933, Caballero moved to the left, and headed the Marxist wings of the PSOE and UGT. He supported the workers' armed uprising of 1934 and, between September 1936 and May 1937, he was prime minister at the head of the Popular Front. Caballero was forced to resign after the May Days, in which republican factions in the civil war fought each other in the streets of Barcelona.

The rebellion in Catalonia was not well organised, and was soon crushed. However, the uprising in Asturias – one of the most industrialised parts of Spain – was much more serious. Asturias was a key coal-mining region, and mine owners had responded to the impact of the Great Depression by drastically cutting wages, increasing working hours and sacking many labourers.

Encouraged by the calls for revolution, left-wing groups began an armed uprising on 5 October 1934. Within a few days, they had overcome the Civil Guard and established control over most of the province. Lerroux responded by sending more than 20,000 troops to Asturias, while the navy and air force bombed towns and villages in the region. After two weeks of bitter fighting, the rebels were defeated by the army – under the command of General **Francisco Franco**. However, the violence did not end there, as the military immediately began a campaign of savage reprisals.

Francisco Franco (1892–1975) Franco was an army officer and a supporter of Rivera's dictatorship. He strongly opposed the reforms introduced at the start of the Second Republic, and after Generals Sanjurjo and Mola were killed in two separate plane crashes in 1936 and 1937, Franco became the leader of the army's nationalist revolt. Although he was not a member of the Falange before 1939, Franco still took the title *caudillo* ('leader') – similar to the titles used by Mussolini and Hitler. After his success in the Spanish Civil War, Franco ruled Spain as an authoritarian leader until his death in 1975.

Why were the years 1934–35 known as the *bienio negro*?

Final steps to war 1935–36

The repression of the Asturias uprising convinced many on the left that they needed to join forces in a coalition to challenge CEDA and confront the rising threat of fascism. This threat seemed confirmed when Gil Robles began openly expressing his admiration for European fascism, and when CEDA adopted elements associated with fascist parties in Italy and Germany, such as uniforms and salutes. In May 1935, Gil Robles became minister of war and one of his first acts in this post was to appoint Franco as chief of the general staff. However, at the end of 1935, corruption scandals led Zamora to dismiss Lerroux's government. New elections were scheduled for February 1936.

The Popular Front 1936

In January 1936, the left finally established its coalition – the Popular Front. Socialists, communists and liberals all joined the coalition, although the anarchists refused to participate. The Popular Front won a narrow victory in the February elections, and Azaña was once again established as prime minister. The new regime – mainly composed of middle-class liberals – was determined to undo the work of the previous government, and immediately announced a political amnesty for the prisoners of the Asturias uprising. It also reintroduced plans for land reform and restored Catalonian autonomy. At the same time, Caballero (see page 137) began calls for a Bolshevik-style revolution in Spain.

These moves naturally caused concern among those on the political right. However, they were even more troubled in April 1936, when the Popular Front found a way of bypassing the constitution to remove Zamora as president and replace him with Azaña. More alarming still was the growth of unrest across the country by workers encouraged by the Popular Front victory.

In rural areas, poor peasants – impatient for land reform – seized land from the aristocracy, and Azaña's government did nothing to stop them. In the cities, the UGT and CNT unions organised strikes to protest against low wages, and these often became violent as the Falange militia tried to break them up. As a result, the government banned the Falange, and José Antonio Primo de Rivera was imprisoned. Despite this, the unrest continued.

The role of the army

Although much of the violence was due to right-wing attacks, CEDA called for a military uprising to restore 'order'. General Emilio Mola began planning a rebellion, which had CEDA's backing as well as support from the Falange and the Carlists (a political organisation that wanted to restore the monarchy). The Falange and the Carlists were particularly important to Mola's plans, as they both had paramilitary forces that could support the army. On 17 July 1936, Mola gave the order for the coup to begin – thus triggering the Spanish Civil War.

How important was foreign intervention in deciding the outcome of the war?

The nature and events of the civil war, which lasted from July 1936 to April 1939, are covered in numerous books, including Hugh Thomas's classic study *The Spanish Civil War* and Antony Beevor's *The War for Spain*. However, when investigating the eventual outcome of the war, two factors emerge as being of particular significance: foreign intervention and the relative unity/disunity within the two camps.

Foreign intervention

The involvement of foreign powers in the Spanish Civil War was a key reason for the republican defeat. It was also an important factor in the impact of the war on international diplomacy and the collapse of collective security by 1939. In 1936, neither side was expecting a lengthy conflict – nor were they equipped for it. Consequently, both sides sought foreign help. The nationalist rebels were provided with a large amount of weapons by Nazi Germany and Fascist Italy; the republicans eventually received aid from the USSR, as well as help from volunteers organised into International Brigades (see page 141).

Support for the nationalists

Initially Mola's army uprising achieved little success, and most major towns and cities – as well as the Spanish navy – remained in republican hands. To gain greater strength, the nationalists needed to bring in Franco's experienced troops, which were currently stationed in Morocco. Hitler provided planes for air cover to allow Franco to move his Army of Africa to the Spanish mainland, and this assistance early on in the civil war turned out to be hugely important for the eventual nationalist victory.

The far-right dictator of Portugal, Salazar, provided some troop support to the nationalists, but most foreign manpower came from Germany and Italy. Italy supplied 40,000 troops to the nationalist cause in Spain (more than three times the number Germany sent, according to historian Harry Browne). Germany's most significant contribution was the Condor Legion – a mixed air and tank unit, which developed a method of combined attacks on the republicans that later became a feature of the *Blitzkrieg* ('lightning war') methods used by Germany in the Second World War. In return for German assistance, Franco joined the Anti-Comintern Pact in April 1939 (see page 212), although he later refused to enter the Second World War on Germany's side.

Support for the republicans

To begin with, the republicans hoped to receive aid from France, where a Popular Front government headed by the socialist Blum (see page 105), had come to power in June 1936. The French did not want a fascist-style state allied with Germany on their southern border, so they initially agreed to sell some aircraft and artillery to the republicans. However, the British government desperately wanted to avoid war breaking out in Europe, so it refused to help the republican government in Spain, and pressured France into reversing its decision. The French knew that they could not fight a war against Germany without British support, so they proposed a Non-Intervention Pact – by which all nations agreed not to become involved in the events unfolding in Spain. In September 1936, Britain, France, Germany, Italy, the USSR and the USA were among the states that signed this pact.

However, it soon became apparent that the Non-Intervention Pact had failed to prevent foreign interference in Spanish matters. When the USSR realised that both Germany and Italy were sending large amounts of equipment to the nationalists, Soviet leader Joseph Stalin ordered that humanitarian aid and military equipment, as well as engineers and military advisors, should be sent to the republicans in Spain. The first consignment of equipment arrived in October 1936, just in time to prevent Madrid falling to the nationalists. Soviet aid – which later included tanks and aircraft – continued until 1939.

In order to prevent Western governments blocking the republic's ability to purchase this military equipment, Spain's gold reserves were transferred to Moscow. Stalin also used the republicans' dependence on the USSR to increase the influence of the Spanish Communist Party (PCE) and Soviet agents working in Spain.

Foreign assistance for the republic also came from the International Brigades, which were made up of men and women from around the world who joined together to oppose fascism. These volunteers were mainly organised by the Communist International (Comintern), but they were a mixture of socialists, communists and democrats. In all, there were about 35,000 volunteers, including about 3500 from Italy and 3000 from Germany. The arrival of the International Brigades certainly boosted republican morale, but in fact there were never more than about 15,000 of them in Spain at any one time, and most had little or no military experience. Soon the effectiveness of the International Brigades was undermined by their communist commanders, who imposed strict military discipline.

SOURCE B

During the course of the whole civil war, between 32,000 and 35,000 men from 53 different countries served in the ranks of the International Brigades. Another 5,000 foreigners served outside, mostly attached to the CNT or the POUM ... [A]lmost 80% of the volunteers from Great Britain were manual workers who either left their jobs or had been unemployed ... Some of them were glad to escape the apathy of unemployment, others had already been fighting Mosley's fascists in street battles, as their French equivalents had fought Action Francaise and the Croix de Feu ...

Most of the volunteers were very unfit, as well as ignorant of the most elementary military skills ... Men who were to be sent against the Army of Africa ... could do little except form ranks, march and turn. Many of them had never even handled a rifle until they were on the way to the front.

Beevor, A. 2006. The Battle for Spain: The Spanish Civil War 1936–1939. London, UK. Weidenfeld & Nicolson. pp. 157–59 and 162.

Unity and disunity

As well as significant differences in the amount of foreign aid each side received during the Spanish Civil War, there were also differences in the structure and unity of each of the sides involved. Both the republicans and the nationalists were made up of a variety of groups, but the republicans were more deeply divided than the nationalists.

The republicans: civil war or revolution?

Supporters of the republic were divided at the most fundamental level – they had different views on the purpose of the war as well as the best way of winning it. Middle-class liberals and the centre-right of the PSOE were opposed to the idea of any workers' revolution. They wanted to defend republican democracy, and believed that a centralised and disciplined army was the only way to defeat Franco's forces. This view was shared by the communist PCE, which followed Stalin's orders. Stalin did not want a revolution in Spain in case it prevented Britain and France from forming an alliance with the USSR to oppose the growing threat from Nazi Germany.

However, many left-wing groups *did* want a revolution, including the anarchists and those on the far left of the PSOE. Also significant – especially in the regions of Catalonia and Valencia – was the Partido Obrero de Unificación Marxista (Workers' Party of Marxist Unification, POUM). The POUM, led by **Andrés Nin** and Joaquin Maurin, was formed in 1935 by the merging of two revolutionary groups, and its membership far outnumbered that of the PCE.

Andrés Nin (1892–1937) Nin was first a member and then leader of the PSOE in Catalonia, after which he helped form the PCE. He supported the Russian revolutionary Leon Trotsky in his struggle against Stalin, and left the PCE to form a Spanish Trotskyist party. However, Nin's decision to form the POUM led Trotsky to withdraw his support for Nin. After the republican in-fighting during the Barcelona May Days of 1937, Nin was arrested and tortured to death by communist agents. A plaque in his honour can be found at the former POUM headquarters site on Las Ramblas, Barcelona.

Activity

Find out more about the various groups that wanted to turn the Spanish Civil War into a revolution. You could read George Orwell's *Homage to Catalonia*, or watch the film *Land and Freedom*. Alternatively, you can find videos on this, and the Spanish Civil War in general, on Youtube. Some examples can be found here:

www.youtube.com/watch?v=JiAFcShrwDM
www.youtube.com/watch?v=VUig0lFHDDw

The POUM believed that an immediate workers' revolution would give the ordinary people of Spain something to fight for, boosting support and going some way towards making up for the republic's relative lack of weapons and experienced troops. For this reason, the POUM favoured the formation of democratic and revolutionary people's militias.

At the start of Mola's military coup, thousands of working-class members of political and trade union groups demanded that the government issue them with weapons so they could resist the nationalists. Initially the government refused, although it later offered weapons to those fighting for the republican cause. Some historians, including Hugh Thomas, believe that the government's reluctance to equip its working-class supporters with weapons to fight the nationalists put it at a disadvantage. They claim that if this had been done immediately, the army coup might have been crushed before a full-scale civil war developed.

POUM militia leave the Lenin barracks in January 1937; George Orwell's International Brigade was attached to these units

In Barcelona, the CNT called a general strike and seized weapons. The CNT and the POUM then formed revolutionary militias that were run on anarchist principles. In areas such as Catalonia and Aragon, these militias encouraged workers and peasants to seize land from landowners and even to set up collective farms. Factories were also taken over by militia groups, and trade unions began organising the production of war materials. Similar developments took place in Asturias, Valencia, the Malaga province of Andalusia, and in and around Madrid. Eventually, on 19 July, the government reluctantly started distributing weapons to the people, and real power in defending the republic passed to armed workers' organisations and factory committees.

However, the government in Madrid opposed this 'dual power' situation, believing it would alienate the middle classes, undermine effective military resistance, and prevent Britain or France from coming to the republic's aid. Consequently, as early as 4 September 1936, the government attempted to reassert its control. Militia groups were broken up and incorporated into regular army units. As the communists became increasingly influential, the police began to repress the more revolutionary organisations, claiming that they were in league with Franco's nationalist forces. In May 1937, the police and pro-communist troops in Barcelona attacked and defeated anarchist and POUM forces.

Activity

'The policies of the revolutionary Marxists and anarchists in 1936–37 offered the best chance for a Popular Front victory in the Spanish Civil War.' Hold a class debate on this assertion, with proposers and seconders for both sides of the argument. These – and the rest of the class – should make sure that all arguments are supported by specific facts and examples.

Many people in Spain felt demoralised by the obvious divisions among left-wing groups, and this reduced the effectiveness of republican forces, making a significant contribution to the republic's eventual defeat.

SOURCE C

After the Civil War, Franco claimed that the Rising had been a pre-emptive strike to prevent a left-wing take-over. Except within nationalist propaganda, no such communist conspiracy had ever existed, yet one of the many ironies of Spain's Civil War was that the army rebellion triggered off a Spanish revolution which was broadly anarchist rather than communist. Throughout Republican Spain, except in the Basque Provinces, the established authorities were swept aside and replaced by workers' committees ...

During the first year of the war, the Revolution became a key question in the political debates within the Republic. To liberals and many socialists the Revolution was divisive and could endanger success against the common enemy; it must therefore be halted, rolled back even ... To most anarchists, however, as to the POUM in Catalonia, the Republic without the Revolution would be void of social content, a liberal political shell whose defence would not win hearts and minds ... The revolution challenged, too, the male chauvinism so strongly entrenched in Spain. In some ways, the liberation of women took giant steps forward in Republican towns, although in the countryside attitudes changed hardly at all.

Browne, H. 1996. Spain's Civil War. London, UK. Longman. pp. 54–55.

How did the political differences amongst the republicans contribute to the nationalist victory?

Franco and the nationalists

The early revolutionary wave after the start of the army rising – and the upheavals that had occurred before 1936 – ensured that the nationalist rebels had the support of the established élites in Spain. Franco was especially keen to win the backing of the Church, as the majority of Spaniards were Catholics. Initially, the army uprising was claimed to be in defence of the fatherland, but Franco soon added defence of the Catholic faith to the alleged aims of the war. In addition, once he became aware of how important the Church was to his supporters, Franco made determined efforts to appear religious himself.

On 1 July 1937, the majority of Spanish bishops signed a document known as the Collective Letter, in which they described the civil war as a 'Christian crusade' of good against the evil of 'godless communism'. This letter – and similar statements made by the Church – helped the nationalists gain the support of Catholics both within Spain and beyond its borders.

Despite a wave of savage repression carried out by the nationalists against republican supporters – known as the 'White Terror' – the Church made no public criticism. Church leaders later claimed that they were unaware of nationalist actions at this time, but in fact it is known that many churchmen took part in acts of repression and, in some cases, participated in the killing of republican supporters.

Discussion point

Can the behaviour of the Catholic Church in Spain during the civil war be justified? Divide the class into two groups: one to support the Church's actions, and one to oppose them. Remember to support your points by using specific details about the events of 1936–39. How different was the role of the Catholic Church in Fascist Italy or Nazi Germany to that in Spain?

Perhaps most importantly, the attitude of Church leaders in Spain eventually helped win the support of the papacy, which had initially condemned the violence on both sides. In 1937, the pope gave in to the calls of the Spanish Church not to support Azaña's appeal for a negotiated peace. Instead, the pope officially recognised the nationalist cause.

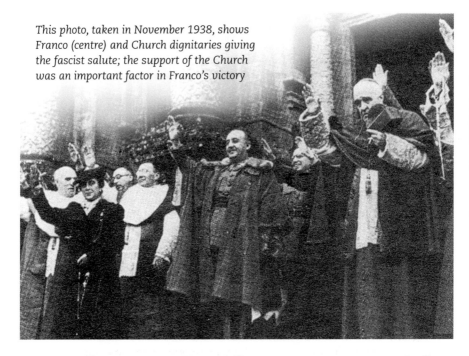

This photo, taken in November 1938, shows Franco (centre) and Church dignitaries giving the fascist salute; the support of the Church was an important factor in Franco's victory

What were the main consequences of the Spanish Civil War?

The Spanish Civil War naturally had a significant impact within the country. However, it also affected international diplomacy in the late 1930s, and contributed to the eventual outbreak of the Second World War.

Franco's dictatorship

After his victory in the civil war, Franco was determined to fully establish his control over Spain. In the early years in particular, this meant brutal repression of any groups or individuals who opposed him.

Franco refused to restore the monarchy, or to give the fascist Falange any real power after 1939, even though both had provided him with valuable support during the civil war. Franco made strenuous efforts to promote his own importance as the 'saviour' of Spain. He was assisted in this by an unofficial alliance with the Church. In 1938 – before the war was won – the nationalists drew up a series of Clerical Laws, promising to give the Church an important position in the new nationalist Spanish state. These included granting a monopoly over primary education and the right to its own independent youth movements, outlawing all non-Christian religions, and severely restricting the rights of Protestants. When the nationalists won the civil war, Franco implemented these laws. In return, the Church endorsed Franco's continuing crusade against atheists and Marxists, and remained silent about the atrocities and executions committed under his regime.

Franco made use of both censorship and propaganda to maintain his personal rule. A Press Law of April 1938 was applied after the nationalist victory in 1939, by which the government reserved the right to authorise all publications, and to shut down those to which it objected. It also had the right to appoint the editors of all newspapers, and to sack journalists.

Franco also used terror to root out potential opponents, to ensure his continued power. In fact, this wave of terror had begun before 1939, as new areas fell into nationalist hands. For example, in February 1937, after the nationalists seized the town of Malaga, 3500 republicans were executed; by 1944, a further 17,000 executions had taken place. After 1939, the police and the Falange militia were placed under military control. The police arrested suspected radicals, who were tried by military courts that required very little evidence to secure a conviction. By 1945, more than 500,000 of these radicals had been found guilty and more than 200,000 were executed by the Falange militia. Those most likely to suffer such punishments were those considered to be 'un-Spanish' – mainly socialists, communists, trade unionists, separatists, liberated women and middle-class radicals who had supported the republic. The arrests and punishments created an atmosphere of fear – the Spanish people called these years 'a time of silence', as few dared speak out against Franco's repression.

Discussion point

Which do you think was more important in the establishment and maintenance of Franco's rule – censorship/propaganda or terror?

The Spanish economy did not recover well after the civil war, and most historians blame Franco's economic policies for this failure. The Falange supported Franco's dictatorship, as he adopted two elements of fascist economic policy – corporatism and autarchy. Corporatism favoured employers and industrialists. No independent trade unions were allowed; instead workers and employers became part of a government-controlled syndicate or corporation. These corporations controlled wage rates, production levels and prices.

Franco hoped that economic controls – especially on imports – would help the Spanish economy recover from both the Great Depression and the civil war. Although this ensured further support from the Falange, it was a disaster for Spain. Living standards for workers declined as wages failed to keep up with price increases.

In addition, Franco's high military spending (between 1939 and 1945, about 50% of the budget went on the armed forces) meant there was less money available to rebuild industry and agriculture.

> ### Activity
>
> Look back at Chapter 4, then make a list of the similarities and differences between Mussolini's regime in Italy and Franco's regime in Spain.

Collective security and the Second World War

The Spanish Civil War also had important consequences for collective security across Europe.

Non-intervention

The two major powers in the League of Nations, Britain and France, proposed that all countries should agree not to intervene in the Spanish Civil War. In September 1936, the Non-Intervention Committee met in London to draw up a pact, which was signed by several countries – including Germany, Italy, the USSR and the USA. Although this effectively blocked the purchase of war materials by the republicans, the nationalists still found it relatively easy to buy such materials from many of the democracies that had signed the pact, including the USA and Britain. According to historian Robert Whealey, in July 1938 alone Franco bought over 30% of his material from British companies, without interference from the British government. Hitler noted the inaction of the British government, and some historians have argued that it helped the German leader reach the conclusion that there would be no serious opposition to his plans for expansion in Central and Eastern Europe.

Importance to the Axis powers

The Spanish Civil War was of great significance to Nazi Germany. In return for German military assistance, Franco provided Hitler with raw materials that greatly aided German rearmament. In addition, Hitler's intervention allowed him to test out his military tactics. This was especially important for the Luftwaffe, which gained valuable experience from the Condor Legion's bombing missions. The efficiency of anti-tank and anti-aircraft guns was also established.

The most significant benefit to Nazi Germany was in fact an assumed one. As Britain and France adopted policies of appeasement and non-intervention, Hitler became convinced that they would take no stand against his own plans for territorial expansion. According to W. C. Frank, Hitler's earlier regard for Britain declined as a result of its inaction. In particular, it gave him the confidence to annex Austria and move against Czechoslovakia in 1938. In fact, Frank believes that it was the experiences gained in the Spanish Civil War that encouraged

Hitler to risk war as early as he did. As well as confirming his views about Britain and France, the experience of the Spanish Civil War also gave Hitler a greater hold over Mussolini. Fascist Italy's intervention further weakened its relationship with Britain, and instead pushed it firmly into Hitler's camp – setting it on course for involvement in the Second World War.

Appeasement and non-intervention

The policy of non-intervention failed and, as noted above, mainly served to expose the weaknesses of Britain and France. Non-intervention only postponed the outbreak of the Second World War – and France was left facing a hostile neighbour in the south, allied to Nazi Germany. The Soviet Union intervened initially to show its support for a democratic republic and its opposition to any revolution in Spain, in the hope that this would result in an anti-fascist alliance with Britain and France. However, Soviet hopes were dashed, and in fact the USSR also came to the conclusion that appeasement meant that Britain and France would not oppose any eastwards expansion by Hitler. Although Stalin continued to press for a grand anti-fascist alliance until April 1939, he also began to consider a temporary deal with Nazi Germany.

SOURCE D

The Spanish Civil War, non-intervention and intervention had an impact on the subsequent fortunes of the world powers. Non-intervention failed to appease the dictators. Intervention hardly benefited Italy and the Soviet Union. Only Germany really gained an advantage, both economically and militarily, from its participation in the Spanish war. Above all, the Civil War can be seen as a rehearsal for, or at least a prelude to, the Second World War … The weaknesses of the democracies were neatly exposed by their refusal to intervene in Spain. According to Mary Habeck, the Spanish war prevented Franco-British unity against the dictators in that it distracted attention from far greater dangers …

Britain's policy of compromise, rather than calming the international situation, only heightened tension between the European powers. The British government failed to understand that Spain was another arena where Germany and Italy were testing how far their aggressive stance could be taken … The Civil War also alienated the Soviet Union from the West. Receiving no response to appeals for collective security, Stalin became increasingly convinced that appeasement would channel Hitler's attention towards the East.

Durgan, A. 2007. *The Spanish Civil War. Basingstoke, UK. Palgrave Macmillan.* pp. 74–76.

Ultimately, the policies of non-intervention and appeasement failed to calm the international situation. Instead, the Spanish Civil War only confirmed the growing ideological divisions between left and right, democracies and dictatorships in Europe. In addition, Hitler's and Mussolini's early fears that Britain would enforce the policy of non-intervention soon disappeared. The British government seemed determined to avoid another European war.

A cartoon published on 14 December 1936 in the British newspaper the Evening Standard, *commenting on the League's inaction during the Spanish Civil War*

Finally, although European tensions over Austria, Abyssinia, the Rhineland and the Sudetenland (see page 177) arguably had a more direct impact on the eventual outbreak of the Second World War, the Spanish Civil War certainly contributed to the growing European crisis. In addition, the bombing of civilian populations in Guernica, Barcelona, Lerida and Madrid gave a taste of the modern and devastating type of war that was about to begin. By the end of the civil war, Europe was divided into two opposed power blocs that would eventually fight in a global conflict.

 ## Theory of knowledge

History, emotion and bias

The American writer William Faulkner (1897–1962) wrote: 'The past is never dead. It's not even past.' The Spanish Civil War – at least in part – involved a life-and-death struggle between fascism and its opponents, and seemed to many to be a precursor for the Second World War. Given that Franco's dictatorship only ended just over 30 years ago, and neo-fascist groups are still active in several countries, are historians who write about the civil war able to avoid bias?

End of chapter activities
Paper 3 exam practice
Question

Analyse the reasons for the outcome of the Spanish Civil War 1936–39.
[20 marks]

Skill focus

Avoiding a narrative-based answer

Examiner's tips

Even once you have read the question carefully (and so avoided the temptation of giving irrelevant material), produced your plan and written your introductory paragraph, it is still possible to go wrong.

By 'writing a narrative answer', history examiners mean providing supporting knowledge that is relevant (and may well be very precise and accurate) **but** that is not clearly linked to the question. Instead of answering the question, it merely **describes** what happened.

The main body of your essay/argument needs to be **analytical**. It must not simply be an answer in which you just 'tell the story'. Your essay must **address the demands/key words of the question**. Ideally, this should be done consistently throughout your essay, by linking each paragraph to the previous one, in order to produce a clear 'joined-up' answer.

> You are especially likely to lapse into a narrative answer when answering your final question – and even more so if you are getting short of time. The 'error' here is that, despite all your good work at the start of the exam, you will lose sight of the question and just produce an **account**, rather than an analysis. So, even if you are short of time, try to write several analytical paragraphs.

Note that if a question asks you to analyse the reasons for something, it expects you to consider a range of reasons and, if possible, to reach a judgement about the relative importance of these factors. Very often, such a question gives you the opportunity to refer to different historians' views (see page 197 for more on this).

A good way of avoiding a narrative approach is to refer back to the question continually, and even to mention it now and again in your answer. This should help you produce an answer that is focused on the specific aspects of the question – rather than just giving information about the broad topic or period.

For this question, you will need to analyse the following aspects:

- the relative military strengths of the two sides at the start of the civil war
- the degree of unity/disunity affecting the two sides
- the military and economic help received by both sides.

You will then need to make a judgement in your concluding paragraph about the relative importance of the factors you have considered.

Common mistake

Every year, even candidates who have clearly revised well, and who therefore have a good knowledge of the topic and of any historical debate surrounding it, still end up producing a mainly narrative-based or descriptive answer. Very often, this is the result of not having drawn up a proper plan.

The extracts of the student's answer below show an approach that essentially just describes the main features of the Spanish Civil War, without any analysis of why certain factors were or were not important in affecting the eventual outcome.

Sample paragraphs of narrative-based approach

This example shows what examiners mean by a narrative answer – it is something you should **not** copy!

At the start of the civil war, the two sides were fairly evenly matched. The bulk of the army was made up of the Peninsular Army, which had about 100,000 soldiers, and the Army of Africa – based in Morocco – which was the élite force and numbered about 45,000. Although the military plotters had the majority of the professional troops at their disposal, their initial plan to capture Madrid and other main cities failed. In five out of the seven places on mainland Spain that they attempted to seize, their forces were defeated by those police and troops who remained loyal to the republic, and by local militias.

In addition, the republic was able to retain control of the navy, which meant that at first the Army of Africa was unable to reach mainland Spain. However, the nationalist rebels were able to take control of parts of western Andalusia in the south, and of parts of the north-west centred on Valladolid.

Nonetheless, the republic held the bulk of Spain's industrial centres and ports – important for production and supplies – and, as the legally elected government, was initially recognised by most countries as the legitimate power. However, this situation began to change over the next few months.

During August and September, Franco was able to bring his Army of Africa over from Morocco, to join the mainland forces of the nationalists. He had been flown from the Canary Islands – where he had been posted by the republican government in February 1936, as it had doubted his loyalty – to Morocco, in a private plane flown by two British MI6 agents. Once there, he took control of the troops – and then received planes from Nazi Germany, which allowed him to transport these troops to Spain.

While Britain and France set up the Non-Intervention Committee in August 1936, and so gave no supplies to the republican government, Germany and Italy began to openly increase the amount of supplies they had been sending to help the nationalists.

The rest of the essay continues in the same way – there are also plenty of accurate/relevant facts about the aid sent by Germany and Italy to the nationalists, and by the USSR to the republicans; the contributions made by the International Brigades, and about the divisions amongst the republicans. However, there is no attempt to answer the question by **analysing** these factors and **explaining** how they affected the eventual outcome. Such an answer would only gain 10 marks at most.

Activity

In this chapter, the focus is on avoiding writing narrative-based answers. Using the information from this chapter, and any other sources of information available to you, try to answer **one** of the following Paper 3 practice questions in a way that avoids simply describing what happened.

Remember to refer to the simplified Paper 3 markscheme on page 225.

Paper 3 practice questions

1   Analyse the causes and consequences of the Spanish Civil War in the years between 1931 and 1939.

2   Compare and contrast the impact of foreign intervention in the Spanish Civil War for the republicans and for the nationalists.

3   Assess the importance of the Spanish Civil War 1936–39 in international diplomacy.

4   Evaluate the impact of the policy of non-intervention on collective security in the period 1936–39.

5   'The Spanish Civil War was a missed opportunity for the democracies to prevent a wider European war.' To what extent do you agree with this statement?

8 Germany and Hitler

Key questions

- How did Hitler establish his Nazi dictatorship?
- What were Hitler's main economic and social policies?
- Did Hitler's foreign policy follow a consistent plan?

In January 1933, Hitler became chancellor of Germany and soon began to create a Nazi dictatorship. Despite promises to establish a new 'classless' community, his Nazi state mainly benefited the wealthier classes, while independent trade unions and strikes were outlawed. Hitler's economic policies for overcoming the effects of the Depression had mixed success, although his attempts to increase Nazi support up to 1939 proved more fruitful. However, Hitler's foreign policy after 1939 eventually brought about his downfall.

Overview

- In January 1933, Hitler was appointed chancellor of a coalition government. He immediately began moves to increase his power and create a Nazi dictatorship.
- After the Reichstag fire and the March 1933 elections, Hitler pushed through the Enabling Act, which gave him emergency powers for four years. By July 1933, trade unions had been banned and Germany had become a one-party state.
- In June 1934, Hitler carried out the Night of the Long Knives, which established his power over the Nazi Party.
- The Nazis followed economic policies designed to overcome the problems arising from the Depression and to make Germany self-sufficient and ready for war. These policies achieved mixed results.
- The Nazis' *Volksgemeinschaft* ('people's community') policy also tried to unite most sections of German society, but some groups were specifically excluded. Jewish people in particular were increasingly persecuted, especially after 1938.
- At first Hitler's foreign policy seemed similar to that pursued by governments during the Weimar Republic. However, after 1934, when his attempt at *Anschluss* with Austria was blocked, Hitler began a more aggressive policy and tried to ally himself with Italy.
- During the years 1935–38, Hitler openly announced rearmament, and took several steps that defied the terms of the Treaty of Versailles. Initially, Britain followed a policy of appeasement and France was not prepared to act without British support.
- Hitler's decision to invade Poland in September 1939 led to the start of the Second World War – and ultimately to his suicide, and the downfall of the Third Reich.

How did Hitler establish his Nazi dictatorship?

With only two other Nazis in his 12-strong coalition cabinet, Hitler's position as chancellor was far from secure. However, one of these Nazis was minister of the interior, which meant that he was in charge of the police; within weeks, therefore, the Nazi Party was able to take control of Germany.

Hitler addresses a crowd of thousands of uniformed men during a Nazi rally in Dortmund in 1933

The road to dictatorship 1933–34

Initially, Hitler and the Nazis set about destroying the Weimar Republic and establishing their dictatorship mainly through legal means.

The March election 1933

Hitler's Nazi–Nationalist coalition lacked a majority in the Reichstag, so Hitler immediately called another election for March 1933. He obtained presidential decrees to ban meetings of any opposition parties and to close down their newspapers so they could not influence public opinion. At the same time, **Hermann Göring** was given sweeping powers to act against the socialist SPD and the communist KPD when Hitler dissolved the provincial parliament. The Nazi election campaign was also helped by large donations from business leaders.

Hermann Göring (1893–1946) Göring joined the Nazi Party in 1923, and by 1933 he had become one Hitler's most trusted senior advisors. Göring helped establish the first concentration camps, arranged (with Himmler) the Night of the Long Knives, and supervised the Four-Year Plan. In 1935, Göring became head of the Luftwaffe and, in 1938, he took control of all the German armed forces. In 1939, he was appointed Hitler's deputy. Göring was convicted of war crimes after the Second World War, but he committed suicide before he could be executed.

The Reichstag fire February 1933

On 27 February, a week before the elections were due to be held, the Reichstag building was set on fire. Hitler immediately claimed that this was the start of a communist revolution. The following day he issued the Decree for the Protection of the People and State, which banned the KPD and gave the government the power to suspend most of the civil and political liberties guaranteed by the Weimar Constitution. Thousands of opponents (especially communists and socialists) were arrested. Although the Nazis only won 43.9% of the vote in the election, they quickly seized control of several state governments where their opponents were in power.

The Enabling Act March 1933

The support of the 52 nationalists of the DNVP gave the Nazis a majority in parliament, but they still lacked the two-thirds majority needed to overthrow the Weimar Constitution. Hitler therefore demanded an Enabling Act, giving him full emergency powers for four years. In addition, to win the support of other centre-right parties, Hitler claimed that the Nazis shared the values of Imperial Germany, and in the first session of the Reichstag Hitler excluded all communist deputies. By promising to respect the rights of the Catholic Church and Christian principles, Hitler persuaded the Centre Party to support his demands. As a result of these political manoeuvrings, Hitler eliminated all opposition except the SPD deputies – and thus won his two-thirds majority.

SOURCE A

The Enabling Act was the constitutional foundation-stone of the Third Reich. In purely legal terms the Weimar constitution was never formally dissolved, but in practice the Enabling Act provided the basis for creating the arbitrary dictatorship which evolved in the course of 1933. The intolerance and violence exhibited by the Nazis along the road to power could now be converted into a tool of government, thus legally sanctioning the creation of a personal and party dictatorship under Hitler and the Nazis. The destruction of Weimar's remaining hallmarks of an open, liberal and pluralist society into the Nazi state system is usually referred to as *Gleichschaltung* – literally 'bringing into line' or, more commonly, 'co-ordination' ... What did *Gleichschaltung* mean in practice? ... it was the deliberate attempt to Nazify the life of Germany ... However, in the spring and summer of 1933 it was the 'co-ordination' of Germany's political system which was the real focus of attention, for the continued existence of the federal states, the political parties and a labour movement were totally at odds with Nazi political aspirations.

Layton, G. 1992. *Germany: The Third Reich 1933–45. London, UK. Hodder & Stoughton. pp. 50–51.*

Why was the Enabling Act such an important step in establishing the Nazi dictatorship?

Gleichschaltung – creating a one-party state

From this point, the Nazis began to establish a one-party totalitarian dictatorship under Hitler's leadership. This was achieved mainly through a process of *Gleichschaltung*, aimed at 'co-ordinating' German political, social and cultural life with Nazi ideology and values. The first targets were local government, trade unions and other political parties.

The provinces

Since February 1933, Nazis in the provinces (*Länder*) had been intimidating their opponents and undermining local governments in order to establish control. In April, Nazi-dominated state governments were granted the authority to make laws without having to obtain the approval of the provincial parliaments (*Landtage*). Hitler then appointed ten Nazi Reich governors (*Reichsstatthälter*), who had almost total control. In January 1934, the Law for the Reconstruction of the Reich abolished the *Landtage*, and all federal governments were placed under the control of the Ministry of the Interior.

The trade unions

Although the trade unions in Germany had a large membership, the effects of mass unemployment eroded their potential power. In addition, many trade union leaders believed that Hitler's government would soon fall, so they tried to avoid provoking the Nazis. Nonetheless, on 2 May, SA and SS members occupied trade union buildings, and most leaders and the more militant activists were arrested. Trade unions were then abolished, and all workers were ordered to join the Nazi Deutsche Arbeitsfront (German Labour Front, DAF), which had no power to negotiate wages or working conditions.

The political parties

The elimination of opposition parties was carried out through a range of actions over a short period of time. The communist KPD was banned after the Reichstag fire; on 22 June 1933, the SPD was also abolished.

In the following weeks, the remaining political parties either merged with the Nazis or disbanded. On 14 July, Hitler imposed the Law Against the Formation of New Parties, which made the NSADP the only legal political party in Germany. Thus, within six months of being appointed chancellor, Hitler had turned Germany into a one-party dictatorship, known as the Third Reich – a great empire intended to last 1000 years.

A cartoon published in the US periodical The Nation *in 1936*

"In these three years I have restored honor and freedom to the German people!"

Discussion point

The Nazis came to power legally, yet they were clearly intent on establishing a dictatorship. How do you think people should have reacted to Nazi policies and actions in the first months of Hitler's rule? Should they have accepted them, as they were technically legal, or should they have organised mass protests to resist the policies and bring down the government?

The Night of the Long Knives June 1934

Although *Gleichschaltung* had gone a long way towards establishing a Nazi dictatorship, Hitler's position was not fully consolidated. The German army had not been 'co-ordinated' and still had the power to overthrow him. Hitler's position was also increasingly threatened by the more militant lower sections of the NSDAP, who wanted a 'second revolution' based on the socialist sections of the party's programme. Ernst Röhm – leader of the 2.5-million strong SA – demanded that the regular army be merged with the SA to form a new People's Army under his command.

Hitler did not want to upset the army commanders, partly because he needed their support for his foreign policy objectives and partly because he feared that Röhm's activities might provoke the army into taking action against the new Nazi regime. He therefore needed to eliminate the threat from Röhm and the SA, and to establish his total control of the NSDAP.

On 30 June 1934, the SS (with weapons and transport provided by the army) arrested and shot many of the SA leaders, including Röhm. This became known as the 'Night of the Long Knives', and over the next few days more than 400 people were murdered. This action secured Hitler's popularity with the army, and when Hindenburg died on 1 August the army supported Hitler's takeover of the post of president and the position's merger with the role of chancellor. On 2 August, the army swore an oath of loyalty to the new Führer and 'supreme commander of the armed forces'.

Building the Nazi state 1935–39

Terror and propaganda both played an important part in allowing the Nazis to consolidate their domination of German politics, and in enhancing Hitler's own power.

Terror and the police state

The cornerstone of the Nazi police state was the SS. By 1939, the SS and the Gestapo (the secret police) had complete power to arrest, torture and execute all 'enemies of the state'. Concentration (detention) camps were set up almost as soon as Hitler became chancellor. The first one was established at Dachau; its inmates were the communists who had been arrested after the Reichstag fire. Nazi officials called *Blockleiters* ('block leaders') supervised urban neighbourhoods, and reported to the police anyone who showed signs of not fully supporting Hitler. Many Germans, therefore, lived in constant fear of being arrested and interned in one of these camps. Documents released after 1945 show that thousands of ordinary Germans denounced their neighbours, work colleagues and even family members to the authorities.

Activity

Historian Daniel Goldhagen has commented that many Germans were Hitler's 'willing executioners', and there is some evidence that many Germans were active participants in support of Nazi policies. Carry out some further research on this. Do your findings suggest that Goldhagen's comments are valid?

The Nazis also pushed through a 'legal revolution', which ended most of the legal rights established by the Weimar Constitution. Only judges who were considered loyal and who were trained in the ideological foundations of Nazism were appointed. As early as March 1933, a parallel Nazi legal system was also created; Special Courts were set up – with no juries – to administer Nazi justice more swiftly.

 Theory of knowledge

History – past and present

According to the historian Bettany Hughes: 'History's job is not just to catalogue the world, but to try to comprehend it. History, can, and should, act as a moral agent.' While history helps us understand why something happened, can it ever teach us any moral lessons that can be applied to the present? In what ways can history act as a 'moral agent'?

Propaganda, censorship and the 'Hitler Myth'

The Nazi propaganda machine was run by Joseph Goebbels (see page 61), who quickly established Nazi control of the mass media and spread Nazi propaganda in order to unite all Germans behind their Führer. One of Goebbels' first acts as minister was to set up the Reich Radio Company, which centralised all broadcasting in Germany. As fewer than 25% of German households had a radio in 1933, the Nazis mass-produced cheap radios; by 1939, over 70% of German households owned one of these *Volksempfänger* ('people's receivers'). Radios and loudspeakers were also set up in all the main public spaces across Germany to ensure that as many people as possible heard the Nazi message.

To begin with, Goebbels banned all newspapers owned by the SPD and the KPD. Then the NSDAP's own publishing house, Eher Verlag, bought many of the other remaining newspapers; by 1939, the Nazis owned more than 60% of all German newspapers. Newspapers were only allowed to print news and pictures that had been officially approved. Finally, in October 1933, the Editors' Law made editors responsible for ensuring that their newspapers' content met with the approval of Goebbels' ministry.

Nazi ideals were also publicised through literature, cinema, music and art – all of which came under the control of Goebbels' Reich Chamber of Culture, established in 1933. Under the Nazis, literature and art had to serve the Nazi state and promote values intended to bind Germans together in the new people's community. Goebbels also organised mass rallies (for example, the Nuremberg rallies) and various public celebrations to widen support for Hitler and the Third Reich. Cinemas showed newsreels covering Hitler's speeches, Nazi rallies and all important announcements.

Historians including David Schoenbaum have argued that these methods allowed the Nazis to change the values and beliefs of the German people after 1933. However, this view has been criticised by historians such as Dick Geary, who point out that – given the fear and terror, and the lack of any alternatives – it is extremely difficult to identify what was genuine support for Nazi aims and values and what was merely passive assent.

The Nazi state and the élites

Until 1938, Hitler avoided antagonising influential élite groups such as the army, the civil service, big business and landowners. The Nazis did not completely take over existing institutions – instead, they either attached themselves to established administrative organisations, or created new groups that worked in parallel with them. The army, in particular, was one organisation that avoided Nazi control throughout most of the Third Reich's rule. However, in 1938, Hitler removed some of the army's top officers and made himself supreme commander.

Personnel changes were not imposed immediately: three key ministries (War, Foreign Affairs and Economics) remained under the leadership of the traditional élites until the late 1930s. It was not until February 1938 that every ministry was headed by a high-ranking Nazi. The German civil service remained largely staffed by conservatives and nationalists, although in 1939 Nazi Party membership was made compulsory for all new recruits.

Hitler as Führer

Historians disagree over exactly how power was distributed in the Nazi state and, especially, the extent to which Hitler was the sole dictator of the Third Reich. The nature of the Nazi state was highly complex, and historians such as Jeremy Noakes regard the different organisations in Nazi Germany as semi-independent empires, acting in competition with one another. For example, although Hjalmar Schacht was minister of economics from 1934 to 1937, after 1936 he often came into conflict with the growing economic 'empire' built up by Göring under his Four-Year Plan (see page 166). The most powerful of these Nazi empires was the SS: its leader, Himmler, was answerable only to Hitler. Confusion has also arisen because Hitler himself never clearly stated what the relationship between the party and the state should be.

Debate about the nature and distribution of power in the Nazi state mainly concerns Hitler's supremacy and style of rule. According to Franz Neumann, although there were four power blocs in Nazi Germany (the party, the army, the bureaucracy and big business), Hitler remained in charge of them all. The importance of the personal oath of loyalty to Hitler, and the *Führerprinzip* ('leadership principle') that prevailed at all levels of party and state, ensured he remained in overall control.

However, historians are divided over whether Hitler was a strong or weak dictator. Although some have argued that he played little part in the development of economic or social policy, most agree that Hitler did play a decisive role in foreign policy, and in decisions involving war and race. Historians in the Intentionalist school (such as Alan Bullock, Klaus Hildebrand and K. D. Bracher) stress that, although there was administrative confusion and rivalry, Hitler was the overall Führer or 'master of the Third Reich' and no important steps were taken without his approval. Sebastian Haffner refers to this as 'controlled chaos'.

Structuralists such as Martin Broszat and Hans Mommsen, on the other hand, believe that Hitler was lazy and weak, and often failed to give clear and consistent directions. The result of this was a chaotic 'polycratic' system. Where many Intentionalists see this as a deliberate attempt by Hitler to 'divide and rule', Structuralists argue that it resulted in Hitler's role being mainly to approve policies pushed by the various power blocs.

Activity

Using the internet, carry out some additional research on the historical debates about whether Hitler was a strong or weak dictator. Then write a couple of paragraphs evaluating the different arguments.

What were Hitler's main economic and social policies?

Nazi promises to create a new order and a classless national society led many Germans to expect a 'second revolution' as soon as power had been established. However, Hitler (like Mussolini in Italy) became ruler of Germany by co-operating with the traditional ruling élites rather than by overthrowing them. Nazi economic and social policies were therefore cautious and conservative.

The economy 1933–39

Hitler had little interest in economic policy, but he wanted the economy to be strong enough for Germany to undertake military conquest. As early as February 1933, he began talking of the need to create a 'military economy'. The Nazis had two broad economic aims: to overcome the effects of the Depression and restart the economy; and to create a *Wehrwirtschaft*, or war economy, in part by achieving German autarchy (economic self-sufficiency).

Dealing with the Depression

An early indication that Nazi economic policy would not follow a revolutionary path was Hitler's appointment of Hjalmar Schacht (see page 48) to oversee economic policy. Schacht was a conservative banker with close ties to Germany's industrialists and bankers. Although he was not a Nazi, he was president of the Reichsbank from 1933 to 1939, and from 1934 to 1937 he was also minister of economics. Schacht's appointment reassured the élites that the Nazis had no intention of harming the interests of big business.

In January 1933, unemployment stood at over 6 million – more than 30% of the labour force. By 1936, this had dropped to 1.7 million and it continued to decline, partly due to government spending on public works schemes. Subsidies and tax concessions were also given to private companies to encourage them to employ more workers. After 1935, conscription and the expansion of the armed forces also helped reduce unemployment. However, it should be noted that some credit for the rise in employment levels lies with programmes that had been set up by the last Weimar governments; in addition, the Nazis benefited from a general improvement in the world economy after 1933.

Previously unemployed men march to begin work on the first Autobahn
(motorway) in September 1933

For all his efforts, Schacht's policies led to inflation and, more
seriously, a balance of payments deficit (that is, imports were
costing Germany more than its exports earned). To overcome these
problems, Schacht was given wide powers to deal with the economy.
In September 1934, he introduced the New Plan, based on total
government control of trade and currency exchange, to prioritise
imports for heavy industry in general and the armaments industry
in particular. He also suspended all interest payments on Germany's
foreign debts. These policies had some success, and by the end of 1935
Germany had achieved a trade surplus, while industrial production
was up by almost 50% from 1933.

However, there was no significant increase in exports or efficiency.
Schacht's policy of printing secret government bonds (known as 'mefo'
bills) to conceal the true expenditure on armaments also contributed
to inflation. In addition, despite efforts to achieve self-sufficiency,
Germany still needed to import raw materials for its rearmament
programme. In 1936, a new economic crisis developed over the balance
of payments – Schacht argued this could only be solved by reducing
spending on rearmament. This ran counter to the Nazis' plans, and
was opposed by the armed forces.

Wehrwirtschaft ('war economy') and the Four-Year Plan

Hitler's response, in September 1936, was to put Göring in charge of a plan designed to make Germany's economy and military forces ready for war in four years' time. The plan outlined the need to control all imports and exports, increase agricultural production, and make Germany self-sufficient in all important raw materials. Göring's plan was supposed to operate alongside Schacht's, but in practice Nazi control over industry increased. Schacht found his position and policies increasingly undermined, and his warnings about the balance of payments problem were ignored. He resigned in November 1937.

Large companies benefited most from Nazi rule during 1933–36. However, the Four-Year Plan reduced the amount of influence big business had after 1936. The massive amounts of state money poured into research and development, and into armaments production, gave the Nazi regime increasing control over several sectors of the economy. There were also some compulsory mergers in order to create monopoly firms which, it was hoped, would be more efficient. In 1933, about 40% of German production was under monopoly control; by 1937, this had risen to over 70%.

Success and failure

Schacht's and Göring's plans did result in big increases in production in some key industries, and by the end of 1938 Germany's total industrial production had increased by just over 100% from its 1933 levels. During the same period, the official number of unemployed dropped to 300,000. However, the Nazis had not carried out an economic miracle, and there were several crucial failures. Firstly, the aim to be self-sufficient in raw materials failed: over 30% of Germany's main raw materials and 20% of its food still had to be imported from abroad. At the same time, rearmament also failed to reach the set targets. By 1939, therefore, Germany was not in a position to fight a long-lasting war.

Activity

Carry out some further research to find out how far Nazi policies against Jewish and female employment (and putting large numbers of opponents in concentration camps) also helped reduce the official unemployment figures by 'creating' jobs for unemployed men.

As Schacht had feared, the cost of rearmament created huge problems regarding exports, gold reserves and foreign currency earnings. By 1939, with the German economy close to collapse, there was therefore a strong temptation to take advantage of weaker states. Göring believed there were two choices: to abandon the rearmament programme, or to carry out several local 'lightning' wars in order to obtain extra resources.

Volksgemeinschaft: the social impact of Nazism

Just as the Nazis' economic policies tended to confirm the existing state of affairs, so too did their social interventions. Despite talk of a *Volksgemeinschaft* ('people's community'), in many ways the Third Reich remained very similar socially to the Weimar Republic.

Nazism and class

There were significant variations in the material benefits received by different social classes in the Third Reich. Overall, the real benefits of the economic recovery after 1933 tended to go to the wealthy élites, and there was a clear redistribution in wealth *away* from the working classes to the upper classes.

The *Mittelstand* (middle classes) had increasingly turned to the Nazis after the Depression began, and following the Nazi victory in 1933 they expected to benefit. However, few of the earlier Nazi promises to help small businesses were carried out. The Law for the Protection of the Retail Trade, which was passed in 1933, placed some general restrictions on further expansion of large department stores. Significantly, however, these were not closed down and, in fact, the five main department store chains experienced a 10% growth in the years 1936–39. Then, in 1937, the Nazis placed restrictions on setting up small businesses.

The farming community had been attracted by Nazi promises of help, yet even here the impact of Nazi policies was somewhat mixed and, overall, the main beneficiaries after 1933 were the owners of larger estates and commercial farms. Nonetheless, smaller farmers did gain in some ways. For example, a significant number had their farm debts written off, and an increase in food prices of about 20% benefited farmers in general in the years 1933–37.

Once trade unions were banned in May 1933, industrial workers had no way of obtaining pay increases or of resisting any decline in working conditions. Although their material situation improved in the period 1933–39 as a result of the reduction in unemployment, national and regional wage rates were abolished and were replaced by individual piece-rates – by which each person's wage depended on how much they produced, rather than the number of hours they worked. The Nazi DAF, which replaced independent trade unions, prevented workers from asking for increased wages; instead, DAF trustees set wage levels that were acceptable to the employers. As a result, industrial workers did not regain the level of real wages that they had enjoyed before the Depression until 1938. Workers did benefit from rent controls, as well as the recreational opportunities provided by the *Kraft durch Freude* (Strength through Joy, KDF) scheme. However, even here the benefits were limited, as these tended to go to white-collar workers and the better-off skilled manual workers.

Young people

The Nazis believed that the long-term future of their *Volksgemeinschaft* lay with the young, and they adopted several different approaches to impress Nazi ideology on young people across Germany.

In 1934, Hitler's government created a centrally controlled system under the Reich Ministry of Education and Science, and changed the school curriculum. In German and history lessons, nationalism, militarism, the different roles of men and women, and the greatness of Hitler and the NSDAP were all emphasised. In biology classes, 'race science' indoctrinated children with the Nazis' racist ideas. The Nazis also purged the teaching professions of any politically unreliable or 'racially unsuitable' members, while others were sent on special 'reconditioning' courses. The universities were also 'Nazified' – in all, over 3000 lecturers and professors were sacked for political or racial reasons.

Central to creating the new *Volksgemeinschaft* generation were the various Nazi youth organisations. These included the Deutsches Jungvolk (German Young People, DJ) and the Hitler Jugend (Hitler Youth, HJ) for boys aged 10–14 and 14–18 respectively. For girls, the corresponding organisations were the Jungmädelbund (League of Young Girls, JM) and the Bund Deutscher Mädel (League of German Girls, BDM). At the end of the 1930s, membership of these groups was made compulsory; however, recent research suggests that many young Germans were not won over by the Nazis, and tried to avoid membership.

Women

Nazi ideology and *Volksgemeinschaft* plans were utterly opposed to social and economic equality for women, and thus to the educational and employment rights that women had gained during the period of the Weimar Republic. The Nazis' attitude to women was summed up in the 'three Ks' slogan: *Kinder, Küche, Kirche* ('children, kitchen, church'). The Nazis believed that women should not be involved in politics or paid employment – the home was their domain, and they should confine themselves to the role of mother and homemaker.

Although women retained the right to vote, they were no longer allowed to be political representatives, and were barred from being judges. The new Nazi government implemented several policies to drive women out of the workplace and back into the home. Between 1933 and 1936, married women were excluded from employment in various professions, and legislation was introduced to dramatically reduce the number of female teachers and university students.

In June 1933, interest-free loans were given to all young women who gave up employment in order to get married. Employers and labour exchanges were told to favour men rather than women.

The slogan 'Emancipation of Women' was invented by Jewish intellectuals and its content was formed by the same spirit. In the really good times of German life the German woman had no need to emancipate herself …

If the man's world is said to be the State, his struggle, his readiness to devote his powers to the service of the community, then it may perhaps be said that the woman's is a smaller world. For her world is her husband, her family, her children and her home … The two worlds … complement each other … We do not consider it correct for the woman to interfere in the world of the man, in his main sphere. We consider it natural if these two worlds remain distinct.

Extracts from Hitler's 'Address to Women' at the Nuremberg Party Rally, 8 September 1934. Quoted in Laver, J. 1991. Nazi Germany 1933–1945. London, UK. Hodder & Stoughton. pp. 63–64.

What are the value and limitations of Source B for finding out about the Nazis' attitude towards women and the role played by women in the Nazi state?

The Nazis then tried to increase Germany's birth rate. Laws against abortion were enforced, birth-control clinics were closed and contraception was increasingly restricted. At the same time, maternity benefits and family allowances were increased. Newlyweds were offered loans, and women who had large families were awarded the Honour Cross of the German Mother.

The results of these Nazi policies were mixed. Although the percentage of women in paid employment in the period 1932–37 dropped from 37% to 31%, the actual numbers increased from about 5 million to 6 million. Then, from 1937 to 1939, both the percentage and the numbers increased – from 31% to 33%, and from 6 million to just over 7 million. In part, this was the result of labour shortages caused by conscription and rearmament after 1935. Women who were well-qualified, however, never regained the position and status they had enjoyed under the Weimar Republic.

The 'outsiders'

While membership of the Nazis' *Volksgemeinschaft* was open to all 'good Aryans', several categories were seen as outsiders or 'a-socials', and were specifically excluded from the Nazi community.

Minority groups increasingly persecuted by the Nazis included people with hereditary physical disabilities or mental problems, Roma and Sinti, gay men and lesbians, and homeless people. More than 300,000 of these people were forcibly sterilised under the Law for the Prevention of Hereditary Disease of 1933. Members of these groups also later became Holocaust victims in the concentration and death camps.

Activity

Divide into groups of four, with each member carrying out some research on how *one* of the non-Jewish minorities identified in this section was persecuted by the Nazis from 1933 to 1939. Each member should then write up their findings and share them with the group.

Right from the start, Jews were specifically excluded from the Nazi community. Anti-Semitism was the central policy of the Nazis' *Volksgemeinschaft*, based on their belief in the 'superiority' of the Aryan race. Hitler's appointment as chancellor allowed him to take action against the Jewish community – although in 1933, there were fewer than 500,000 Jewish people in Germany (about 1% of the population).

From 1933 to 1938, the Nazis moved cautiously, mainly restricting themselves to legislative measures. In April 1933, Hitler announced an official boycott of all Jewish shops and professional services. Although this was not widely supported – and was quickly dropped because of opposition and ineffectiveness – it was almost immediately followed by the Law for the Restoration of the Professional Civil Service, which removed all Jewish people from government posts. Jews were also officially classified as 'non-Aryans'. Further laws in 1934 banned them from other professions and from the media.

The Nuremberg Race Laws of 1935 took anti-Semitic policies even further. The Reich Citizenship Act deprived German Jews of all civil rights, while another law banned sexual relations or marriage between Jews and other German citizens. In 1937, measures were taken to remove Jewish people from the professions and from business – this was known as 'Aryanisation'. Propaganda depicting Jewish people as the 'polluters' of the Aryan race increased, and Jewish children were humiliated in front of their classmates in schools.

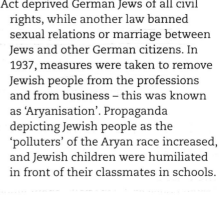

A scene from a US documentary showing two German Jewish boys next to a blackboard, which reads 'The Jews are our greatest enemy! Beware of the Jews!'

What can you learn from the photograph on page 170 about Nazi policies towards Jewish people, and how other Germans responded to such policies?

After 1938, the Nazi campaign became more violent. First, over 15,000 Polish Jews living in Germany were expelled and, in July, Jewish people were banned from all commerce. At the same time, all Jews were forced to have 'Jewish' forenames such as Israel or Sarah, to register all the wealth or property they possessed, and to carry identity cards and internal passports.

In November 1938, the Nazis led an attack on the Jews that became known as *Kristallnacht* ('Night of the Broken Glass', after all the smashed windows). Thousands of Jewish homes, shops and synagogues were destroyed and more than 100 Jews were killed; 25,000 more were sent to concentration camps. Later that month, all Jewish pupils were expelled from state schools. In December, Jewish businesses were closed and sold off, and all Jews in skilled jobs were sacked.

By 1938, almost 150,000 Jewish people had emigrated; yet around 300,000 stayed on, in the hope that the persecution might eventually lessen. When all Jewish valuables were confiscated in April 1939, leaving the country became much more difficult as Jews could no longer buy or bribe their way out. In addition, few countries were prepared to accept any significant number of impoverished immigrants. By 1939, Jewish people had been 'eliminated' from economic, political, social, cultural and legal life of Germany. After the outbreak of the Second World War in 1939, Nazi treatment of Jewish people worsened. As early as January 1939, Hitler threatened that any outbreak of war in Europe would result in the 'annihilation of the Jewish race'. Ultimately, almost 6 million Jews and 5 million others (including Roma and Sinti, gay men and lesbians) were slaughtered in the Holocaust under the Nazi regime.

Activity

Carry out some further research on Nazi anti-Semitic policies in the period 1933–39. Then draw up a timeline, giving details of the dates, main laws and events, and the terms of those laws.

Did Hitler's foreign policy follow a consistent plan?

There has been a great deal of historical debate about the aims of Nazi foreign policy and, especially, about whether Hitler always intended to launch a world war – or at least a major war. In general, it is possible to divide German foreign policy from 1933 to 1939 into two periods: a 'continuity' phase from 1933–36; and an increasingly aggressive phase from 1937 to 1939.

Continuity and 'revisionism' 1933–36

After Hitler's appointment as chancellor in 1933, German foreign policy did not immediately change significantly. From 1923 to 1933, Germany had followed a policy of peacefully attempting to revise parts of the Treaty of Versailles. This approach continued after 1933 for a number of reasons: the German economy was still suffering from the Depression, Hitler's domestic political position was not yet secure, and Germany's armed forces were weak.

International relations in 1933

On becoming chancellor, Hitler kept the conservative nationalist **Konstantin von Neurath** as foreign minister. In part, this was to reassure Germany's neighbours that there would be no dramatic changes to foreign policy, but it was also because Hitler's key aim at this time was to establish Nazi control of Germany itself. Thus, Hitler tried to maintain good relations with Britain and Italy. However, on 3 February 1933, Hitler informed German army officers of his intention to make Germany's military the most powerful in Europe by 1938; after that, Germany would seek *Lebensraum* ('living space') in the east – mainly at the expense of the Soviet Union. and Poland

Konstantin von Neurath (1873–1956) Neurath was German foreign minister from 1932 to 1938 but, although he joined the Nazi Party in 1937, he was replaced by Ribbentrop, a more committed Nazi. From 1939 to 1943, Neurath was *Reichsprotektor* of Bohemia and Moravia. At the end of the war, he was tried for war crimes at Nuremberg, and was sentenced to 15 years' imprisonment.

Hitler noted the League of Nations' lack of effective action against aggression when Japan invaded Manchuria in 1931 (see page 206). Britain and France were the leading powers in the organisation. However, Britain was more concerned about the effects of global events on its own empire than about containing unrest in other parts of the world, and it was reluctant for the League to act as the 'world's policeman'. At the same time, growing political instability in France weakened its ability to pursue a vigorous foreign policy. For the first few years of his regime, Hitler took advantage of this situation.

The League and isolating France

When Hitler came to power, Germany was already attending the World Disarmament Conference that had begun in 1932. In 1933, Germany proposed that either all nations should disarm to the level imposed on Germany by the Treaty of Versailles or, alternatively, Germany should be allowed to rearm to the level of France. Although Britain supported this, France blocked Germany's call for equal treatment. Hitler

immediately withdrew Germany from the conference – and then from
the League of Nations. To some, particularly Britain, it seemed that
France had acted unreasonably and they understood Hitler's reaction.

France was further isolated by Hitler's decision in January 1934 to
sign a ten-year non-aggression pact with Poland. This undermined
the earlier defensive system of alliances that France had made with
Poland and some other Eastern European states, which was designed
to put pressure on Germany's eastern frontier and so deter a future
invasion of France. Once again, Hitler came across as a reasonable
statesman, while France seemed petulant.

Austria and the Stresa Front 1934–35

Although there was some sympathy in Britain for Germany's desire to
revise parts of the Treaty of Versailles, Hitler's backing of an attempted
coup by the Austrian Nazis later in 1934 alienated both Britain and
Italy. The relationship declined further in March 1935, when Hitler
announced that Germany once more had an air force, and that he
was introducing conscription in order to build up the German army
to a strength of 550,000 troops. Consequently, Britain, France and Italy
met at Stresa in Italy, and formed the Stresa Front to resist any further
moves by Germany to overturn the treaty without negotiation.

However, the Stresa Front unity did not last long. In June 1935, Britain
(unhappy about France's hardline position over Germany and its pact
with the USSR) signed a naval agreement with Germany. This allowed
the German navy to expand beyond the limits set in 1919, as long as it
remained at no more than 35% the strength of the British navy. Britain
had not discussed this agreement with France or Italy, and relations
between the Stresa Front allies began to decline.

Hitler was further helped when Mussolini invaded Abyssinia in October
1935. Through the League of Nations, Britain and France eventually – if
reluctantly – opposed this, although France in particular was concerned
not to alienate Mussolini. Hitler offered his support to his fellow fascist,
and Italy left the Stresa Front and moved closer to Nazi Germany.

> Why was isolating France diplomatically – and breaking up the Stresa Front
> – important for Hitler's foreign policy?

The reoccupation of the Rhineland 1936

Encouraged by yet another weak League response to aggression, in
March 1936, Hitler decided to send German troops into the Rhineland.
This had been a demilitarised zone since 1919, and reoccupying
the area was also in breach of the Locarno Treaty (see page 53).

In fact, the German army was still not strong enough to fight Britain or France should either of these countries make a military response, and the German Foreign Ministry and the Army High Command warned against this move. Eventually, Hitler was persuaded to allow German troops to retreat at the first sign of opposition from the Allies. Hitler, however, correctly calculated that there would be no resistance – and indeed Britain persuaded France to take no action. This success weakened Hitler's critics, and strengthened his resolve to take a more aggressive stance in the near future.

The Four-Year Plan and the Rome–Berlin Axis 1936

Despite the successful reoccupation of the Rhineland, the traditional élites in the Foreign Ministry and the army wanted to pursue a more conservative way of creating a stronger Germany. In addition, the economic crisis of 1936 showed that Germany was not yet able to fight any sustained war. One response to this was the Four-Year Plan, designed to prepare Germany for war. However, leading Nazis were divided over which diplomatic course to follow: some wanted to reach a closer understanding with Britain, while the foreign minister, **Joachim von Ribbentrop**, wanted Germany to join forces with Italy and Japan.

Joachim von Ribbentrop (1893–1946) Ribbentrop served as German foreign minister from 1938–45. He joined the Nazis in 1932, and was extremely anti-Semitic. Between 1936 and 1938, he was ambassador to Britain. Despite his personal preference for an alliance with Italy and Japan, he worked hard with members of Britain's establishment to obtain an Anglo–German alliance, in accordance with Hitler's wishes. These élites included King Edward VIII and his then mistress Wallis Simpson who, according to recently released FBI files, was also Ribbentrop's lover and passed on secret information to him. Ribbentrop was later found guilty of war crimes at the Nuremberg Trials, and was hanged in October 1946.

Although Hitler preferred the option of a closer relationship with Britain (mainly in the hope of destroying the Soviet Union), he was doubtful that Britain would be amenable. Hitler was also keen to secure Italy's acceptance of his plan to annex Austria. Thus, in November 1936, Nazi Germany signed the Rome–Berlin Axis with Fascist Italy. The two countries had been co-operating since July 1936 in giving military assistance to the nationalists in the Spanish Civil War (see Chapter 7).

Thus, by the end of 1936, Nazi Germany had succeeded in overturning most of the terms of the Treaty of Versailles that related to its western borders, without suffering any military consequences. As a result, Hitler now felt able to turn his attentions to winning *Lebensraum* in the east.

Increasing aggression: the road to war 1937–39

By 1937, Hitler had been able to achieve many of his territorial ambitions without having to resort to military force, and Germany appeared to be in a stronger position. Rearmament was well underway, the economic crisis of 1936 was mainly over, and Göring's Four-Year Plan seemed to be producing results. In addition, the Anti-Comintern Pact, which Germany had signed with Japan in 1936, was joined by Italy in 1937.

The Hossbach Memorandum 1937

On 5 November 1937, Hitler called a meeting with Neurath, Werner von Blomberg (war minister) and the three commanders-in-chief of the armed forces. Historians are divided on the significance of this meeting, and on what claims to be a record of what occurred at the meeting. One of those present was Colonel Hossbach, Hitler's adjutant (administrative officer); although he took no notes during the meeting, he made a summary of the main points the following day. This has become known as the Hossbach Memorandum. According to Hossbach, Hitler told those present at the meeting to get Germany ready for conquests in Eastern Europe, to be completed by 1943–45. The Hossbach Memorandum included plans to seize Austria and Czechoslovakia – even if it provoked war with Britain and France.

Historians such as A. J. P. Taylor have questioned the reliability of this document, and whether 1937 was really a turning point in Hitler's foreign policy. Some believe this meeting was simply a way for Hitler to justify his rearmament programme to doubting conservatives, rather than a definite plan. Nonetheless, Hitler's intentions were further encouraged in November 1937, when the British prime minister Neville Chamberlain declared that Britain would support legitimate revisions to Germany's borders with Austria and Czechoslovakia, as long as they were carried out peacefully.

Hitler's increasing control of foreign policy

Hitler's foreign policy became more adventurous in the years 1938–39, after he had made several personnel changes in an attempt to ensure greater personal control of the Foreign Ministry and the army. In January 1938, the moderate war minister Blomberg and Werner von Fritsch, the commander-in-chief of the army, were dismissed. Hitler himself took over the post of minister for war and declared himself to be the supreme commander of the armed forces. He also created a new personal High Command for the armed forces, under General Wilhelm Keitel, a known supporter of Nazi plans. Göring was promoted to field marshal. Other leading positions were filled by hardline Nazis, and later Ribbentrop replaced Neurath as foreign minister.

Anschluss with Austria 1938

"Why should we take a stand about someone pushing someone else when it's all so far away .."

Since the failed attempt to achieve *Anschluss* with Austria in 1934, Hitler and Mussolini had become allies, and this gave Hitler the confidence to try once more to unite Germany and Austria. By making use of the Austrian Nazi Party, Hitler was able to bring about a crisis in Austria that he 'solved' by sending in German troops in March 1938, after being invited to do so by the Nazi members of the Austrian coalition government. Neither Britain nor France opposed this move.

A British cartoon called 'Increasing Pressure', commenting on the German Anschluss *with Austria, published in 1938*

What is the message of this cartoon? How does the cartoonist get the message across?

SOURCE C

In 1936 when Hitler ordered German troops into the demilitarized Rhineland there was little international protest ... Few in Germany bothered to read *Mein Kampf* to discover Hitler's real motives and his obsession with territorial expansion. Nazi propaganda portrayed Hitler as a man of peace pursuing justifiable revisions of the humiliating Versailles Treaty.

The treaty that led to the Rome-Berlin Axis in November 1936 had changed the balance of power in Europe, and Austria, in particular, was left isolated as a result. Previously, Austria had depended on an alliance with Britain, France and Italy to secure her independence in the face of German demands. With Italy now on Germany's side, the balance of power in central Europe had shifted dramatically ... As a result of the Rome-Berlin Axis, Hitler was now in a stronger position ... The German invasion of Austria [on 12 March 1938] was Hitler's first move outside German territory in defiance of the Treaty of Versailles ... The Anschluss of Austria not only revealed the extent of Hitler's imperial ambitions, it also dealt a strategic blow at Czechoslovakia which could now be attacked from the south as well as from the west and north.

Welch, D. 1998. Hitler. London, UK. UCL Press. pp. 58–59.

Munich and Czechoslovakia 1938–39

Hitler next turned his attention to the 3.5 million German-speakers living in the Sudetenland, the border region of Czechoslovakia. These former citizens of the Austrian Empire, stirred up by the pro-Nazi Sudeten German Party, provided Hitler with another excuse for military action. With Britain following a policy of appeasement, Hitler calculated that France would not act against him without British support.

It seems that Hitler initially intended a complete takeover of Czechoslovakia in one swift move. However, Czechoslovakia and France had signed a defence treaty in 1924, and France and the USSR also had a mutual assistance pact that included an undertaking to protect Czech independence. In addition, the Czechs had a small but efficient army and seemed prepared to resist German aggression. These factors caused the crisis to build to such an extent that by September 1938 the prospect of war seemed a reality. Hitler's military advisors continued to warn him that Germany was not yet prepared to undertake a European war.

In September 1938, at a conference held in Munich, Britain, France, Germany and Italy agreed that the Czech government should hand over the Sudetenland to Nazi Germany. In return, Hitler promised that this would be his last territorial demand. The Czechs were not present at the conference, and without any offer of help from France or the USSR despite their treaty obligations, the Czech government was forced to comply. Later in the month, Poland and Hungary also seized land from Czechoslovakia.

Once again, Nazi Germany had increased its population and added significantly to its agricultural and industrial resources without having to take up arms. In addition, with its former border defences in German hands, Czechoslovakia's ability to resist future aggression was severely reduced. Within three weeks of occupying the Sudetenland, Hitler ordered his armies to prepare to invade the rest of Czechoslovakia.

By the end of 1938, Hitler was ready to carry out his plans for achieving *Lebensraum* in the east by invading the USSR – correctly calculating that Britain was more concerned about containing communism than German ambitions in the east. At the same time, Stalin accepted that his attempts to build an anti-Nazi alliance with Britain and France were doomed to failure. In February, Britain signed a military alliance with France. Nonetheless, the system of European diplomatic alliances remained uncertain, so Hitler ordered the invasion of the rest of Czechoslovakia in March 1939. This, too, was achieved without any opposition from Britain or France.

The Nazi–Soviet Non-Aggression Pact and Poland 1939

Hitler's plans to move against Poland without facing opposition on Germany's western borders were undermined when Britain and France announced that they had signed a pact with Poland, guaranteeing its independence. To counter this, Hitler decided to strengthen his military alliance with Fascist Italy and, in May 1939, Hitler and Mussolini signed the Pact of Steel (see page 89).

More importantly, Hitler also decided to pursue negotiations with the USSR, so that there would be no ally for Britain and France in the east. It was not until July/August that Britain began to consider a pact with the USSR to limit Nazi aggression. Trade talks began between Germany and the Soviet Union in July 1939 and, in August, a ten-year Non-Aggression Pact was signed between these two states. The agreement contained a secret clause that outlined the break-up of Poland for their joint benefit.

On 1 September 1939 – confident that Britain and France would not honour their pledges – Nazi Germany invaded Poland.

SOURCE D

On 23 August Hitler gave instructions for the invasion of Poland to begin at 4.30 a.m. on 26 August. Two things caused him to countermand the order. On 25 August Britain ratified the Anglo-Polish Agreement of 31 March and Mussolini informed Hitler that Italy was not ready to fight. That afternoon Hitler postponed the attack. But on 26 August he again ordered the invasion to take place, this time on 1 September. The intervening delay of five days can be interpreted as a final attempt on Hitler's part either to secure a compromise or to split Britain and France from Poland, or simply as a loss of nerve on Hitler's part. According to A. J. P. Taylor, war broke out because Hitler launched 'on 29 August a diplomatic manoeuvre which he ought to have launched on 28 August' (*Origins of the Second World War*, 1964, p. 336). The manoeuvre in question was an offer on Hitler's part to negotiate directly with the Poles, provided that a plenipotentiary arrived in Berlin within twenty-four hours. The Poles refused to be coerced, and on this occasion neither Britain nor France (unlike the case of Czechoslovakia) were prepared to abandon Poland.

Simpson, W. 1991. Hitler and Germany. *Cambridge, UK. Cambridge University Press. p. 110.*

To Hitler's surprise, Britain and France finally took action. On 3 September, they declared war on Germany. Germany's Four-Year Plan and rearmament programme had still not achieved full economic and military readiness, and Hitler found himself facing a war in September 1939 that he had not anticipated. After early German successes, the combined strength of the Allies led to increasing defeats and, on 30 April 1945, with the Soviet Red Army in Berlin, Hitler committed suicide.

Activity

Carry out some further research on the actions of the British and French governments up to August 1939. Then write two newspaper articles – one praising them for averting war, and one blaming them for not acting against Hitler. In your articles, you should quote different historians and assess their arguments.

Interpretations of Hitler's foreign policy

Historians are divided over whether German foreign policy after 1933 was merely a more aggressive continuation of previous policies, or whether it showed a distinct break arising from Hitler's personal priorities. Divisions have also emerged over another aspect of Hitler's foreign policy, with two broad schools of thought: the Orthodox/Intentionalist school, and the Revisionist/Structuralist school. The former – including historians such as Hugh Trevor-Roper, Alan Bullock, Andreas Hillgruber and Klaus Hildebrand – have argued that Hitler deliberately planned for such a war even before he came to power, and that he consistently pursued a *Stufenplan* (master plan). Such historians have pointed to his statements in *Mein Kampf*, and to the Hossbach Memorandum. However, Intentionalists are themselves divided, with 'globalists' arguing that he aimed for world domination, while 'continentalists' see his aim as being restricted to *European* dominance.

Revisionist/Structuralist historians – such as A. J. P. Taylor, K. D. Bracher and Martin Broszat – have criticised these 'Intentionalist' views. A. J. P. Taylor, for example, questioned the reliability of the Hossbach Memorandum. Instead, he argued that Hitler's foreign policy was essentially improvised and based on making the most of opportunities when they arose. Later historians have also pointed out how Hitler's foreign policy was at times a response to internal economic problems, as well as external opportunities.

End of chapter activities

Summary activity

Copy the spider diagram below to show the main aspects of domestic and foreign policy developments in Hitler's Germany during the period 1933–39. Then, using the information from this chapter, and any other sources available to you, complete the diagram. Make sure you include, where relevant, brief comments about different historical debates/interpretations.

Establishment of the Nazi dictatorship

Social policies

Hitler's Germany 1933–39

Economic policies

Foreign policies

Paper 3 practice questions

1 Assess the importance of terror in maintaining Nazi control in Germany under the Third Reich between 1933 and 1939.

2 Evaluate the success of Hitler's economic and social policies between 1933 and 1939.

3 How far did Hitler's actions and policies between 1933 and 1939 show that foreign policy was his main concern?

4 'Hitler's foreign policy was based on the long-term aim of achieving European and even global domination.' To what extent do you agree with this view?

5 Compare and contrast the foreign policies of Mussolini and Hitler.

9 The League of Nations 1919–29

Timeline

1919 Jun: Conference of Ambassadors established

1920 Jan: League of Nations begins work

Sep: war between Turkey and Greece begins

1920–21 Aaland dispute between Finland and Sweden; dispute between Poland and Lithuania over Vilna; Russo–Polish War

1921 Mar: dispute over Upper Silesia between Germany and Poland

1921–22 Washington Naval Treaties

1922 Apr–May: Genoa Conference on Disarmament

1923 Jan: invasion of Ruhr by France and Belgium

Aug: Corfu Incident between Italy and Greece

1924 Jan: alliance between France and Czechoslovakia

Aug: Dawes Plan

Sep: Geneva Protocol drawn up

1925 Oct: Geneva Protocol rejected; Locarno Treaty; war between Greece and Bulgaria

1926 Sep: Germany becomes member of the League of Nations

1928 Aug: Kellogg–Briand Pact

1929 Jun: Young Plan

Key questions

- What were the initial weaknesses of the League of Nations?
- How successful was the League in the period 1919–29?
- What were the main diplomatic agreements in the period 1919–29?

US president Woodrow Wilson considered the traditional secrecy of European diplomacy to have been a major cause of the First World War. He believed that the USA should use its new global economic and military power to create a new international order – not just to ensure that no conflict such as the First World War would occur in the future, but also to address Allied concerns arising from the 1917 Bolshevik Revolution in Russia. Consequently, his Fourteen Points included a call for the establishment of a general association of nations to guarantee the political independence and territorial integrity of all nations. This was the origin of the League of Nations.

Overview

- Although the idea for a League of Nations was raised by US president Woodrow Wilson, the US never joined the League. In addition, Germany was not allowed to become a member when it was first established and communist Russia was not invited to join.
- As a result, Britain and France were left as the League's main members. This made the League appear as a 'club of victors' to the defeated countries. Britain and France, however, did not always agree with each other on the actions that the League should take.
- Where conflicts arose between relatively weak states, the League had some success in the years 1919–29. However, where the interests of a strong country clashed with those of a weaker one, the League was much less successful.
- The League also carried out humanitarian work – dealing with refugees, health and working conditions. In these areas it was largely successful.
- Much international diplomacy during 1919–29 was carried out independently of the League. In particular, the Conference of Ambassadors frequently settled disputes or negotiated agreements during this period.
- Diplomatic attempts to guarantee the peace of Europe (such as the Locarno Treaty and the Kellogg–Briand Pact) had limited success.
- Nonetheless, the 1920s can be seen as a time of improving international relations, with several important agreements – including the 1922 Washington Naval Treaty, and the Dawes and Young plans.

What were the initial weaknesses of the League of Nations?

In January 1919, the Big Five (the USA, Britain, France, Italy and Japan), along with nine smaller states, met to draft a constitution for the League of Nations. Although all of them agreed that the prevention of war should be the main aim of the League, there was disagreement about how this should be achieved. Despite this, a constitution (the League of Nations Covenant) was successfully drawn up, and became the first 26 articles in all of the peace treaties of 1919–20.

Organisation and membership

The League was established as a permanent international conference, with a variety of functions. The four most important ones were:

- to guarantee the territory of states through collective security
- to prevent conflicts
- to settle disputes peacefully
- to act as an agency for disarmament.

Additionally, the League was to supervise the former colonies or provinces of Germany and Turkey. It would also have an economic and social role – for example, helping to stabilise currencies and assisting with world health issues, the problem of illegal drugs, and slavery.

The League was based at Geneva, in neutral Switzerland, and its founder members were 32 Allied states and 13 neutral powers – all of which had their own national interests. An Assembly was established as the body to which any members would bring disputes, so that they could be resolved without resorting to violence. If the Assembly proved unable to prevent a conflict breaking out, then the smaller Council – made up of the Big Four (Britain, France, Italy and Japan) as permanent members, plus four smaller countries elected at intervals by the Assembly – would take action to implement collective security. Initially, this would take the form of economic sanctions against countries resorting to aggression.

The routine administration and secretarial work was carried out by the Secretariat. In addition, the League had several special commissions to administer the former territories of the defeated powers and special geographical areas such as Danzig and the Saar, which fell under League control. Finally, in order to carry out its economic and social roles, the League established various internal organisations and committees.

The structure of the League of Nations

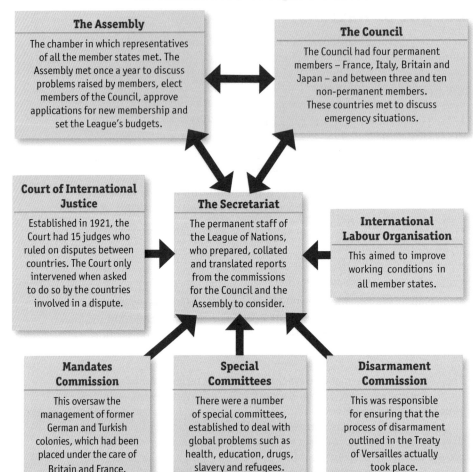

The Assembly

The chamber in which representatives of all the member states met. The Assembly met once a year to discuss problems raised by members, elect members of the Council, approve applications for new membership and set the League's budgets.

The Council

The Council had four permanent members – France, Italy, Britain and Japan – and between three and ten non-permanent members. These countries met to discuss emergency situations.

Court of International Justice

Established in 1921, the Court had 15 judges who ruled on disputes between countries. The Court only intervened when asked to do so by the countries involved in a dispute.

The Secretariat

The permanent staff of the League of Nations, who prepared, collated and translated reports from the commissions for the Council and the Assembly to consider.

International Labour Organisation

This aimed to improve working conditions in all member states.

Mandates Commission

This oversaw the management of former German and Turkish colonies, which had been placed under the care of Britain and France.

Special Committees

There were a number of special committees, established to deal with global problems such as health, education, drugs, slavery and refugees.

Disarmament Commission

This was responsible for ensuring that the process of disarmament outlined in the Treaty of Versailles actually took place.

Weaknesses and problems

Although the number of Council members elected by the Assembly increased to six in 1926 and nine in 1929, this institution was essentially seen as a European club. Furthermore, the League had several specific weaknesses and practical problems that undermined its chances of successfully carrying out its aims.

Non-membership

One of the most significant weaknesses of the League of Nations was that right from the start, three of the most powerful nations in the world were not members. Germany was not permitted membership when the League was first formed, and even after it joined in 1926 (and became a permanent member of the Council), the League was still seen as a 'club of victors', designed to further the interests of the major Allies. Fear of communism meant that the USSR was also not allowed to join – in fact, the Soviet government condemned the League as a capitalist club dominated by imperialist powers.

The USA's refusal to join the League was a serious blow at the outset. Although Wilson wanted the US to be a member, the Republican Party won the 1918 US midterm elections, and the Republicans preferred to stay out of European affairs. However, although historians such as Ruth Henig claim that the absence of the US undermined the League, this viewpoint is challenged by others – such as R. J. Overy – who believe that in the 1920s, Britain and France were both strong enough to uphold the treaties without US support.

Enforcing the peace treaties

Wilson had intended that the League would guarantee – by collective action – the territorial integrity and political independence of all members against external aggression. Several states (including Britain) had tried unsuccessfully to get Wilson to drop this intention, as they had no desire to become the 'world's policemen'. In addition, any revisions to the new frontiers drawn by the 1919–20 treaties would prove difficult, as it soon became clear that Britain and France had different priorities and concerns.

SOURCE A

The persistence of internationalist idealism in the 1920s masked important weaknesses in the international order. In the first place, there was a certain moral ambiguity about the British and French position. While they preached the virtues of self-determination and democracy, they strenuously denied granting either to the subject peoples of their empires. Although liberal enough at home, both states could be thoroughly illiberal in the colonies when they were dealing with nationalist forces hostile to European imperialism. When Britain adhered to the Kellogg-Briand Pact, it was only on the condition that it could still resort to force in its own empire. When the League tried to outlaw aerial bombing in 1931, Britain refused to abandon it as an instrument of colonial control ... The moral authority of the League suffered from what was perceived to be the hypocrisy and self-serving of the 'satiated' powers. This situation made it difficult for Britain and France to resist the claims of other states in the 1930s that wanted to build an empire, or to ignore the strident demands for self-determination from the national minorities created by the peace settlement.

Overy, R. J. 1994. *The Inter-War Crisis 1919–1939. London, UK. Longman.* pp. 74–75.

Finally, at the same time as the League was established, a separate organisation – the Conference of Ambassadors, consisting of Britain, France, Italy and Japan – was set up to supervise the peace treaties. This group met at regular intervals in Paris, and there was often uncertainty about which of these two institutions should address particular issues.

Dealing with aggression

There were two main practical problems with the process the League followed in preventing aggression.

Firstly, member states had to submit any dispute to the Council. However, Council decisions had to be unanimous, and as the Council was dominated by Britain and France – which had quite different views about the role of the League – unanimous agreement was often difficult to reach.

Secondly, if a member failed to comply with League procedures or rulings, economic sanctions (such as trade boycotts and the banning of financial relations with an aggressor) could be imposed. However, many League members were reluctant to become involved in trade boycotts, in case non-member states such as the USA simply took over trade with the boycotted country. If economic sanctions failed, the Council could recommend military action, using troops provided by member states.

France strongly supported the idea that the League should have its own armed forces so that it could undertake direct military intervention. However, several nations – most notably Britain – opposed this. In reality, therefore, if a country refused to abide by the rules of the League, there was little the organisation could do to enforce its ruling.

Disarmament

Disarmament also proved to be an extremely contentious issue. In the immediate post-war years, the situation in Europe was very unstable. Russia had recently emerged as a communist state, and there was a power vacuum in much of Central and Eastern Europe. As a result, nations such as Poland and Czechoslovakia were reluctant to disarm in case they found themselves in a position where they were required to defend themselves against other countries.

More importantly, France was extremely concerned about disarming. The League had no real military power, and neither Britain nor the USA would pledge military support to France in the case of future aggression from Germany. In fact, Britain expressed a willingness to reduce its level of weaponry, and encouraged the establishment of a commission to draw up a disarmament convention, but it was not until 1926 that a Preparatory Disarmament Commission was formally set up in Geneva.

Activity

Carry out some additional research into the various factors contributing to the weakness of the League. Then draw up a table listing these factors – ranked in order of importance, and giving brief details about each. Finally, write a short paragraph justifying what you consider to be the most important factor.

How successful was the League in the period 1919–29?

Formally established in 1919, the League officially began its work in January 1920. Despite the problems it faced, it did achieve several successes between this time and 1929. However, even before the Depression, its value as a peacekeeping organisation proved limited.

General work

Among the League's general successes in the period 1920–29 was its administration of the Saar (a region on the border between France and Germany) and Danzig (a port city on the Baltic Sea). The League also assisted the Austrian and Hungarian economies in the 1920s, helping to stabilise their failing their currencies. In addition, the League helped revive the global economy by arranging world conferences on tariffs and trade agreements. In the late 1920s, it also examined proposals from France's **Aristide Briand** for closer European economic and political co-operation. Its humanitarian work with refugees and prisoners of war (especially after the Russo–Polish war of 1920–21 and the Greco–Turkish War 1920–22) was also a significant achievement.

Aristide Briand (1862–1932) Briand was a radical socialist politician who served as prime minister of France 11 times between 1909 and 1929. He was also foreign minister in this period. Briand was best known for his call for international co-operation in the interwar years. He strongly supported Germany's admittance to the League of Nations in 1926, and helped bring about the Locarno Treaty of 1925 (for which he shared the 1926 Nobel Peace Price) and the Kellogg–Briand Pact in 1928.

However, the League was less successful in supervising the mandates given to Britain, France and Japan to administer the former German and Turkish territories. Similarly, the League was unable to exert much authority in protecting the rights of ethnic minorities in the new successor states (those that had been created after the break-up of the Austro-Hungarian Empire). More importantly, attempts to strengthen the League's ability to guarantee the 1919–20 peace treaties also failed. In 1923, France suggested a Draft Treaty of Mutual Assistance to give the League powers to take rapid military action in the event of unprovoked aggression, but this was blocked by Britain.

In 1924, France tried to gain the League more military power again through the Geneva Protocol, which aimed to commit all members to undertake collective military action. This was supported by the new Labour prime minister of Britain, Ramsay MacDonald, who took office in January 1924. He said that Labour's foreign policy would be based on the League's Covenant. The Geneva Protocol was put forward in September 1924, but MacDonald lost the October 1924 election and the new Conservative government did not support the scheme. It was blocked in March 1925.

Dealing with disputes and aggression

The League had a mixed record when it came to dealing with disputes between countries.

Successes

In 1920, the League of Nations persuaded Yugoslavia to withdraw the troops it had stationed in Albania, and also settled a dispute between Finland and Sweden over possession of the Aaland Islands. In 1921, the League successfully resolved a dispute between Poland and Germany over the region of Upper Silesia, by dividing it between the two countries. During 1924–25, the League resolved a dispute between Iraq and Turkey over Mosul (an important oil-rich area) in Iraq's favour – significantly, however, Iraq was a British mandate so in reality Mosul came under British control. Also in 1925, the League settled a conflict between Greece and Bulgaria, forcing Greece to withdraw its troops from the disputed area and pay compensation to Bulgaria.

Failures

In 1920, Poland seized the city of Vilna from Lithuania, and Lithuania appealed to the League to intervene. Vilna had a significant Polish population, and there was some sympathy for Poland's claim to the city. However, having staged the invasion it was clear that Poland was the aggressor and the League ordered the Poles to withdraw. They refused. Eventually, in 1922, the Conference of Ambassadors agreed to Polish control of Vilna, which caused a great deal of resentment in Lithuania.

The League was also unable to prevent the Russo–Polish War of 1920–21, which began when Poland – dissatisfied with its eastern borders as agreed by the peace treaties of 1919–20 – seized parts of Russia, including Ukraine. In fact, Poland was backed by Britain and France in this action.

The opera house in Athens, transformed into living quarters for homeless Greek families in 1925

The Greco–Turkish War also began in 1920. Turkish nationalists were unhappy that the Treaty of Sèvres had given most of Turkey's European lands to Greece. They overthrew their sultan for signing the treaty, and announced their determination to reverse the terms of the treaty. Greece invaded Turkey to prevent this. The League failed either to prevent the war breaking out or to halt its progress once it had started, largely because Britain supported Greece while France backed Turkey. Ultimately, the fighting was ended not by the League, but by a new treaty – the 1923 Treaty of Lausanne – drawn up to replace the Treaty of Sèvres. However, the League's Refugee Committee and Health Organisation did much useful work in assisting the 1.4 million Greek civilians who were driven from their homes during the conflict.

 # Theory of knowledge

History, language and bias

A particular problem in history is national bias, which makes it difficult for people to deal objectively with sensitive issues involving their countries. According to most historians, an Armenian genocide took place between 1915 and 1923. However, Turkish governments have rejected this term, and some writers have been prosecuted for calling attention to these events. Is it possible for historians to avoid bias when writing about such controversial issues?

Discussion point

In August 1939, just before the invasion of Poland, Hitler delivered a speech to German army officers, in which he reputedly said: 'Who, after all, speaks today of the annihilation of the Armenians?' In view of what Hitler's regime went on to do, should international bodies take action over developments in different countries, or is it always too difficult to gain a full appreciation of what is going on? Do you think such interventions are usually undertaken for national interests rather than for humanitarian reasons?

In 1923, the League failed to prevent Lithuania seizing the port of Memel and the surrounding land, which had been placed under League administration by the Treaty of Versailles. Eventually, the League persuaded Lithuania to accept a compromise in which the port itself would become an 'international zone', but Lithuania would keep the surrounding area.

The League suffered two other, more serious, failures in 1923. Firstly, it was unable to prevent France and Belgium invading the Ruhr after Germany failed to meet its reparations payments (see page 36). In fact, France did not even consult the League before it took action.

Later in the year, the League also failed to stop Italy – another of its leading members – from invading the Greek island of Corfu (see page 72). Greece approached the League for help after this act of Italian aggression, but Mussolini simply ignored the League's instruction for him to withdraw his troops. The Conference of Ambassadors eventually resolved the conflict in Italy's favour. The main reasons for this lay with the personal interests of France and Britain. France regarded Italy as a potential ally against Germany, while Britain had no desire to apply sanctions against Italy in case they damaged British interests. These two disputes revealed the League's serious weaknesses when attempting to resolve problems that involved the larger and more powerful nations.

Activity

Carry out some additional research on these various disputes. Then draw up a table, with sub-headings for 'successes' and 'failures', and give some brief details of each dispute.

SOURCE B

During the 1920s the League enjoyed mixed success as an effective peace-keeper. On the one hand, a few minor disputes were settled by the League, most notably the withdrawal of Yugoslav troops from Albania and the resolution of a territorial dispute over the Aaland Islands, between Finland and Sweden. Successful arbitration was achieved in disputes between Germany and Poland over Upper Silesia, Britain and Turkey over the administration of oil fields in Mosul, and between Greece and Bulgaria over disputed territory in the Balkans. On the other hand, the League could not prevent Poland annexing Vilnius in 1922, [or] Italians occupying Corfu in 1923.

McDonough, F. 2001. *Conflict, Communism and Fascism: Europe 1890–1945.* Cambridge, UK. Cambridge University Press. p. 61.

What were the main diplomatic agreements in the period 1919–29?

For most of this period, direct diplomacy between nations was more significant than the work of the League of Nations. In particular, much was done by the Conference of Ambassadors. This body – set up to resolve any problems arising from the peace treaties – was often able to reach limited practical agreements on issues that the League found difficult to resolve.

Diplomacy in the 1920s

Largely because of the League's weaknesses, the Conference of Ambassadors frequently made decisions independently of the League. Non-League agreements made during the period 1919–29 included the Dawes Plan of 1924 (see page 48) and the Young Plan of 1929 (see page 55), both of which addressed Germany's reparations payments. The League was further undermined in the 1920s when it became clear that both Italy and Japan were determined to follow expansionist policies in defiance of the League.

Activity

Using the internet and any other sources available to you, find out more about the Conference of Ambassadors, its role and the actions it took during the 1920s. Then write a paragraph on how the activities of the Conference might have affected the credibility of the League of Nations.

The Washington Naval Treaties 1921–22

The Washington Naval Treaties were largely the result of the initiative of a non-League member, the USA, which was concerned about growing tensions with Japan in the Pacific. In 1921 and 1922, the Washington Conferences took place between the USA, Britain, France and Japan, along with Belgium, Portugal, the Netherlands and China. The talks resulted in three agreements, all of which aimed to limit naval expansion.

The Locarno Treaty 1925

The invasion of the Ruhr, and the subsequent Dawes Plan, resulted in improved diplomatic relations between France and Germany – largely due to the policies and work of Aristide Briand of France and Gustav Stresemann of Germany. Once again, though, this came about independently of the League. In 1925, in order to alleviate French fears of a German attack, Stresemann offered to guarantee Germany's acceptance of its western frontiers, as established at Versailles.

In September 1925, the Locarno Conference gave rise to a series of treaties in which Germany, France and Belgium promised not to use force to change their borders with each other. Germany also promised to accept the demilitarisation of the Rhineland. Britain and Italy guaranteed these agreements. The Locarno Treaty was a key factor in Germany being allowed to join the League of Nations the following year.

SOURCE C

The Locarno Pact was greeted with exuberant relief as the dawning of a new world order ... But amidst all the jubilation, no one noticed that the statesmen had sidestepped the real issues: Locarno had not so much pacified Europe as it had defined the next battlefield.

The reassurance felt by the democracies at Germany's formal recognition of its Western frontiers showed the extent of the demoralization and the confusion that had been caused by the [mix] of old and new views on international affairs. For within that recognition was implicit that the Treaty of Versailles, which had ended a victorious war, had been unable to command compliance with the victors' peace terms, and that Germany had acquired the option of observing only those provisions which it chose to reaffirm. In this sense, Stresemann's unwillingness to recognise Germany's Eastern frontiers was ominous; while Great Britain's refusal to guarantee even the arbitration treaties gave international sanction to two classes of frontier in Europe – those accepted by Germany and guaranteed by other powers, and those neither accepted by Germany nor guaranteed by the other powers.

Kissinger, H. 1995. Diplomacy. *New York, USA. Touchstone. p. 274.*

The Kellogg–Briand Pact 1928

In 1927, as tensions eased after Germany joined the League, the USA and France – represented by **Frank Kellogg** and Briand respectively – renounced the use of force for national objectives. In 1928, 15 countries, including Britain and Germany, signed this Kellogg–Briand Pact. However, the pact contained no details of what action would be taken should a country act in defiance of it, and attempts to have the terms of the pact incorporated into the League of Nations Covenant failed.

Frank Kellogg (1856–1937) Kellogg was a Republican politician, and became a US senator in 1916. He took part in the Paris Peace Conferences in 1919, and was one of the few Republicans who supported US ratification of the Treaty of Versailles. In 1929, he was awarded the Nobel Peace Prize for his work in promoting world peace.

Unresolved problems

Although direct diplomacy was frequently more successful than League action in dealing with post-war issues, the 1920s revealed three main underlying problems. These were:

- how to resolve armed conflicts involving at least one strong power
- how to achieve disarmament
- how to guarantee the borders between Germany and the successor states.

It became increasingly clear that Britain and France had very different aims and policies. Both nations faced competition from an economically strong USA, but Britain was also dealing with rising nationalism in its empire, especially in Egypt and India. Thus, Britain sought political and economic stability in Europe so it could concentrate on protecting its possessions further afield.

Successive British governments believed that the best way of ensuring German acceptance of the main terms of the Treaty of Versailles was to agree to some revisions. In the absence of any form of Anglo–American military commitment, however, France refused to consider even the slightest changes to the treaty, afraid that this might strengthen Germany and pose a future threat to French security.

Armed conflicts

As noted on page 190, two major uses of armed force occurred in 1923, one involving France (the invasion of the Ruhr) and the other Italy (the Corfu Incident). Both these countries were important members of the League and the Conference of Ambassadors. These conflicts were resolved through direct diplomacy rather than League action, but they revealed serious problems, which became even more apparent in the Depression-hit Europe of the 1930s. Such problems also highlighted the differences between Britain and France in their views on how to ensure compliance with the terms of the peace treaties.

Disarmament

Achieving global disarmament was a key objective of the League, and was closely linked to enforcing the terms of the peace treaties as well as France's fears of what might happen if Germany regained its political and military strength. France was given no real help in restoring its war-devastated provinces, and the US continued to press France for repayment of its war debts despite the weak French economy. In addition, the French were offered no significant support in pressuring Germany for reparations, while France's proposals for military and economic co-operation to strengthen the treaties were always rejected by Britain and the United States.

SOURCE D

The Ruhr invasion of 1923–4, which triggered off the spectacular collapse in value of the German mark, finally brought about United States intervention in Europe's economic affairs, but as one American historian, William MacDougall, observed in *France's Rhineland Diplomacy 1914–24* (1978), United States policy in the Dawes Plan consisted of 'financing Germany's return to industrial dominance, lending her far more than she would pay in reparations, while simultaneously squeezing France to pay her war debts, disarm and hasten the dismantling of Versailles'. France is now seen by historians as having been badly treated by her allies after 1919, left to restore her war-torn provinces and weakened economy as best she could, and forced to battle with Germany alone for the reparations due to her. Her suggestions for schemes of broad economic co-operation ... were rejected by Britain and the United States, neither of whom wished to be financially or militarily involved in ongoing European schemes which might necessitate security obligations to France. Her invasion of the Ruhr is now seen by historians as evidence of France's growing weakness and isolation, a desperate act to seize the reparations due to her and to try to strangle the inexorable German political and economic recovery and prevent a further military conflict.

Henig, R. 1995. *Versailles and After, 1919–1933. London, UK. Routledge.*
pp. 64–65.

In 1919, security concerns had led France to push for the transformation of the Rhineland into a separate state. Britain and the US had overcome this by supporting the demilitarisation of the Rhineland (see page 13), and by proposing a treaty guaranteeing military support – under League supervision – if France suffered unprovoked aggression. However, Britain insisted on an escape clause that would cancel the treaty in the event that the USA refused to ratify it. When the US Senate rejected the treaty, Britain used this escape clause. Consequently, France continued to refuse disarmament within Europe until it received guaranteed military support from Britain. A draft disarmament treaty drawn up in January 1922 failed when Britain refused to make any firm commitments.

Throughout April and May 1922, the question of disarmament, as well as economic issues, were discussed at the Genoa Conference. However, the different interests of Britain and France meant that no significant agreement was possible. The question of disarmament was complicated by the signing of the Treaty of Rapallo between Germany and the USSR in April 1922. Besides establishing friendly relations between the two countries, this treaty contained clauses on military co-operation.

This strengthened British willingness to make concessions to Germany, while France became even more determined to keep Germany weak and to reject calls for disarmament.

Britain and France moved further apart in their attitudes towards the treatment of Germany in general – and disarmament in particular – as a result of France and Belgium's occupation of the Ruhr. Even after Locarno, France remained concerned about security and thus opposed any serious disarmament. These fears multiplied in the period 1926–29, when German statesmen (including Stresemann) repeatedly indicated their desire to revise the Treaty of Versailles. Consequently, the League's Preparatory Disarmament Commission failed to produce an agreed agenda for discussion until 1931.

A British cartoon from December 1925, commenting on disarmament

The security of the successor states

The collapse of the Austro-Hungarian and Turkish empires in Central and Eastern Europe led to fragmentation, disorder and a political vacuum. This situation was further complicated by the political threat posed by the communist USSR. With the League of Nations denied real military capability, and the refusal of Britain and the USA to give France the military guarantees it felt it needed, French governments turned more and more to negotiating military pacts with countries on Germany's eastern borders. Czechoslovakia and Poland, in particular, owed their existence to the defeat of Germany and the break-up of the Austro-Hungarian and Russian empires. These states were not in favour of any increase in Germany's strength and, like France, wanted the peace treaties to remain as they were. As early as 1921, Czechoslovakia, Romania and Yugoslavia united in the Little Entente.

Britain felt that a strengthened Germany would be better able to resist the spread of communist revolutions than the weak and often divided states of Eastern Europe, so the British were not opposed to some revisions to the treaty in the east. However, with the loss of the Soviet Union as an ally (shunned because of its communist government), France felt that alliance with the successor states would provide some sort of check on Germany. Consequently, a series of mutual assistance treaties were signed by France with these states – Poland (1921), Czechoslovakia (1924), Romania (1926) and Yugoslavia (1927).

Conclusion

According to historians such as J. Jacobson, Locarno – and diplomacy in the years 1925–29 – failed to resolve the main causes of bitterness and rivalry between the major powers. In particular, even after 1925, there was still no agreement about what Germany's power and role in Europe should be. However, although the diplomacy of the 1920s did not solve all the problems of post-war Europe, it did help to reduce the risk of war.

According to historians such as Overy, it took the impact of the Depression, and the rise of Hitler and the Nazis, to plunge Europe into a Second World War. This view is challenged by historians such as Henig, who see the differences between Britain and France as more significant in explaining the ultimate failure of the League and collective security.

Activity

Divide into pairs. Each pair should carry out some additional research on the attempts at keeping the peace in the period 1919–29. One of you should then write a front-page newspaper article claiming that events since 1919 made another war unlikely; the other member of the pair should write an article arguing the opposite. Ensure your points are supported by precise and accurate facts. Display the articles in the classroom and hold a class discussion on which view you find most convincing.

End of chapter activities
Paper 3 exam practice
Question

Assess the success of the League of Nations in resolving post-war problems between 1919 and 1929.
[20 marks]

Skill focus

Using your own knowledge analytically and combining it with awareness of historical debate

Examiner's tips

Always remember that historical knowledge and analysis should be the *core* of your answer – aspects of historical debate are desirable extras. However, where it is relevant, the integration of relevant knowledge about historical debates/interpretations, with reference to individual historians, will help push your answer up into the higher bands.

Assuming that you have read the question carefully, drawn up a plan, worked out your line of argument/approach and written your introductory paragraph, you should be able to avoid both irrelevant material and simple narrative. Your task now is to follow your plan by writing a series of linked paragraphs that contain relevant analysis, precise supporting own knowledge and, where relevant, brief references to historical debate interpretations.

For this question, you will need to:

- give a brief explanation of the historical context (i.e. the reasons for the establishment of the League of Nations; its strengths/ weaknesses)
- supply an outline of the immediate problems confronting Europe and the League at the end of the First World War
- provide a consistently analytical examination of the disputes and problems the League attempted to solve from 1919 to 1929, and the reasons for the outcomes.

Such a topic, which has been the subject of some historical debate, will also give you the chance to refer to different historians' views.

Common mistakes

Some students, being aware of an existing historical debate (and knowing that extra marks can be gained by showing this), simply write things like: 'Historian X says … and historian Y says …' However, they make no attempt to **evaluate** the different views (for example, has one historian had access to more/better information than another, perhaps because he/she was writing at a later date?); nor is this information **integrated** into the answer by being pinned to the question. Another weak use of historical debate is to write things like: 'Historian X is biased because she is American.' Such comments will not be given credit.

Sample paragraphs containing analysis and historical debate

The following is a reasonable example of how to use historians' views. The **main** focus of the answer is properly concerned with using precise own knowledge to address the demands of the question. However, although the candidate has also provided some brief but relevant knowledge of historical debate, which is **smoothly integrated** into the answer, there is no evaluation of different views. Consequently, such an answer would probably be awarded a mark at the bottom rather than the top of Band 2.

The situation in Europe after 1919, resulting both from the impact of the First World War and from the various peace treaties, was a potentially dangerous mix of economic disruption, displaced populations and bitter resentments. Thus, the new League of Nations, which formally began its operations in January 1920, faced a very difficult set of tasks. The work of the League was made even more difficult by the fact that the two main members of the League – Britain and France – had different post-war aims. As a result of this, antagonism between the two nations began to grow. In addition, two other important League members – Japan and Italy – soon had governments that were determined to follow aggressive expansionist policies to further their interests. Finally, three important states – Germany, the USA and the USSR – were, for different reasons, not members at all. Thus, the League was not a truly worldwide organisation.

These problems have led historians such as Ruth Henig to argue that it is hardly surprising that the League should have ultimately failed to have any significant successes. Yet this view is challenged to an extent by other historians, such as R. J. Overy, who don't see the absence of the US as being very critical – arguing, instead, that both Britain and France were still world powers in 1920, with strong military forces. Furthermore, they had both been strengthened by taking over the former German and Turkish colonies – albeit under mandates from the League. They were thus strong enough, at least in the 1920s, to enforce the treaty and run the League – and, as noted by Overy, had a vested interest in upholding the treaties and maintaining peace.

Certainly, during the 1920s, the League was successful in dealing with a variety of problems – including the vast refugee and homelessness problems arising from the war, and in preventing or ending aggression.

[There follows analysis and precise own knowledge regarding these problems – such as refugees and homeless people, particularly as a result of the Greco–Turkish War (1920–22) and the Russo–Polish War (1920–21) – and the role played by the League in dealing with them.]

However, the success or failure of the League is usually judged in terms of its work in preventing or halting aggression – and it is in this area that historians have different opinions concerning the 1920s. Most historians accept that its record here was mixed. As regards success, the League was able to end or resolve a number of disputes during this period – these include disputes between Yugoslavia and Albania, and Finland and Sweden (both in 1920); Poland and Germany (1921); Iraq and Turkey, and Greece and Bulgaria (both in 1925).

[There follows more precise own knowledge and analysis about these disputes, and the League's success in ending them.]

Yet these instances of successful peacekeeping had two things in common – they mostly involved smaller and/or weaker countries, and the disputes did not seriously concern the national interests of Britain or France. When it came to matters involving larger states, or those affecting Britain and France, the League was seriously undermined. In particular, the League experienced several failures between 1920 and 1929. These include disputes between Poland and Lithuania (1920–22); Poland and Soviet Russia (1920–21); Turkey and Greece (1920–22); Italy and Greece (1923); France and Germany (1923).

[There follows precise own knowledge about these disputes, and explanations of why the League was generally unsuccessful.]

Despite these failures – and the failure of the League's attempts to increase its ability to impose its decisions (via the draft Treaty of Mutual Assistance in 1923, and the Geneva Protocol in 1924) – the League was successful in a more general sense. As noted by the historian Frank McDonough, the League helped promote a greater level of international co-operation in the 1920s, which resulted in some positive achievements. These include the Washington Naval Agreements (1921–22), which attempted to limit naval expansion and warfare; and diplomatic agreements – such as the Locarno Treaty (1925) and the Kellogg-Briand Pact (1928) – which attempted to safeguard the terms of the peace treaties and limit the possibility of aggression. Thus, the League can be seen as overall being successful up to 1929, and it can be argued that it was only the impact of the Depression after 1929 that ended the chances of maintaining peace in Europe. However, this is disputed by Ruth Henig, who argues that the crucial factor was the growing difference between Britain and France, the two most important members of the League.

Activity

In this chapter, the focus is on writing an answer that is analytical and well supported by precise own knowledge, and one which – where relevant – refers to historical interpretations/debates. Using the information from this chapter, and any other sources of information available to you, try to answer **one** of the following Paper 3 practice questions using these skills.

Remember to refer to the simplified Paper 3 markscheme on page 225.

Paper 3 practice questions

1   Evaluate the reasons for the formation of the League of Nations and the results of its actions up to 1929.

2   Analyse the attempts by the League of Nations to uphold the Paris Peace Treaties between 1919 and 1929.

3   Compare and contrast attempts by the League of Nations to solve **two** disputes in the years 1919–29.

4   Discuss the attempts to achieve collective security between 1919 and 1929.

5   In what ways, and with what results, did the Conference of Ambassadors deal with European disputes in the years 1919 to 1929?

6   'The main reason that attempts to achieve collective security in the period 1919–29 failed was the USA's absence from the League of Nations.' To what extent do you agree with this view?

10 The collapse of collective security 1929–39

Key questions

- What impact did the Depression have on international relations?
- How effective was the League in the period 1929–37?
- How important was appeasement in the road to war?

Although the League's attempts at ensuring collective security and enforcing the peace treaties had mixed results in the 1920s, the situation changed dramatically after the Wall Street Crash in October 1929. From this point on, the League was increasingly marginalised, international co-operation declined, and several countries adopted more aggressive foreign policies. Britain's attempt after 1937 to avoid another war by following a policy of appeasement towards Germany ended in failure.

Overview

- The Depression affected most countries throughout the 1930s, although to varying degrees. Its impact soon shattered the hopes for continued European peace that had been raised by the Locarno Treaty of 1925 and the Kellogg–Briand Pact of 1928.
- Several countries, most significantly Japan and Italy, began to adopt aggressive foreign policies as a way of solving their economic problems. Other nations chose to ignore foreign developments and instead focused on their own economic situations. As a result, the League of Nations became increasingly ineffective.
- In a series of crises from 1934 to 1937 – in particular the Italian invasion of Abyssinia, the Spanish Civil War, and Hitler's many violations of the Treaty of Versailles – the League was shown to be powerless and irrelevant.
- At the same time, Britain, France and the Soviet Union pursued quite different foreign policy objectives. In particular, Britain pursued a policy of appeasement in an attempt to avoid war. Meanwhile, despite condemning some German acts of aggression, the USA tried to avoid involvement in any new European war by passing a series of Neutrality Acts.
- From 1938, when the solution to the Czech crisis failed to satisfy Hitler's ambitions, it became clear that the next crisis would be over Poland. In September 1939, Germany invaded Poland, thus beginning the Second World War.

This page, from the British newspaper the Daily Mirror, *4 September 1939, places the blame for the start of the Second World War on Hitler*

What impact did the Depression have on international relations?

The collapse of the US stock market, which began with the Wall Street Crash on 24 October 1929, not only caused economic chaos in the USA, it also began an economic crisis that affected the whole world. Its impact on both international diplomacy and on countries' domestic policies was tremendous. In general, most nations set aside diplomatic issues while trying to deal with the economic effects of the Depression at home.

SOURCE A

The role of the Great Depression in encouraging international instability must be considered when evaluating the causes of the Second World War ... The most damaging consequences of the depression were felt in Germany. It was in the midst of the depression that Adolf Hitler's Nazi Party rose to become the largest party in Germany, which greatly aided Hitler's accession to office in 1933.

It is very important to recognise the significance of the Great Depression on the unstable international relations of the 1930s. The optimism for peace in the 1920s gave way to the self-preservation of the 'hungry' 1930s. The depression plunged the free market into a major crisis. Most countries adopted protectionism and turned inwards to deal with social and economic problems. Democratic government was also challenged by new dynamic totalitarian regimes, with state-run economies, ruled by charismatic dictators such as Stalin, Hitler, Mussolini and Franco. In comparison, democratic leaders looked dull and ineffective.

McDonough, F. 2001. Conflict, Communism and Fascism: Europe 1890–1945. Cambridge, UK. Cambridge University Press. pp. 105–6.

The effects of the Depression in the USA and Europe

In the USA, national income dropped by almost 50% in the years 1929–32 and as a result, the country became increasingly protectionist. In addition, US foreign policy towards Europe became even more isolationist than it had been before 1929.

The impact of the Depression was even greater in Europe, especially in Germany. Chancellor Brüning (see page 116) attempted to divert attention from the domestic problems caused by the Depression by turning to foreign affairs. In March 1931, he suggested the idea of economic union with Austria. However, this was in breach of the Treaty of Versailles, and was blocked by the International Court of Justice.

In 1932, Brüning unilaterally stopped all reparations payments. Later that year, an International Conference met at Lausanne in Switzerland, where Britain and France agreed to accept the moratorium on reparations in light of the Depression. (As it turned out, Germany never resumed the payments.) Britain and France also requested that the USA scale down their own repayments for war debts, but the US refused to consider this.

Later, a more nationalist German government headed by Papen, increased tariffs on British goods by 300% and demanded the return of Germany's former colonies and the Saar region. Politically, the impact of the Depression was one of the main factors contributing to the rise of the Nazis, and in January 1933 Hitler was appointed chancellor of Germany.

In 1932, Britain imposed protectionist policies and cut government spending, including defence spending. As chancellor of the Exchequer, **Neville Chamberlain** drew up the lowest arms estimates for the entire period 1919–39. In the main, British governments after 1929 wished to avoid any risk of involvement in a European conflict, as they were more concerned about protecting the British Empire. Japan's growth was seen as a particularly serious threat.

Neville Chamberlain (1868–1940) Chamberlain was a Conservative British politician who became prime minister in 1937. He is best remembered for his pursuit of the policy of appeasement with Hitler before the outbreak of the Second World War. At the time, Chamberlain believed that Hitler's demands were reasonable and – to begin with at least – he totally rejected the idea of an alliance with the Soviet Union. Despite the failure of appeasement, Chamberlain remained prime minister for the first eight months of the war. He resigned in May 1940, but was a member of the new prime minister Winston Churchill's War Cabinet. He died of cancer in November 1940.

Developments in Japan

Japan fought with the Allies in the First World War, but was disappointed by its gains from the 1919–20 peace settlements. When the Depression hit in the early 1930s, Japan was particularly badly affected, and nationalists in the country began to press for Japanese conquests to aid the economy.

Given Japan's geographical position, Asia seemed the natural area for expansion. However, this brought Japan into potential conflict with those European nations that already had Asian colonies – in particular Britain, France and the Netherlands. Japanese imperialist ambitions also concerned the USA, which was trying to extend its own influence in the Pacific region.

The Japanese army – already a powerful force by the late 1920s – was linked to the *zaibatsu* (the largest industrial companies), which also urged a more aggressive foreign policy as a way of dealing with the Depression. The army increasingly dominated or ignored the civilian governments of Japan. Military influence increased even further after 1930, when a serious drop in exports led to a political crisis.

 ## Theory of knowledge

History, theories and causation

The American historian Bernard de Voto (1897–1955) wrote: 'History abhors [hates] determinism, but cannot tolerate chance.' Are historians who see the Great Depression as the main reason for the eventual outbreak of war being deterministic, or are they pointing out the importance of unpredictable events?

How effective was the League in the period 1929–37?

Although the League of Nations enjoyed occasional successes in the period 1929–37, the impact of the Depression on international diplomacy meant that earlier League weaknesses became increasingly apparent.

The League's actions 1929–32

In 1932, the League was able to stop a border dispute between Colombia and Peru from erupting into war. However, it had little effect in alleviating longstanding tensions between Bolivia and Paraguay over the Chaco border area, and in 1932 a full-scale war broke out that continued until 1935. The League's failure to deal with an issue that involved two minor states indicated its growing ineffectiveness. Two other failures – Manchuria, and attempts at disarmament – were particularly significant.

The Japanese invasion of Manchuria 1931–32

Japan had occupied Korea in 1905 and formally annexed it in 1910. Since then, Japanese nationalists and various economic interests had wanted to expand into Manchuria, most of which was ruled by China. By 1927, Japanese firms owned most of Manchuria's mines, factories and ports, and to protect these interests Japan was allowed a large army based in the Kwantung area of southern Manchuria. In 1927, civil war broke out in China between the nationalists and the influential warlords, and this caused instability in Manchuria. By 1928, a new nationalist government was established in China, and Japan feared that it would want to re-establish Chinese control over Manchuria.

On 18 September 1931, the officers of the Japanese Kwantung army staged an attack near the town of Mukden on the Japanese-owned South Manchurian Railway, which ran through Manchuria. The Mukden Incident was used to justify sending in a Japanese army of occupation. Japan's civilian government tried to get the military to withdraw, but the army refused.

This Japanese invasion was in breach of the League's collective security system, and both China and Japan were League members. The invasion of Manchuria also defied the Washington Naval Treaty of 1922, in which Japan had promised not to attack China. China appealed to the League's Council to stop this Japanese aggression.

At Japan's suggestion, the League set up a Commission of Enquiry – headed by Britain's Lord Lytton – to investigate the situation. The Lytton Commission did not report until November 1932, 11 months after Japan had established complete control of Manchuria. The report criticised both China and Japan, and did not recommend either economic or military sanctions. The League accepted the report in February 1933, admitting the validity of Japanese claims that they were protecting their own interests in Manchuria but stating that Japan was wrong to have used force and should therefore withdraw its troops. As a result, Japan withdrew from the League of Nations.

> What action did the League take over Japan's invasion of Manchuria?

Reasons for the League's ineffectiveness 1931–32

The Manchurian crisis clearly showed that the idea of collective security was not working in practice. According to historians such as Gaetano Salvemini, the reason for the League's inability to solve the problem in Manchuria was that the crisis occurred just as the Depression reached its peak. The USA and countries in Europe were more concerned with domestic economic problems than in resolving a crisis thousands of miles away.

The League might have been more effective if the USA and the USSR had been members, as both these countries had interests in Asia. Despite having significant trade links with Japan, however, US president Herbert Hoover's Republican government was reluctant to get involved in the conflict between China and Japan, and refused to consider economic sanctions (although it did state that the US would not accept any territorial changes resulting from military aggression). As a result, most League members feared that any trade ban imposed on Japan would merely result in losing that trade to the USA.

The USSR considered the Japanese act of aggression to be a direct threat to its Asian territories, and was willing to act. However, no Western European state was prepared to co-operate with the communist regime in any military action, and the Soviet Union would not risk intervening on its own.

In addition, the main League members could not agree on what action to take. Neither Italy nor Germany really objected to the Japanese invasion: Italy was not interested in Asia, and was already planning the enlargement of its own empire. In fact, Mussolini was so encouraged by the lack of effective League action during the Manchurian crisis that from 1932, he began detailed planning of the conquest of Abyssinia. Meanwhile, despite significant investments in China, Germany was waiting to see what the League would do in response to Japan's use of force.

Britain and France remained divided. Britain did not want to risk a naval conflict as, under the Washington Naval Treaty, Japan had a naval superiority in the Far East, and military advisors informed the British government that such a conflict might be lost. This would endanger important imperial territories such as India, Singapore and Hong Kong. Britain also had important trade links with Japan that it did not want to lose. The British National Government did ban the sale of arms to both sides, but this boycott had a greater effect on China than Japan, and was soon ended.

France had its own Asian colony of Indochina (comprising Vietnam, Laos and Cambodia), and disapproved of Japan's actions. However, France was already dealing with an armed communist–nationalist insurrection there, and was anyway more concerned with the possible threat from Germany closer to home. France thus wished to avoid any conflict with Japan. Publicly, France condemned the Japanese aggression, but a secret note was sent stating that France sympathised with the 'difficulties' Japan was dealing with in China.

The World Disarmament Conference 1932

Although the crisis over Manchuria led to continued instability in the Asian and Pacific regions, this was not highly significant for later developments in Europe. More important was the World Disarmament Conference in Geneva, organised by the League of Nations in an attempt to agree limits on army, naval and air-force weapons. The conference was attended by 61 nations of the League and five non-members, including both the USA and the USSR. France again unsuccessfully attempted to give the League its own army. A British proposal to limit offensive weapons such as tanks, bombs, submarines and chemical weapons obtained a 41-vote majority, but Germany and the Soviet Union refused to agree.

This British cartoon from 1933 refers to the failure of the World Disarmament Conference

What is the message of this cartoon? How does the cartoonist get this message across?

Of more immediate significance was the fact that Germany insisted on 'equality of treatment' – demanding that all nations should either disarm to the German level set by the Treaty of Versailles, or that Germany should be allowed to rearm to the levels of other major powers. In fact, Germany had never fully complied with the disarmament restrictions of Versailles, and had begun some limited rearmament via the Treaties of Rapallo and Berlin with the Soviet Union. In 1932 – *before* Hitler became chancellor – German delegates walked out of the conference, and said they would not return until they had been granted this equality. The conference continued without them.

What did German delegates at the World Disarmament Conference mean by 'equality of treatment'?

Collective security 1933–37

The rise of Hitler and the Nazis had a significant impact on international affairs in this period. Although Hitler was mostly concerned with establishing internal control until 1934, he soon moved to a more aggressive foreign policy.

Hitler's foreign policy

Initially, Hitler's foreign policy was quite cautious. At the Disarmament Conference, he stressed the German desire for peace, but repeated the earlier request for 'equality of treatment'. However, the French insistence on a German guarantee that the Versailles limitations would be respected for the next four years led Germany to formally withdraw from the conference and then from the League in October 1933.

In 1934, Hitler signed a non-aggression pact with Poland. This eased general European concerns over Germany's intentions, but it also prevented closer Polish ties with France, as well as bringing Poland under greater German influence. Britain welcomed this development, but France remained suspicious and pursued its security independently of Britain.

SOURCE B

While Britain was therefore pressing for an arms limitation agreement with Germany and trying to pressurize France into making substantial concessions, France was preoccupied with the construction of an east European agreement along the lines of the Locarno treaty of 1925 which would include Germany ... However, if Germany's agreement could not be secured, [Britain] feared the construction of a bloc of states encircling Germany. They warned that such encirclement might drive Hitler to some desperate act of aggression. Without British co-operation on measures of security, the French would not agree to further concessions on arms limitation. On 14 October 1933, Germany withdrew from the Disarmament Conference, denouncing it as a sham, and Hitler announced Germany's intention of withdrawing from the League. He would, however, consider returning when Germany's grievances were recognized and serious proposals put forward to meet them. There was worse news to come. In January 1934 Poland, fearing that treaty revision would be concluded at her expense in some agreement between France and Germany, became the first country to conclude a non-aggression pact with Germany. It would run in the first instance for ten years. Clearly, German rearmament was having its effect on the political calculations of east European leaders.

Henig, R. 1985. *The Origins of the Second World War 1933–1939.* London, UK. Routledge. pp. 17–18.

Although Germany's departure from the League was a setback for the organisation and for international relations in general, a new member soon joined its ranks. The Soviet Union, increasingly disturbed by Hitler's rise to power, had begun to fear Nazi Germany's intentions and put aside its distaste of this 'capitalist club' to become a member of the League in 1934.

Hitler's first aggressive foreign policy action was an attempt to bring about *Anschluss* with Austria in 1934. However, Hitler was forced to back down from this after being warned that the German army was not ready for a serious military conflict. In January 1935, the important Saar area – ruled by Britain and France under a League of Nations' mandate since 1920 – voted to return to Germany. In March, Hitler announced that Germany was no longer bound by the military terms of Versailles. Germany began openly rearming and reintroduced conscription. Britain, France and Italy formed the Stresa Front in April 1935 to oppose further German actions (see page 86). The League took no action against these clear breaches of the peace settlements.

Hitler immediately began taking steps to weaken the Stresa Front. He made speeches in which he expressed Germany's desire for both peace and rearmament. The effect was to further widen the gulf between British and French policies – Britain was impressed by these statements, while France remained unconvinced. As a result, France negotiated a mutual assistance pact with the Soviet Union, which included a joint promise to protect Czechoslovakia from German aggression. Britain disapproved of these links with the communist USSR and, in June 1935, signed the Anglo–German Naval Treaty, in an attempt to limit Hitler's planned naval expansion.

Activity

Using the internet, and any other resources available to you, find out more about the Franco–Soviet agreements of 1935. Then list their main points and highlight their weaknesses.

Italy's invasion of Abyssinia 1935

In October 1935, with allied foreign policy already undermined by the Anglo–German Naval Treaty, Italy invaded Abyssinia. This was the first serious act of aggression by a major European power since 1920. The limited sanctions imposed by the League effectively demonstrated its weaknesses and irrelevance when it came to solving serious crises, while many non-League members continued to trade with Italy. France in particular was reluctant to provoke an argument with Mussolini, as it wished to maintain the Stresa Front in order to resist future German threats.

After the secret Hoare–Laval Pact was dropped (see page 87), the League began to take a tougher line. In March 1936, it decided to ban the sale of oil and petrol to Italy. However, this was not fully implemented until May 1936, by which time the Italian conquest was complete. The British and French reaction had succeeded in both alienating Mussolini (and so destroying the Stresa Front), and in discrediting the League which, in July, ended all sanctions against Italy.

When neither Britain nor France approved his invasion of Abyssinia, Mussolini moved away from the allies and closer to Germany. As early as January 1936, Mussolini let Hitler know that he no longer had any objections to Austria coming under German control, and hinted that he would not prevent any reoccupation of the Rhineland. On 6 March 1936, Mussolini withdrew Italy from the League of Nations. With the loss of Italy as an ally, Britain and France were forced to rely on each other.

The reoccupation of the Rhineland

On 7 March 1936, Hitler ordered German troops to enter the Rhineland which, according to the Treaty of Versailles, was supposed to remain a demilitarised zone. Despite the collapse of the Stresa Front and the need to support each other, Britain and France continued to follow quite different policies. Anthony Eden, the British foreign secretary, was prepared to 'appease' what the British government believed were justified German grievances. Although Britain promised to support France if Germany launched an unprovoked attack, France still felt isolated. A request to US president Franklin D. Roosevelt to condemn the German remilitarisation of the Rhineland was refused, and France felt unequal to opposing the action alone. The League made no attempt at all to stop Germany.

> What was the significance of Germany's reoccupation of the Rhineland in March 1936?

The Spanish Civil War

The total ineffectiveness of the League was highlighted once again when civil war broke out in Spain in July 1936. Despite the German and Italian military assistance to the Spanish nationalists, Britain and France responded by forming an ineffective Non-Intervention Committee (see page 140). Hitler and Mussolini then established the Rome–Berlin Axis, which confirmed to the world where Italy's loyalties now lay. The following month, Hitler signed the Anti-Comintern Pact with Japan, designed to confront the Soviet Union. During this time, the League remained silent over Germany's rearmament programme.

Japan's invasion of China 1937

In the Pacific, Japan greatly increased its armaments expenditure and military influence in the country grew. The Asia–Pacific region came to be seen as Japan's natural sphere of influence, in which it had a right to expand. In 1936, this was formalised by a policy statement ('Fundamentals of Future National Policy'), which made it clear that Japanese interests in Southeast Asia would continue to expand in the immediate future. Japan refused to renew the Washington Naval Treaty of 1922 or the more recent Treaty of London, in which Britain, Japan, Italy and the USA had set limits on submarines and agreed to scrap some warships. In July 1937 – in clear defiance of the League – Japan invaded China. As a League member, China appealed to the organisation for help. The League's response was to call an international conference. Britain and France gave China some financial aid, but no offer of military assistance was forthcoming.

How important was appeasement in the road to war?

By 1937, there was conflict in China, civil war in Spain and growing threats from Germany and Italy. It was clear that the League of Nations was no longer effective. In this tense period of decline in international co-operation, Neville Chamberlain became prime minister of Britain. Chamberlain hoped that a policy of appeasement would calm international relations and bring about a lasting peace.

Reasons for appeasement

For decades, appeasement has been criticised as a short-sighted policy and an encouragement to Hitler to continue his aggressive actions. As such, it has been regarded as a major factor contributing to the outbreak of the Second World War. Yet many contemporaries saw it as the only practical policy for averting war. A few key politicians at the time, including Winston Churchill, suggested an alternative policy of forming a grand anti-fascist alliance. However, the only significant European power capable of resisting Nazi Germany was the Soviet Union. Many Western governments rejected Stalin's Russia as a potential ally, mainly because of its commitment to communism and world revolution. Chamberlain was not alone in his extreme anti-communist stance.

Another alternative – reviving the collective-security role of the League of Nations – seemed totally unrealistic given the non-membership of Germany, Italy and Japan, and the League's failure to act effectively in the years since 1929. By 1937, the League was weak and discredited. Many British politicians regarded France as their only possible ally, but this was also problematic. The Stresa Front had collapsed, Germany was openly ignoring the conditions of the Versailles and Locarno treaties, and it seemed likely that a pro-Axis state would soon be established on France's southern borders.

More importantly, in 1937 Chamberlain was informed by his advisors that British armed forces were in no state to give effective military support to France, or even to defend British cities from air raids. In addition, Chamberlain was told that the British navy could not adequately protect British colonies in the Far East, in view of Japan's increasing military strength. The majority of British citizens were also opposed to rearmament, and many believed that some revision of the peace settlements was legitimate. Those who had lived through the horrors of the First World War sought any alternative to another global conflict.

Consequently, most British government ministers supported Chamberlain's policy of appeasement, designed to avoid war by negotiating a mutually acceptable revision of the Treaty of Versailles. In November 1937, Lord Halifax was sent to Germany to meet Nazi officials and to tell them that Britain would support legitimate German claims in Europe, as long as they were negotiated peacefully.

The historical debate about appeasement

There has been considerable debate about appeasement and Chamberlain's role in pursuing this policy. The early orthodox view believed he was following a morally dubious and ineffective campaign; this was essentially the view of historians from the late 1940s, such as John Wheeler-Bennett.

However, from the late 1960s various revisionist historians, such as John Charmley, portrayed Chamberlain as having a good grasp of Britain's economic and military weaknesses, and claimed he was trying to maintain peace while preparing for war. Keith Feiling, among others, focused on Chamberlain's doubts about the USSR as a potential ally. These revisionist historians based their arguments on the structural problems facing Britain in the late 1930s, the threat posed by Japanese expansion in Asia, the strength of public opinion against rearmament, and documents that became available under the 30-year rule. All this, they argued, showed that the British government did not have any choice but to pursue appeasement.

These views later came under attack by post-revisionists, who argued that revisionists had placed too much reliance on official documents, which had been drafted and selected by the supporters of appeasement, and had overlooked intelligence reports that warned Chamberlain of Hitler's intention to dominate Europe. Keith Middlemas and R. A. C. Parker, for example, see Chamberlain as persisting in a misguided policy, deliberately misleading the public and ignoring viable alternatives. Some – such as Anthony Adamthwaite – believe that the decision not to consider an alliance with the USSR until it was too late was part of the élite's inherent hostility to communism.

Later views have accepted that Chamberlain had limited options, and R. J. Overy has argued that when the circumstances changed, so did Chamberlain's policy. However, such arguments have been criticised on the grounds that even after the declaration of war in 1939, Chamberlain still seems to have attempted to keep appeasement alive.

Appeasement and the final steps to war

Despite the aims of Chamberlain's policy of appeasement, the years after 1937 saw Hitler taking an increasingly aggressive approach to foreign policy objectives.

Anschluss with Austria March 1938

Anschluss with Austria remained Hitler's objective, despite his failure in 1934. In July 1936, he persuaded the Austrian government to accept German supervision of its foreign policy in return for German promises to guarantee Austria's sovereignty. However, in February 1938 the Austrian chancellor called a referendum on Austrian independence. When it looked as if the vote might reject union with Germany, Hitler insisted that a new government be formed, dominated by Austrian Nazis. This new government then invited German soldiers to enter Austria to help deal with the unrest. On 12 March 1938, therefore, German troops crossed into Austria and *Anschluss* was finally achieved. France later denounced this action, but did not threaten any military response at the time; Britain maintained its policy of appeasement.

The crisis over Czechoslovakia 1938

As well as breaching Versailles, the *Anschluss* also strengthened Nazi Germany's ability to threaten Czechoslovakia. The Czech prime minister, Edvard Beneš, had been an active supporter of the League of Nations and the enforcement of the peace treaties. However, Czechoslovakia faced unrest among the 3.5 million German-speakers who lived in the Sudetenland along its borders with Austria. In May 1938, the Czech government claimed that Hitler was planning to invade. Hitler denied this, and Chamberlain sent Lord Runciman to mediate between the Czech government and the Sudeten Germans. Runciman concluded that the Sudeten Germans were an oppressed minority and that they should be allowed to become part of Germany.

The situation in Czechoslovakia continued to deteriorate, and in September 1938 Chamberlain decided to negotiate with Hitler in person. On 15 September, they met at Berchtesgaden, and on 22 September at Bad Godesburg. Each time, Hitler increased his demands until eventually Mussolini tried to convince the Führer to be more moderate. Ultimately, Britain and France informed the Czech government that it should hand over the Sudetenland to Germany or risk fighting a war on its own. The Soviet Union, which had signed a treaty with France to protect Czechoslovakia in 1935, was not even consulted.

The Munich Agreement

Chamberlain met Hitler for the third time on 29 September 1938, at Munich. Here, Germany, Britain, France and Italy finally agreed that the Sudetenland should be handed to Germany, on the basis that self-determination had been denied these German-speakers in 1919.

Once again, neither Czechoslovakia nor the Soviet Union was consulted. On 10 October, the Sudetenland became part of Germany. Without firing a shot, Hitler obtained the part of Czechoslovakia that contained its border defences and the important Skoda armaments works. In return, Hitler made vague promises to leave the rest of Czechoslovakia alone, and signed a document with Chamberlain stating that Germany and Britain would never go to war against each other – the infamous 'peace in our time' pledge.

The front page of the British newspaper the Daily Sketch, *1 October 1938*

SOURCE C

For Chamberlain, appeasement meant taking the initiative and showing Hitler that 'reasonable' claims could be achieved by negotiation and not force. Chamberlain and Daladier, the new French Prime Minister, feared that the Czech crisis could precipitate a wider conflict and decided that Czechoslovakia was simply not worth a European war. The Czech President, Benes, was urged therefore to make concessions to the Sudeten Germans. Chamberlain had three meetings with Hitler: at Berchtesgarden on 15 September, at Bad Godesberg on 22–23 September, and at Munich on 29–30 September. At the first meeting, Hitler stated his intention to annex the Sudetenland on the principle of self-determination. At Bad Godesberg he insisted on immediate German occupation, and finally at Munich he was persuaded to accept a phased occupation with an international commission to arbitrate over disputed boundaries ...

On 29 September 1938, an international conference was held at Munich. The participants were Germany, Italy, Britain and France. Conspicuous by their absence were Czechoslovakia, whose fate was to be decided, and the Soviet Union, which was not invited.

Welch, D. 1998. Hitler. *London, UK. UCL Press. pp. 59–60.*

How valid do you think Soviet fears were that their exclusion from the Munich Conference indicated British and French support for Hitler's expansion eastwards? What other explanations are there for their exclusion from this conference?

At the time, many people believed that Chamberlain's policy of appeasement had peacefully resolved some of the 'unfair' conditions of the 1919–20 settlements, and Chamberlain was nominated for the 1938 Nobel Peace Prize. However, in November 1938, the anti-Jewish violence of *Kristallnacht* (see page 171) added to growing concern over Hitler's real intentions (intelligence reports also suggested a possible invasion of the Netherlands). So, in February 1939, Britain promised to support France. Britain then began to create a large British Expeditionary Force in order to be able to meet this obligation, and discussions took place between British and French military leaders.

Why did losing the Sudetenland weaken Czechoslovakia so much?

The invasion of Czechoslovakia 1939

Hitler's foreign policy now centred on seizing the rest of Czechoslovakia. The Slovaks were bullied into declaring their independence, while Poland and Hungary were encouraged to make their own territorial demands. On 15 March 1939, Nazi Germany finally invaded Czechoslovakia.

A map showing the territorial expansion of Germany by March 1939

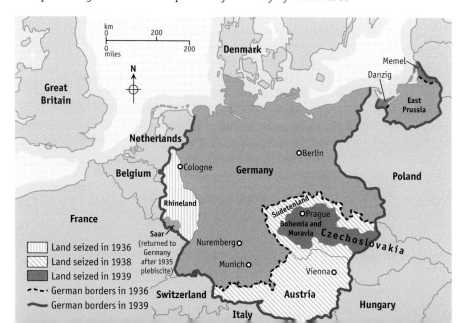

217

Although the French prime minister **Edouard Daladier** put his country on a war footing, no action was taken by either Britain or France. As a result, Hitler confidently turned his attention to the Lithuanian port of Memel, where the German inhabitants were demanding to be returned to Germany.

Edouard Daladier (1884–1970) Daladier was a radical, and served as prime minister of France in 1933, 1934 and from 1938 to 1940. He signed the Munich Agreement in 1938, and declared war on Germany in September 1939. Daladier was imprisoned by the Vichy government in France (which, with German permission, ruled part of the country following France's defeat in 1940). He was then deported to Germany, where he remained a prisoner until the end of the war in Europe in 1945.

The Nazi–Soviet Non-Aggression Pact

The Soviet Union had been offering an anti-Nazi alliance for some time, but Chamberlain – a strong anti-communist – was opposed to this, partly because it might provoke Germany, but also because Poland objected to it. Despite a second British rejection in May 1939, by the middle of the year there was strong public support in both Britain and France for such an alliance. Chamberlain reluctantly agreed to open negotiations – but only at a low level. Anthony Eden, who had offered to conduct them, was excluded from the initial negotiations.

Since the Munich Conference in September 1938, however, Stalin had come to suspect that Britain and France were prepared to accept German conquests in the east. Britain's slow response to these low-level negotiations in the summer of 1939 seemed to confirm this fear, so Stalin also began to respond to German requests for negotiations.

Hitler had already set the date for the invasion of Poland, convinced that with no Soviet ally, Britain and France would not honour their pledges to Poland. At the same time, with no firm alliance with Britain or France, Stalin hoped that a non-aggression agreement with Germany would give him time to prepare his defences against an invasion. While the negotiations with Britain seemed to stall, therefore, the Molotov–Ribbentrop Pact was concluded on 23 August 1939. This included secret clauses for the division of Poland and a Soviet takeover of the Baltic States.

Activity

Carry out some additional research on the reasons why Britain was so reluctant to ally with the Soviet Union before 1939. Then rank them in order of importance, and write a paragraph explaining your first choice.

SOURCE D

The notion of 'concept pluralism' – that there were a number of different views among the leaders of the Third Reich about the foreign policy Germany should pursue – has recently been taken further by Wolfgang Michalka in his analysis of Ribbentrop's own foreign policy ideas and influence upon Hitler. Michalka argues that from the mid-1930s onwards an anti-English rather than essentially anti-Russian policy provided the main thrust of Ribbentrop's own conception of foreign policy ... He demonstrates how, in the later 1930s, Hitler's increasing recognition of the failure to win over England allowed Ribbentrop a considerable scope for exerting influence, culminating in the signing of the Non-Aggression Pact with the Soviet Union in 1939 ...

None of the 'structural-functionalist', 'concept pluralist', or 'polycratic' approaches to foreign policy ... has shaken the conviction of the 'intentionalists' (or 'programmatists') that the character and consistency of Hitler's ideology was the crucial and determining element in the equation. Indeed ... the leading studies of the varying centres of influence in the formation of foreign policy all come down ultimately to similar or compatible conclusions.

Kershaw, I. 1993. The Nazi Dictatorship: Problems and Perspectives of Interpretation. London, UK. Arnold. p. 115.

Poland

Soon after the Munich Conference, Germany began to request the return of Danzig (run by the League of Nations as an International Free City), and the building of road and rail links across the Polish Corridor to East Prussia. Once Czechoslovakia and Memel had been taken, it became clear that Poland was Hitler's next target. By the end of March, both Britain and France had made a significant policy change and had guaranteed to protect Polish independence (similar promises were made to Greece following Italy's invasion of Albania in April 1939). However, Hitler was not convinced that these guarantees would be honoured, even when the US moved a battle fleet from the Atlantic to the Pacific (allowing British and French fleets to move to the North Sea), or when Britain announced conscription for all males aged 20–21.

On 29 August, Hitler offered Poland the 'choice' of peaceful dismemberment by negotiation – or war. Poland refused to negotiate, and on 1 September Germany invaded. Two days later, on 3 September, Britain and France declared war on Germany. Appeasement had failed. The Second World War had begun.

End of chapter activities

Paper 3 exam practice

Question

Analyse the reasons for the outbreak of the Second World War in 1939.
[20 marks]

Skill focus

Writing a conclusion to your essay

Examiner's tips

Provided you have carried out all the steps recommended so far, it should be relatively easy to write one or two concluding paragraphs.

For this question, you will need to cover the following possible reasons:

- the long-term problems resulting from the peace treaties of 1919–20
- the weaknesses and failures of the League of Nations
- the impact of the Great Depression on diplomacy and collective security
- the foreign policies of Italy, Japan and Germany after 1929
- the reasons for, and role of, appeasement
- the significance of the Nazi–Soviet Non-Aggression Pact, and the Anglo–French guarantee given to Poland.

This question requires you to consider a **range** of different reasons/factors, and to support your analysis with **precise and specific** supporting knowledge – so you need to avoid generalisations. Also, the date at the end of the question requires some consideration of 1939 – i.e. why did war break out then and not in 1938?

Finally, such a question implicitly offers you the chance to consider different views, and to come to some kind of **judgement** about which reason(s) was/were most important.

Common mistakes

Sometimes, candidates simply rehash in their conclusion what they have written earlier – making the examiner read the same things twice. Generally, concluding paragraphs should be relatively short. The aim should be to come to an overall judgement/conclusion that is clearly based on what has already been written. If possible, a short but relevant quotation is a good way to round off an argument.

Sample student conclusion

After examining the various possible reasons for the outbreak of war in 1939, it is difficult to come to a decision about whether any particular factor was most important. While long-term factors – such as the peace treaties of 1919-20, or the weaknesses of the League – clearly played a role, events after 1929 were probably more important. In particular, the Depression resulted in many countries placing their national interests above the maintenance of collective security during the 1930s. This applied to the democracies as well as to the dictatorships. In addition, the long-standing suspicions between the capitalist West and the communist USSR meant that Britain – if not necessarily France – ruled out the Soviet Union as a possible ally until it was too late. This, in part, explains the policy of appeasement that some historians have seen as giving Hitler the expectation that there would never be any opposition to his eastward expansion.

However, the main reason for the outbreak of the Second World War was Hitler's determination to obtain 'Lebensraum' – and his willingness to risk military conflict to do so. In the end, other major powers only had two choices: to accept Nazi Germany's domination of Europe, or to oppose it. As Ruth Henig has suggested: 'Whenever resistance came – whether over the Sudetenland or over the Polish Corridor – it was likely to provoke war.'

> This is a good conclusion because it briefly pulls together the main threads of the argument (without simply repeating/summarising them), and then also makes a clear judgement. In addition, there is an intelligent final comment that rounds off the whole conclusion – and no doubt the core of the essay – in a memorable way.

Activity

In this chapter, the focus is on writing a useful conclusion. Using the information from this chapter, and any other sources of information available to you, write concluding paragraphs for **at least two** of the Paper 3 practice questions on page 222. Remember: to do this, you will need to create full plans for the questions you choose.

Remember to refer to the simplified Paper 3 markscheme on page 225.

Paper 3 practice questions

1 'International diplomacy failed to prevent the outbreak of the Second World War mainly because of the impact of the Depression.' To what extent do you agree with this statement?

2 Why did the League of Nations fail to take action against Japan's invasion of Manchuria in 1931 and Italy's invasion of Abyssinia in 1935?

3 For what reasons, and with what results, did attempts to achieve collective security between 1929 and 1939 fail?

4 To what extent was the British policy of appeasement the main reason for the collapse of collective security in the late 1930s?

5 Discuss the relative importance of Chamberlain's policy of appeasement and Hitler's policy of *Lebensraum* as causes of the Second World War.

11 Exam practice

Introduction

You have now completed your study of the main diplomatic developments and political events during the period 1919–39, and have seen how these developments contributed to the outbreak of the Second World War. You have also had the chance to examine some of the various historical debates and differing historical interpretations that surround these developments.

In the earlier chapters, you have encountered examples of Paper 3-type essay questions, with examiner's tips. You have also had some basic practice in answering such questions. In this chapter, these tips and skills will be developed in more depth. Longer examples of possible student answers are provided, accompanied by examiner's comments that should increase your understanding of what examiners are looking for when they mark your essays. Following each question and answer, you will find tasks to give you further practice in the skills needed to gain the higher marks in this exam.

IB History Paper 3 exam questions and skills

Those of you following Route 2, HL Option 5 – *Aspects of the History of Europe and the Middle East* – will have studied in depth **three** of the 12 sections available for this HL Option. *Interwar Years: Conflict and Cooperation 1919–39* is one of those sections. For Paper 3, two questions are set from each of the 12 sections, giving 24 questions in total; and you have to answer **three** of these.

Each question has a specific markscheme. However the 'generic' markscheme in the IB *History Guide* gives you a good general idea of what examiners are looking for in order to be able to put answers into the higher bands. In particular, you will need to acquire reasonably precise historical knowledge so that you can address issues such as cause and effect, and change and continuity. This knowledge will be required in order to explain historical developments in a clear, coherent, well-supported and relevant way. You will also need to understand relevant historical debates and interpretations, and be able to refer to these and critically evaluate them.

Essay planning

Make sure you read each question **carefully**, noting all the important key or 'command' words. You might find it useful to highlight them on your question paper. You can then produce a rough plan (for example, a spider diagram) for **each** of the three essays you intend to attempt, **before** you start to write your answers. That way, you will soon know whether you have enough own knowledge to answer them adequately. Next, refer back to the wording of each question – this will help you see whether or not you are responding to **all** its various demands/aspects. In addition, if you run short of time towards the end of your exam, you will at least be able to write some brief condensed sentences to show the key issues/points and arguments you would have presented. It is therefore far better to do the planning at the **start** of the exam; that is, **before** you panic if you suddenly realise you don't have time to finish your last essay.

Relevance to the question

Remember, too, to keep your answers relevant and focused on the question. Don't go outside the dates mentioned in the question, or write answers on subjects not identified in that question. Also, don't just describe the events or developments. Sometimes students simply focus on one key word, date or individual, and then write down everything they know about it. Instead, select your own knowledge carefully, and pin the relevant information to the key features raised by the question. Finally, if the question asks for 'causes/reasons' and 'results', 'continuity and change', 'successes and failures', or 'nature and development', make sure you deal with **all** the parts of the question. Otherwise, you will limit yourself to half marks at best.

Examiner's tips

For Paper 3 answers, examiners are looking for well-structured arguments that:

- are consistently relevant/linked to the question
- offer clear/precise analysis
- are supported by the use of accurate, precise and relevant own knowledge
- offer a balanced judgement
- refer to different historical debates/interpretations or to relevant historians and, where relevant, offer some critical evaluation of these.

Simplified markscheme

Band		Marks
1	**Consistently analytical/explanatory** in approach, with very explicit focus on all demands of the question. **Understanding and evaluation of different historical interpretations**; good synthesis of **plentiful and precise own knowledge** with different interpretations/approaches. **Argument is clear, well-supported and well-structured** throughout.	17–20
2	**Clear/explicit focus** on all the demands of the question, with **consistently relevant analysis/explanation**. Very **detailed own knowledge**. Argument in the main is **well-structured and supported**. Some **awareness of different historical interpretations**, and **some attempts at evaluation**.	14–16
3	**Some relevant analysis/argument**, mainly linked to the question, with **relevant and precise supporting own knowledge. Reasonable structure, with some explanation** and **some awareness of different historical views** – but not all aspects of the question addressed.	11–13
4	Mainly **narrative in approach**, with **reasonable accurate knowledge**; but **limited focus**, and **no real analysis/ explanation. Some structure**, but **links to the question are mainly unclear/implicit**.	8–10
5	**Limited relevant knowledge**, with a **few unsupported comments/assertions. Not well-structured**; and **not linked effectively to the question**, which is not really understood.	0–7

Student answers

The following extracts from student answers have brief examiner's comments in the margins, and a longer overall comment at the end. Those parts of student answers that are particularly strong and well-focused (such as demonstrations of precise and relevant own knowledge, or examination of historical interpretations) will be *highlighted in purple*. Errors/confusions/irrelevance/loss of focus will be *highlighted in white*. In this way, you should find it easier to follow why marks were awarded or withheld.

Question 1

'Hitler's desire for *Lebensraum* was the main reason for the outbreak of the Second World War in 1939.' To what extent do you agree with this view?
[20 marks]

Skills

- Factual knowledge and understanding
- Structured, analytical and **balanced** argument
- Awareness/understanding/evaluation of historical interpretations
- Clear and balanced judgement.

Examiner's tip

Look carefully at the wording of this question, which asks you to consider the various reasons, including *Lebensraum*, for the outbreak of the Second World War in 1939. This means you need to identify and analyse a **range** of causes – including Hitler's foreign policy aims – **and** attempt a judgement about which reason(s) you think was/were most important. Remember, it is perfectly acceptable to disagree with the view, as long as you support your arguments with relevant and precise own knowledge. All aspects of the question will need to be addressed in order to achieve high marks. Remember – don't just list or describe the various reasons. You need to provide explicit analysis and explanation of these reasons, **and** how they contributed to the outbreak of war.

Student answer

There are many reasons for the outbreak of the Second World War in 1939 – and these have been the subject of considerable debate amongst historians. For a long time, the orthodox view was that the war was the result of Hitler's actions – in particular, his aim to obtain Lebensraum in the east. This aim was first stated in his book Mein Kampf and, according to orthodox historians, formed the basis of the foreign policy he followed from 1933 to 1939. However, revisionist historians, such as Overy, have argued that war broke out in 1939 as a result of various factors that undermined the international diplomatic system established after 1919 – Hitler's foreign policy objectives were just one of those factors. Others include the problems resulting from the peace treaties, the weaknesses of the League of Nations, the impact of the Great Depression, the rise of authoritarian regimes, and the policy of appeasement pursued by Britain and France.

Examiner's comment

This is a clear and well-focused introduction, showing some awareness of the views of historians, and identifying a range of different factors/reasons for the outbreak of war.

The orthodox argument that Hitler's determination to secure Lebensraum was the main reason for the outbreak of war in 1939 is based, in part, on his book Mein Kampf and, especially on the Four-Year Plan that Hitler asked Göring to oversee in 1936, after the successful reoccupation of the Rhineland in March 1936. Although the Four-Year Plan was in part a response to an economic crisis, it was also designed to get Germany ready – economically and militarily – to fight a war by 1940. A further argument in support of the prime importance of Hitler's foreign policy is the Hossbach Memorandum of November 1937. This was notes made by Hitler's adjutant, Colonel Hossbach, a day after a meeting called by Hitler in early November. Those present were the foreign and war ministers, and the three commanders-in-chief of the armed forces. According to Hossbach's notes, Hitler told these people that they had to get Germany ready to make conquests in the east – and that these should be completed by 1943–45. Hitler is also supposed to have made specific references to taking Austria and Czechoslovakia, even if this resulted in war with Britain. However, historians are divided about the significance of this meeting and about the reliability of the notes made by Hossbach, especially as he made no notes during the meeting itself. Some revisionist historians see the meeting as more of a way of justifying his rearmament programme to cautious conservative ministers than as a definite war plan.

Examiner's comment

There is some accurate own knowledge about aspects of Hitler's foreign policy aims, and some general understanding of the arguments surrounding this factor, although no specific historians are mentioned.

Another reason for the outbreak of war in 1939 was that the peace treaties of 1919–20 had failed to solve the problems that had led to the outbreak of the First World War. These included economic and imperial rivalries between Britain, France and the new state of Germany – especially in relation to the Scramble for Africa. There had been two Moroccan crises before 1914, which had been provoked largely by Germany, and which had pushed Britain and France closer together. This had resulted in the formation of two rival alliance systems – the Triple Alliance and the Triple Entente – which had also played a part in the outbreak of war in 1914. Associated with these tensions was an arms race between the main European states. Britain and Germany competed over their respective navies, while France and Germany focused on their armies.

Even after the war, the countries of Europe – especially Britain and France – saw their continued prosperity and power as being based on maintaining their empires. Germany – which had lost its colonies and some of its European lands – saw this as a weakness to be overcome. Significantly, this view was part of German foreign policy before Hitler came to power in 1933. Even Stresemann, who did so much to improve Germany's standing in Europe, pursued a revisionist foreign policy in relation to Germany's eastern borders. For instance, the Locarno Treaty of 1925 said nothing about these eastern borders. However, it is important to note that he tried to carry out this 'revision' of Versailles peacefully, in co-operation with Britain and France.

Examiner's comment

While this paragraph has some relevant general comments about German foreign policy before 1933, there is also some largely irrelevant material on the causes of the First World War. This material will not score any marks, so the candidate is wasting time by giving this detail.

[There then follow several more paragraphs giving accurate and reasonably detailed facts on how League weaknesses, the Great Depression, and the rise of right-wing dictators, also helped cause the Second World War.]

Finally, appeasement also contributed to the outbreak of war in 1939. In many ways, it was a policy of desperation resulting from the problems of Europe in the 1930s. Britain in particular, which had always favoured a revision of the Treaty of Versailles, was reluctant to stand against aggressive dictators such as Mussolini and Hitler in case this resulted in war. France, which had suffered economic and military decline as a result of the First World War, was only prepared to take a stand if Britain took the lead – this was something that Britain's National and then Conservative governments of the 1930s were not prepared to do. Although the USSR joined the League in 1934, and from then until 1939 offered to join an alliance to oppose Germany's breaches of the Versailles Treaty, Britain was not prepared to listen, and France (though interested in such an alliance) would not act without Britain. Consequently, Hitler was allowed to rearm, and then reoccupy the Rhineland, without any opposition. He was also allowed to force Anschluss on Austria in 1938. Even when he extended his demands to the Sudeten area of Czechoslovakia – which had never been German territory – the British prime minister, Neville Chamberlain, preferred to appease Hitler rather than stand with the USSR against Hitler's demands. In this way, Hitler came to believe that his actions would never be opposed. Even when Britain promised to protect Poland, Hitler believed this was likely to be as much honoured as the earlier understanding to protect Czechoslovakia. As Overy has stated, all these successes before 1939 put Germany in a much stronger position.

Examiner's comment

Another reason has been identified, and there is some relevant supporting information. However, although there is some analysis, the answer tends to read as a 'list', with no real attempt to comment on relative importance.

So, in conclusion, I think the view expressed in the question is wrong. There is no single reason why war broke out in 1939 – they were all important.

Examiner's comment

This is a brief conclusion; while it is perfectly acceptable to disagree with the view, there has been no real attempt to make a valid judgement about the relative importance of the other reasons.

Overall examiner's comments

There is accurate own knowledge (although some of it is largely irrelevant), with some hints of analysis. However, while a range of reasons is considered, there are limited attempts to **explicitly link** the material closely to the question. Thus it tends to be a list of factors, which doesn't always make it clear how they contributed to war in 1939. Nonetheless, the answer has possibly done just about enough to reach the bottom of Band 3 and earn about 11 marks. What was needed was an answer that analysed various reasons, and that clearly evaluated their relative importance – allowing a judgement to be reached. In addition, the candidate has not examined the role of Japan and Hitler's alliances, nor has the candidate really dealt with 1939 itself. For example, there is no mention of the Nazi–Soviet Pact, or any attempt to explain why Britain opposed Hitler in 1939 but not in 1938. Finally, although there is some awareness of historical debate/historians' views, it is rather dated, limited and not evaluative.

Activity

Look again at the simplified markscheme and the student answer on pages 226–29. Now draw up a plan focused on the demands of the question. Then write several paragraphs which will be good enough to get into Band 1, and so obtain the full 20 marks. As well as making sure you address **all** aspects of the question, try to integrate into your answer some references **and** evaluation of relevant historians/historical interpretations.

Question 2

Analyse the strengths and weaknesses of the Weimar Republic between January 1919 and October 1929.
[20 marks]

Skills

- Factual knowledge and understanding
- Structured, analytical and **balanced** argument
- Awareness/understanding/evaluation of historical interpretations
- Clear and balanced judgement.

Examiner's tip

Look carefully at the wording of this question, which asks you to evaluate the strengths and weaknesses of the Weimar Republic and also provides very specific dates for consideration. You will not only need to consider what strengths and weaknesses the republic possessed, you will also have to decide whether the strengths outweighed the weaknesses or vice versa.

You would also be advised to go further and consider the relative importance of the various strengths and weaknesses that you refer to. Remember to stick closely to the dates given in the question. It is important not merely to describe features and events, but use them to support an argument. In making your plan, you will be able to decide whether you can produce more evidence on one side than the other, and thus decide what that argument will be. It does not matter what view you adopt, as long as you have a 'thesis' and can write analytically and convincingly.

Student answer

The Weimar Republic was set up in Germany at the end of the First World War. Its home was in Weimar rather than Berlin because Spartacist riots there made the capital too dangerous for the government. However, it established a new constitution for Germany that was one of the most democratic in Europe, and thus the Weimar Republic started out with many high hopes. However, many historians have suggested that it was 'doomed from the start', because the constitution contained flaws and the new republic had many enemies. This essay will consider whether or not that was true.

Examiner's comment

This is a poor introduction and suggests limited reflection before writing. It shows some knowledge of the establishment of the Weimar Republic and so identifies the topic that the question is asking about. However, it fails to offer a view in relation to the question and also becomes slightly sidetracked by a related, but slightly different question – 'Was the Weimar Republic doomed from the start?' The final sentence is unnecessary and the reference to 'many historians' suggests a lack of precise knowledge.

The Weimar Republic had a poor start. It was the product of a revolution that never really quite succeeded. The socialists in the SPD wanted to bring about change in Germany at the end of the war, but they were horrified at the outbreaks of mutiny and communist-inspired rioting that occurred throughout the country in October/November 1918. The risings and establishment of workers' councils frightened the socialists, who believed things were going too far. So, when they proclaimed the republic and the kaiser was forced to abdicate, they made a pact with the army called the Ebert–Groener Pact. This was both a strength and a weakness.

Examiner's comment

These paragraphs offer some useful information, but the candidate has made the mistake of ignoring the question dates and providing too much detail pre-1919. This also gives a rather narrative feel to the answer. Mention of the Ebert–Groener Pact is relevant, and its part in crushing the Spartacists is important to any consideration of the republic's strengths and weaknesses. The knowledge given at the end of this paragraph is excellent, but what this candidate fails to do is to offer any judgement. This merely sets out views on both sides.

It gave Ebert, the socialist leader of the new government, the power he needed to crush the rebellions. He was also able to use the army and the Freikorps when the Spartacists rebelled in January 1919. However, it made the socialists reliant on the right-wing army. This was a weakness, because Noske, who commanded the troops, behaved brutally towards the communists, whose beliefs were actually nearer to those of the socialists than the nationalist views of the army were. The SPD was therefore accused of 'selling out' by some of its own supporters and the more left-wing USPD.

The Weimar Republic was 'doomed from the start' because of its constitution. This gave a lot of power to the president, who appointed and dismissed the chancellor, could dissolve the Reichstag, commanded the army and could, in emergencies, rule by decree under Article 48. This was a major weakness, which allowed for the use of dictatorial powers. However, the constitution also had its strengths. Everyone over the age of 20 could vote every four years, and there were both local state assemblies and a central government, thus dispersing power. They also had the right to arrange plebiscites, giving still greater people-power. Having a Reichsrat that could give advice and reject new laws (even though it could be overridden by the Reichstag) provided a check on what laws were made, and the Supreme Court was kept separate from the legislature and executive. Although the proportional representation system was in some ways a weakness, because it produced coalition governments and allowed extremist parties into the Reichstag, it was also a strength because it allowed all voices to be heard. Finally, the constitution guaranteed the basic rights of German citizens.

The Weimar Republic has been criticised by historians such as Lee because the underlying social, administrative and judicial structures remained unchanged. Big business and the large landowners, for example, continued much as before and the judiciary were notorious for favouring the right wing. When left-wing opponents were brought to trial they were treated very harshly, but members of the right wing were given lenient sentences and treated sympathetically. The army was also unchanged and hostile to the republic and so were many of the civil servants and teachers, especially in the universities. However, Carr says that all of this was also a strength because by leaving the key structures and people alone, the republic could function. Had most of the civil servants been dismissed, for example, the republic might have collapsed immediately.

Examiner's comment

These paragraphs shows some excellent knowledge and understanding, but the candidate still fails to advance any particular view. Whilst the link to historians in the second paragraph shows further awareness, it is a shame that no individual judgement is offered. The first paragraph perpetuates the mistake of focusing on words that are different from the question at the beginning (probably trying to adapt a previously prepared answer), but there is also some consideration of strengths and weaknesses, which could have gone further. Article 48, for example is alleged to be a 'major weakness' but this is not fully explained – or questioned – and the final sentence of paragraph one is undeveloped. The second paragraph shows some depth of awareness, but is again a little limited in development. It would have been relatively easy to add a specific case of right-wing judicial leniency, or left-wing prejudice.

In June 1919, the German government was forced to sign the Treaty of Versailles. This was regarded as a 'diktat' because there had been no German representatives invited to Versailles, where the negotiations took place. The Germans had expected a lenient peace based on Wilson's Fourteen Points, but what they got was extremely harsh on their country and they were horrified and humiliated. The Weimar politicians who signed it were soon known as the 'November Criminals' (because they had also agreed the armistice) and they were accused of 'stabbing Germany in the back' by agreeing to a peace while the German army was still undefeated.

The treaty weakened the Weimar Republic because Germany lost land, including Alsace-Lorraine and the Polish Corridor, as well as all its colonies. It was also left with a tiny army of 100,000, no air force and only six battleships. The war guilt clause and reparations were particularly hated. The treaty encouraged opposition to the republic. The only strength of the treaty was that it ended the war and there were hopes among some politicians who believed that it could be changed in future years if Germany co-operated with it. Not all Germans understood this idea though, and many remained hostile.

Examiner's comment

This paragraph introduces another major factor weakening the republic, although the way it is presented offers detail followed by comment rather than directly addressing its strengths and weaknesses for the republic. There is an admirable attempt to identify some strengths at the end, however, and the knowledge and overall understanding are again good.

[There then follow several paragraphs considering the attempted risings of both left and right wings, and the economic problems and hyperinflation 1919–23. Both show how the republic displayed strengths and weaknesses in their handling of these developments.]

Between 1924 and 1929, the republic showed more strengths than weaknesses. Politically, the country became much more stable and the democratic parties performed better in the elections; there were no more putsches or assassinations. Inflation was cured and thanks to the Dawes Plan of 1924 and the Young Plan of 1929, reparations were made easier to cope with. American and other foreign money flowed into Germany to aid the development of industry, and this also helped the government to set up an extensive welfare system. Furthermore, the country gained greater credit internationally in the hands of Stresemann, who negotiated the Locarno Treaty and oversaw Germany's entry into the League of Nations. As well as an economic revival there was a flowering of culture, which has led to this period being known as a 'golden age'. These years of Weimar Germany produced exciting new 'modernist' art, architecture and thought-provoking literature and plays. Berlin became the centre for a liberating new night-life and young people enjoyed greater freedom. Feuchtwanger has described the 'feel-good factor' of these years. However …

[This is followed by a paragraph considering the limitations of the 1924–29 period, with specific reference to the views of the historians Layton, Nicholls and Peukert. The essay ends with a conclusion that emphasises that the republic had both strengths and weaknesses – it was not entirely 'doomed from the start' but had problems that would make it difficult to cope in a crisis like that experienced after 1929.]

Examiner's comment

These paragraphs provide a good, balanced appraisal of the strengths and weaknesses of the later years of the republic, and also show some historiographical understanding. There is some limitation to the depth of detail (for example, there is no explanation of the Dawes Plan or the Locarno Treaty), but a lot of useful and relevant material is conveyed in a short space, together with a good overall focus. Once again, points on both sides are presented rather than judged and even the conclusion, which still perpetuates the 'alternative' question theme – 'was the republic doomed?' – does not make a clear judgement about the relative importance of strengths and weaknesses.

Overall examiner's comments

This answer displays a good understanding of the strengths and weaknesses of the Weimar Republic, addressing all aspects of the question and providing a good deal of accurate supporting knowledge. There is little that is irrelevant, for example. The essay also shows an awareness of historiography and differing historical interpretations, although there is scope for the range of interpretation to be developed further. The answer is, on the whole, well-structured and there are some attempts at evaluation, even though the synthesis of views in support of an individual judgement is limited. The essay is not without its faults. It has a weak introduction, it provides a little too much background information, sometimes the comment on strengths and weaknesses grows out of the information supplied rather than being presented first and then supported by the detail and, most importantly, the conclusion is rather bland. However, there is definitely enough here for an award in Band 2, with 15 marks.

Activity

Look again at the simplified markscheme and the student answer on pages 231–34. Now try to draw up your own plan and rewrite the answer in a way that would reach the criteria for Band 1 and so obtain the full 20 marks. You will need to offer a clearer judgement, provide a little more supporting detail and evaluate a greater range of alternative interpretations. Make sure your introduction (theses) and conclusion match!

Further information

Sources and quotations in this book have been taken from the following publications.

Beevor, Antony. 2006. *The Battle for Spain: The Spanish Civil War 1936–1939*. London, UK. Weidenfeld & Nicolson.

Blinkhorn, Martin. 2006. *Mussolini and Fascist Italy*. London, UK. Routledge.

Browne, Harry. 1996. *Spain's Civil War*. London, UK. Longman.

Carr, William. 1991. *A History of Germany, 1815–1990*. London, UK. Bloomsbury Academic.

Clark, Martin. 2005. *Mussolini*. Harlow, UK. Pearson.

Durgan, Andy. 2007. *The Spanish Civil War*. Basingstoke, UK. Palgrave Macmillan.

Eddy, Steve and Lancaster, Tony. 2004. *Germany 1866–1945*. London, UK. Causeway Press.

Findley, Carter Vaughan and Rothney, John. 1986. *Twentieth Century World*. Boston, USA. Houghton Mifflin Company.

Gregor, A. J. 1979. *Italian Fascism and Developmental Dictatorship*. Princeton, USA. Princeton University Press.

Haffner, Sebastian. 1973. *Failure of a Revolution: Germany 1918–1919*. Berne, Switzerland. Andre Deutsch.

Henig, Ruth. 1995. *Versailles and After, 1919–1933*. London, UK. Routledge.

Henig, Ruth. 1998. *The Weimar Republic 1919–1933*. London, UK. Routledge.

Hiden, John. 1996. *The Weimar Republic*. London, UK. Longman.

Hite, John, and Hinton, Chris. 2000. *Weimar and Nazi Germany*. London, UK. John Murray.

Hobsbawm, Eric. 1994. *Age of Extremes*. London, UK. Abacus.

Kershaw, Ian. 1993. *The Nazi Dictatorship*. London, UK. Arnold.

Kindleberger, Charles P., 1992, *The World in Depression 1929–1939*. Berkeley, USA. University of California Press

Kissinger, Henry. 1995. *Diplomacy*. New York, USA. Touchstone.

Laver, John. 1991. *Nazi Germany 1933–1945*. London, UK. Hodder & Stoughton.

Layton, Geoff. 1992. *Germany: The Third Reich 1933–45*. London, UK. Hodder.

Layton, Geoff. 2005. *Weimar and the Rise of Nazi Germany 1918–1933*. London, UK. Hodder Murray.

Lee, Stephen J. 1987. *The European Dictatorships, 1918–1945*. London, UK. Routledge.

Macdonald, H. 1999. *Mussolini and Italian Fascism*. Cheltenham, UK. Nelson Thornes.

McDonough, Frank. 2001. *Conflict, Communism and Fascism*. Cambridge, UK. Cambridge University Press.

McKay, John, and Hill, Bennett and Buckler, John. 1988. *A History of World Societies*. Boston, USA. Houghton Mifflin Company.

McKichan, Finlay. 1992. *Germany 1815–1939*. Edinburgh, UK. Oliver and Boyd.

Mommsen, Hans. 1998. *The Rise and Fall of Weimar Democracy*. Chapel Hill, USA. University of North Carolina Press.

Nicholls, A. J. 2000. *Weimar and the Rise of Hitler*. Basingstoke, UK. Palgrave Macmillan.

Overy, R. J. 1994. *The Inter-War Crisis 1919–1939*. London, UK. Longman.

Paxton, Robert O. 1997. *Europe in the Twentieth Century (3rd Edition)*. Fort Worth, USA. Harcourt Brace College Publishers.

Preston, Paul. 2006. *The Spanish Civil War*. London, UK. Harper Perennial.

Robson, Mark. 1992. *Italy: Liberalism and Fascism 1870–1945*. London, UK. Hodder.

Simpson, William. 1991. *Hitler and Germany*. Cambridge, UK. Cambridge University Press.

Tampke, Jürgen. 1988. *Twentieth Century Germany: Quest for Power*. Southbank, Australia. Thomson Learning Australia.

Waller, Sally. 2009. *The Development of Germany, 1871–1925*. Cheltenham, UK. Nelson Thornes.

Weitz, Eric D. 2007. *Weimar Germany: Promise and Tragedy*. Princeton, USA. Princeton University Press.

Welch, David. 1998. *Hitler*. London, UK. UCL Press.

Wood, Anthony. 1986. *Europe 1815–1960*. London, UK. Longman.

Index

Acknowledgements

The volume editor and publishers acknowledge the following sources of copyright material and are grateful for the permissions granted. While every effort has been made, it has not always been possible to trace all copyright holders. If any omissions are brought to our notice we will be happy to include the appropriate acknowledgement on reprinting.

Picture credits

Cover © 2006 Alinari/Topfoto.co.uk; p. 10 Underwood & Underwood/ Corbis; p. 11 Trinity Mirror/Mirrorpix/Alamy; p. 19 Mary Evans Picture Library/Alamy; p. 25 Mary Evans Picture Library/Alamy; p. 39 Interfoto/ Alamy; p. 47 The Image Works/Topfoto; p. 53 Associated Newspapers Ltd/Solo Syndication; p. 58 dpa/Corbis; p. 67 Topham Picturepoint/ Topfoto; p. 73 Topham Picturepoint/Topfoto; p. 87 Associated Newspapers Ltd/Solo Syndication; p. 93 Topfoto; p. 101 Hulton-Deutsch Collection/Corbis; p. 103 Popperfoto/Getty Images; p. 106 Getty Images; p. 113 The Granger Collection/Topfoto; p. 117 Ullstein Bild/Topfoto; p. 123 Getty Images; p. 130 Topfoto; p. 136 Agencia EFE; p. 143 UCL Library Services; p. 150 Associated Newspapers Ltd/Solo Syndication; p. 157 Getty Images; p. 160 The Nation; p. 165 Getty Images; p. 170 Yad Vashem; p. 176 Associated Newspapers Ltd/Solo Syndication; p. 189 Getty Images; p. 195 Associated Newspapers Ltd/Solo Syndication; p. 203 John Frost Newspapers; p. 209 Express Syndication Ltd; p. 216 John Frost Newspapers.

Produced for Cambridge University Press by

White-Thomson Publishing
+44 (0)843 208 7460
www.wtpub.co.uk

Series editor: Allan Todd
Development editor: Margaret Haynes
Reviewer: Neil Tetley
Editor: Sonya Newland
Designer: Clare Nicholas
Picture researcher: Sonya Newland
Illustrator: Stefan Chabluk